Urban Life and Urban Landscape
Zane L. Miller, Series Editor

LAKE EFFECTS
*A History of Urban Policy Making
in Cleveland, 1825–1929*

~

RONALD R. WEINER

The Ohio State University Press
Columbus

Copyright © 2005 by The Ohio State University.
All rights reserved.

Library of Congress Cataloging-in-Publication Data

Weiner, Ronald R.
Lake effects : a history of urban policy making in Cleveland, 1825–1929
/ Ronald R. Weiner.
p. cm.—(Urban life and urban landscape)
Includes bibliographical references and index.
ISBN 0–8142–0989–0 (cloth : alk. paper)—ISBN 0–8142–9064–7 (cd-rom) 1. Urban policy—Ohio—Cleveland—History—19th century. 2. Urban policy—Ohio—Cleveland—History—20th century. 3. Cleveland (Ohio)—Politics and government —19th century. 4. Cleveland (Ohio)—Politics and government—20th century.
I. Title. II. Urban life and urban landscape series.
HN80.C6W45 2005
330.9771'3203—dc22
2004029399

Cover art and design by Jason Moore
Type set in Adobe Minion

The paper used in this publication meets the minimum requirements of the American National Standard for Information Sciences—Permanence of Paper for Printed Library Materials. ANSI Z39.48-1992.

9 8 7 6 5 4 3 2 1

In memory of
Lorraine A. Weiner (1918–1989)
Henry D. Shapiro (1937–2004)

CONTENTS

List of Illustrations	ix
Acknowledgments	xi
Introduction: Regimes and Urban Policy: An Overview	1

PART ONE
The Merchant Regime, 1825–1878

    Chapter 1   Merchant Regime Urban Policy, 1825–1878   11

PART TWO
The Populist Regime, 1878–1895

    Chapter 2   Ideals and Policy Making Institutions   37

    Chapter 3   Economic Development and Urban Growth Devalued   48

    Chapter 4   The Realignment of Policy Priorities   65

PART THREE
The Corporate Regime, 1895–1919

    Chapter 5   Ideals, Institutions, and Policies   85

    Chapter 6   Urban Growth Policy I: Land Use Controls at the Periphery   102

    Chapter 7   Urban Growth Policy II: Land Use Controls at the Center   116

    Chapter 8   The Professional Ideal Triumphant   133

PART FOUR
The Realty Regime, 1919–1929

    Chapter 9   Origins of the Realty Regime   153

Chapter 10 Getting Down to Business:
Economic Development and the Financing of Urban
Growth Policy   171

Chapter 11 Land Use Controls in an Era of Changing City Structure 187

Chapter 12 The Balkanized Metropolis: The Realty Regime Victorious 202

Conclusion: Paths to the Present: A Post Mortem   214

Appendix A: Mayors of Cleveland   221

Appendix B: Annexations by Regime   223

Methodological Notes   225

Notes to Chapters   233

Index   263

LIST OF ILLUSTRATIONS

Figures

Figure 1.1	Cleveland and Ohio City, 1836	17
Figure 6.1	Cleveland Park System and Cleveland Metropolitan Park System, 1930	109
Figure 7.1	Cleveland central business district, 1900	118
Figure 7.2	Group Plan of public buildings (downtown civic center), 1903	123
Figure 7.3	Artist's rendering of University Circle, ca. 1930—Cleveland Trust Bank advertising	125
Figure 9.1	Map of Euclid Corridor, E. 18th to E. 105th (ca. 1929)	159

Tables

Table 3.1	Municipal budgets, 1870 and 1880 (values in $1,000)	49
Table 3.2	VAPE for durable and nondurable goods by decade: the United States and Cleveland, 1860–1920	52
Table 3.3	Employees in durable vs. nondurable goods industries by decade, 1860–1920	54
Table 3.4	VAPE for primary metals vs. metals fabricating by decade, 1860–1920	57

ACKNOWLEDGMENTS

Years ago, when my children were young, we vacationed in the pointed-fir country of northern Wisconsin, a two-day journey by car from Cleveland. Somewhere near Elyria, Ohio, the first query would come: "Are we there yet?" The children are grown and scattered now; but in more recent years, at holiday gatherings, I hear echoes of the earlier interrogatory: "The book, is it finished yet?" Now I can finally answer: "Yes, it is finished at last." But not without the help of many people.

Cleveland is a city blessed with world-class cultural institutions, some the enduring legacy of the Corporate Regime. I have drawn on several of these in the preparation of this book. I am grateful for the assistance of the librarians at Case Western Reserve University, the Western Reserve Historical Society, Cleveland State University, Cuyahoga Community College, the Cuyahoga County Archives, and the staff of the city's crown jewel, the Cleveland Public Library.

Many individuals, knowingly or unknowingly, contributed to my understanding of Cleveland's past and taught me various ways to unearth it. I discussed the ideas expressed in this book and much else with my friend and colleague, David P. Shriver. Richard Parish, Richard Karberg, Mark and Sally Lewine, Carol Beal, and Harry McGee shared with me their knowledge of geography, art history, anthropology, local business history, and historical methodology. Karberg, in particular, alerted me early on to the importance of suburban real-estate agents in the development of Cleveland, and Beal to the impact of national merger waves on Cleveland businesses.

Anyone with an interest in Cleveland history soon became a friend of the late Thomas F. Campbell. I was no exception. We spent many convivial hours discussing Cleveland's past and present. Tom was a man of great good humor and uncommon generosity. He is missed by his family, friends, colleagues, students, and, no small matter, by Cleveland historiography.

This book is a volume in the Urban Life and Urban Landscape Series of The Ohio State University Press. When this project began, Henry D. Shapiro was the co-editor of the series. Shapiro worked with me and provided editorial advice and commentary (some forty thousand words of it), and in the process he became a good friend. If this book has any merit, it is because of him. Henry died in January 2004 of lung cancer. The book is dedicated to him, a small payment on the debt owed.

When the manuscript proved overlong for the economics of university press publishing, Zane L. Miller (the other co-editor of the series) stepped into the breach, blue pencil in hand (red pen, actually) and cut the manuscript by sixty thousand words. After recovering from the initial shock of seeing so much of my work littering the cutting room floor, I now grudgingly concede that this streamlined version is better. Editing is an art, and Zane Miller is a master of it. Robert B. Fairbanks read both longer and shorter versions of the manuscript and made helpful and timely suggestions on both.

Thanks also to Park Dixon Goist for being a pal, luncheon companion (with Shapiro), poker adversary, neophyte horseplayer, and faithful source of merriment.

Last, I thank my wife Sue for her loving support and ongoing instruction in social welfare policy.

INTRODUCTION

REGIMES AND URBAN POLICY
An Overview

Some readers may wonder why a book that appears to be a political history has so little "politics" in it. One could write a very long and mildly entertaining political history about the ignorance, myopia, venality, and stupidity of Cleveland's politicians past and present. But this book is about policy rather than politics. Policy is what happens after elections are decided. Policy is the long view of political decision making. Politics is short term and is typically about electioneering and partisan combat. Politics distorts long-term reality by focusing on individual elections, personalities, and conflict.[1]

Mayors, city councilmen, school boards, party leaders, and public servants repeatedly failed the citizens of Cleveland. Nonetheless, Cleveland's political history has typically been written as a story of "good guys vs. bad guys." Except for Mayor Johnson (and a few others), however, there were hardly any good guys at all. Moreover, no political party was more committed to serving the public interest than any other, and no political party was more effective in serving the public interest than any other. As a result, no amount of careful attention to party platforms, campaign rhetoric, or the changing balance of party control over public offices can explain how Cleveland got to be the way it is.

Indeed, throughout the nineteenth and almost all of the twentieth centuries, the parties and the candidates were virtually interchangeable. In Cuyahoga County, and in Cleveland in particular, affiliation with the two parties crossed economic and social lines, although membership in the county (as opposed to the city) Republican Party skewed toward the affluent. Ideologically, the two parties stood for nothing of substance and nothing that would distinguish one from the other. Both employed a rhetoric of fiscal frugality and low taxes and feigned alarm at the corruption and incompetence of the other. Campaigns, coming at much too frequent two-year intervals, merely involved charges and counter charges of fiscal irresponsibility, increased taxes, corruption, and incompetence. In the 1980s municipal elections became quadrennial, but they remained mud fights nonetheless.

Urban policy differs. It aims to cultivate, maintain, and defend the local region's particular geography of production and consumption by the creation of a loose coalition of disparate groups and organizations—the urban regimes discussed below.[2] A policy-making regime may exist for a considerable period of time, as did the four regimes under consideration here. Although they appear stable and unified, urban regimes are in the still longer run unstable because they crumble when the geography of production and consumption changes.

The somewhat labored phrase "geographies of production and consumption" is intended to serve as a code signifying several things. The phrase means, in general, that economic activities, such as production and consumption, are perceptible in urban space. Cleveland's geography of production, that is, the places in and about the city where goods were actually produced, changed as Cleveland's economy evolved from agricultural, to commercial, to industrial modes of production. This meant that Cleveland's production occurred, sequentially, on farms, and in warehouses, steel mills, and factories at shifting locations within the urban region. Markets for goods flowing from Cleveland's farms, warehouses, mills, and factories may be distant or local, but consumption of goods and services was bound by an existing mode of transportation—horse, wagon, canal boat or steam ship, railroad car, auto, or truck. Geographies of consumption also changed in response to the spending and travel patterns of individuals. When production shifts from farms to warehouses to mills to factories, and consumers move from farms to cities to suburbs, the "where" of individual spending changes as well. Cleveland's geographical configuration at any given time was that of the agricultural village, the commercial entrepot, or the industrial metropolis. The shorthand phrase that summarizes all of this activity is "geographies of production and consumption."

ON URBAN REGIMES

Urban regimes are political and institutional adaptations to changing geographies of production and consumption. The participating groups in a regime at any given time possess differing degrees of power, vary in stages of growth or decline, possess distinct value systems, and promote both comprehensive and parochial policy goals. The inability of all member organizations to adapt to changing external and internal conditions makes urban regimes discontinuous. Each regime adapts to a changing social geography in its own way, sets policies, and aligns priorities among them until spatial conditions again change and a new round of adaptive behavior becomes necessary. Urban regimes come apart because organizations change and because society offers new challenges to which an existing coalition of organizations cannot adapt.[3]

Urban policy in Cleveland, from 1825 until 1929, was set by four discontinuous local regimes.[4] The first of these, the Merchant Regime (1825–1878), was composed of business, governmental, and social organizations created by the city's original settlers. As legatees of a common value system, they seldom disagreed over policy means and ends, and the policies of the regime transformed the city's geography of production and consumption. But Merchant Regime organizations failed to adapt to the changed geography of production and consumption that their regime occasioned, and a new regime, the Populist Regime (1878–1895), replaced it.

The Populist Regime was a diverse coalition of organizations striving to cope with the early industrial era geography of production and consumption. Some of these carried over from the preceding regime, while others, such as immigrant churches, mutual aid societies, immigrant clubs, and ward organizations, were entirely new. These diverse Populist Regime organizations coalesced around two contradictory value systems: a universalist professional ideal held by an emerging class of organization men, and a particularized neighborhood-based value system held by newcomers to the city. In its heyday, the Populist Regime reordered policy priorities and charted entirely new policy directions for the city of Cleveland.

The strengths of the Populist Regime were also its weakness. It tried to be all things to all people and in so doing made unpopular policy choices. These choices were aggravated by the conflict in ideals between the regime's professionals, who sought to bring order and efficiency to city operations, and the residents of working class neighborhoods, who viewed the regime's leaders as benefactors who would reliably provide material rewards in exchange for political support.

The Corporate Regime rose from the Populist Regime's inability to manage the industrial era geography of production and consumption. The Corporate Regime overhauled old organizations, built new organizations in the image of the modern industrial business organization, and merged all into a hierarchical policy setting network, which included divisions for each type of policy. The Corporate Regime was composed of entrepreneurs, corporate managers, and professionals alienated from the Populist

Regime. At the outset, the values of entrepreneurs, managers, and professionals appeared to be compatible. In the end, the dramatic ad hoc projects favored by the entrepreneurs could not be reconciled with the long-term institutionalization of policy favored by managers and professionals.

For all its organizational brilliance and policy achievements, the Corporate Regime failed to respond adequately to the challenges of the automobile era geography of production and consumption. Its replacement, the Realty Regime, was composed of new and old organizations staffed by local businessmen not affiliated with the industrial era corporation. These were new people with a more expansive, regional vision of social geography and new, self-interested policy priorities. The Realty Regime did not see policy as a comprehensive whole and instead concentrated on a narrow range of policy objectives. The Realty Regime was, however, attuned to the automobile era geography of production and consumption and implemented its narrow range of policies on the scale of the metropolitan region rather than that of the central city.

URBAN POLICY DEFINED

Urban policy is the sum of four elements: economic development, urban growth, service distribution, and wealth redistribution.[5] Regimes define what their goals are in each of the four areas of policy, establish priorities among them, and then work within a specific coalition of organizations toward policy implementation. Policy culminates in the building of physical and social infrastructure necessary to sustain an existing geography of production and consumption.

Economic Development Policy

Economic development policy is the deceptively simple activity of adding new work to old work. But where that work is added and how decisions get made to add new work are crucial. The issue of where new work is added is crucial because urban economies are composed of two distinct but related elements: an export sector and a local sector. The export sector is the more critical of the two and is the object of economic development policy because it produces goods and services for sale outside the community. Export sector activity has the desirable outcome of bringing new money into the urban economy, rather than recycling money already in the local economy. Economic development policy, then, is about schemes which bring new money into the economy by adding new work to old work in the export sector.⁶

Cleveland began its economic history as an agricultural village, processing locally grown crops (e.g., wheat to flour) for sale outside the community, the city's initial export sector activity. The new work it added in the mid-nineteenth century to the old work in the agricultural export base was in commerce—transportation services, warehousing, and banking. In its next stage of export sector development, Cleveland added new work in manufacturing to its commercial export sector base, so once again new work was added to old work in the export sector and the new money made from the sale of manufactured goods outside the community continued to flow into Cleveland as the nineteenth century ended. In the early twentieth century, more diverse forms of export sector manufacturing activity were added, continuing the cycle.

It is vital for the reader to note that new work does not get added to old export sector work by accident. These gains are the result of conscious organizational decision making. How and whether each of the four regimes defined economic development policy and what priority status was assigned to it will be important matters for later discussion.

The other half of the urban economy, the local sector, produces goods and services for those living in the locality and is, in most ways, dependent on the export sector. Export sector businesses buy goods and services produced locally, and export sector workers must have food, housing, clothing, medical care, education, and other services. The local sector of the urban economy exists to provide them.

Urban Growth Policy

Urban growth policy seeks to sort out and manage the mass of tangled land use issues created by the export and local sectors of the economy. All businesses, export sector and local, have spatial requirements and therefore are competitors for the land required to meet the spatial needs of their businesses. People, obviously, also inhabit the city, and people have housing requirements but also a more modest ability to stand the cost of competing for land and paying for the structures built upon it. Businesses and citizens alike have transportation needs that generate geographies of consumption as businesses move their goods in and about the city and citizens travel to work and to purveyors of goods and services.

Urban growth policy and city structure are braided strands. From their colonial beginnings, American cities evolved through at least three structural stages, correlating roughly to the changing geographies of production and consumption: (1) the commercial era walking city of the Merchant Regime, (2) the industrial era hub and spoke streetcar city of the Populist and Corporate regimes, and (3) the multiple-nuclei or automobile city of the Realty Regime. Cleveland between 1825 and 1930 progressed through all three stages of urban structure. Urban regimes were adaptations to changing city structure.

Service Distribution Policy

Services are deemed "distributive" because everyone in theory benefits from public safety, public health, municipal housekeeping, and public education. Caveats become necessary because increasingly, with passage of time and growing public sophistication, distributive services became matters of qualitative public choice, choices which frequently provoked debates over priority status because services cost taxpayers money and add little to the city's economic development and contribute only indirectly to its growth.

Policies governing service distribution were (and are) mostly answers to three questions: what services are demanded, how much is the public willing to pay, and "who benefits." The answers to these questions varied markedly from regime to regime. Services taken for granted in a 1920s suburb would have been considered wildly extravagant by the merchants and populists.

Wealth Redistribution Policy

The "who benefits" issue also underlies wealth redistribution policy. Redistribution is a one-way transfer or grant of wealth from one individual or group to another and is tolerated in an exchange economy because it is a reflection of two elemental human traits: benevolence and fear. Benevolent impulses run deep in the American psyche, but the wellspring of benevolence must flow toward clearly defined and deserving beneficiaries, such as the aged, the infirm, widows and orphans, or victims of natural disaster. When ambiguity creeps into the definition of deserving, Americans become wary and insist on accountability and reciprocity. The able-bodied poor, for example, are ambiguous as beneficiaries; they should work or at least show willingness to work in exchange for their one-way grant. As one-way transfers of wealth have become an increasingly common element in

American economic and social relations, they have also become increasingly more controversial.[7]

THE POLICY PRIORITIES OF THE FOUR REGIMES

Each of the regimes shaped its own economic development, urban growth, service distribution, and wealth redistribution policies, brought different perspectives to the policies, and ordered them on a descending scale of priorities.

The Merchant Regime established economic development as its primary policy priority and pursued it with dogged energy and good results. Urban growth issues also ranked high with the merchants, but service distribution and wealth redistribution cost actual dollars and political capital which the regime was disinclined to spend.

The Populist Regime emerged because of the merchants' failure to satisfactorily address service distribution issues. Service distribution became the highest priority of the new regime and the one on which the populists would eventually impale themselves. Economic development was not understood by the regime, but urban growth was. The goal of the regime was to bring spatial growth to a halt. Wealth redistribution and service distribution in the Populist Regime were yoked issues, and the unpopularity of the latter leached into the former.

The top policy priorities of the Corporate Regime were urban growth and wealth redistribution. But in all policy areas, the corporate leaders would transfer the planning and management efficiencies of modern business organization to policy making and policy implementation. The lone policy area where this methodology failed was economic development.

Urban growth was far and away the highest policy priority of the Realty Regime. The realtors' growth policy created suburbia, and each politically independent suburb would chart its own direction in service distribution and wealth redistribution. The Realty Regime not only created the geographically expansive urban region, but it also created in its politically independent suburbs balkanized urban policy making.

As this is written, local leadership and the media are much vexed by the Cleveland region's economic decline. Initially, this was blamed on "structural" changes taking place in the economy, that is, the shift in economic activity and employment from a receding manufacturing sector to both high- and low-grade services. To avoid being trapped as low-wage burger flippers in fast food restaurants, locals were advised to reinvent themselves as skilled high-tech information processors and financial services wizards. More bad news followed. The combination of outsourcing and off-shore production expanded to include not only blue collar manufacturing but most recently back office functions and information processing, the work initially defined as high tech, high wage, highly reliable, and reliably middle class. The local leadership laments the fact that the city's ability to control its economic destiny is withering.

This study aims to show, among other policy matters, that Cleveland has not controlled its economic destiny for many decades. This is a result not only of shortsighted policy making but also of institutional forces outside the city's control, the past meeting the present. Past and present also suggest that local leadership has often confused economic development with urban growth policy, mistakenly holding the belief that rearranging the deck chairs in the form of novel land uses, sports stadiums, and convention centers is a substitute for a well-designed economic vessel, one able to follow a safe course through dangerous waters.[8]

PART ONE
The Merchant Regime, 1825–1878

1

MERCHANT REGIME URBAN POLICY, 1825–1878

Urban policy making began in Cleveland during the first half of the nineteenth century when a policy setting regime composed of local merchants guided the destiny of the fledgling settlement. Stimulated by a vision of a boundless economic future, yet more often badgered by the press of daily events, the Merchant Regime stitched together an informal network of private and public institutions from which came policies for economic development, urban growth, service distribution, and wealth redistribution.

The Merchant Regime's initial policy issue, and the matter of highest priority concern, was economic development, a policy pursued with a singleness of purpose unmatched since. An expansive urban growth policy of wholesale annexations was also pursued with enthusiasm and vigor, so much so that distributive services and wealth redistribution policies were merely reflexive responses to the unanticipated consequences of economic development and growth policies. In the 1880s, Cleveland's population size, its advance into an industrial stage of economic development, and its increasing social heterogeneity rendered obsolete the merchants' institutional policy setting network.[1]

ECONOMIC DEVELOPMENT POLICY, 1825–1878

The Old Northwest in the decades before the Civil War was a grain producing region. The region's scattered urban centers were chiefly grain transshipment points, and transshipment was confined to such regional river cities as Cincinnati until the canal era of the 1820s awakened the first stirrings of urbanization in such Great Lakes centers as Cleveland.[2]

Although founded in 1796, Cleveland[3] grew slowly because silt blocked the Cuyahoga River, creating a malarial swamp which spooked even the most pioneering of potential settlers. Only in the 1820s, at the dawn of the canal era, did Cleveland attract a steady stream of settlers who arrived by waterborne transportation after the Erie Canal opened in October of 1825.[4]

Cleveland's more promising growth after 1825 was triggered by the Merchant Regime's aggressive economic development policy, which added new work to old work in the export sector of the city's economy.[5] In the 1820s, the city was a minor transshipment center, a funnel through which grains harvested in the surrounding hinterland passed on their way to larger urban processing centers. Cleveland did not develop a strong export sector until the Merchant Regime connected the town with reliable transportation arteries to larger centers and until it acquired a store of capital necessary for building local export-sector enterprises.

Because institutional structures were embryonic, Merchant Regime economic development policy was a highly personal enterprise forged primarily by Alfred Kelley. Born in Middlefield, Connecticut in 1789, Kelley was educated in the Fairfield, Connecticut Common Schools and later read law in the offices of New York Supreme Court Justice Jonas Platt before moving to Ohio in 1810. Within five years, Kelley was a growing presence in Cleveland, serving as the first president of the village of Cleveland and president of the Commercial Bank of Lake Erie. Kelly's father and brothers joined him in Cleveland and they too became business and civic leaders. One Kelly brother served as postmaster while the senior Kelley and other siblings were aspiring merchants and shippers. But Alfred Kelley, alone, saw that his family's mercantile aspirations were tied to the economic development of the village through public policy. For this purpose Alfred Kelley entered politics and added a succession of state offices to his resume—member of the state house of representatives, state senator, and state canal commissioner—and used them to design and implement Cleveland's economic development policy.[6]

By the end of the decade, public programs promoted by Kelley connected Cleveland by water to downstate Ohio, the Great Lakes ports, and New York City via the Erie Canal. In 1823, state representative Kelley introduced legislation targeting Cleveland as the northern terminus of the Ohio and Erie Canal, linking the city to Portsmouth and the valuable grain hinterland in between. The next victory came when Kelley, now a canal commissioner, persuaded his commission colleagues to site the terminus of the Ohio Canal on the east bank of the Cuyahoga River at Cleveland rather than the rival west bank settlement of Ohio City. Two years later, businessman Kelley, with backing from fellow Cleveland merchants, secured a

$5000 federal harbor improvement grant to dredge the mouth of the Cuyahoga River and open the way for shipping.[7]

These water transit solutions fulfilled Kelley's expectations, for Cleveland grew as a banking, warehousing, and lake transshipment center, and the population rose from five hundred in 1825 to seven thousand in 1840.[8] Nevertheless, the Merchant Regime in the mid 1840s found itself prodded by newspaper editorials to do even more. Editorial writers warned that the economic development policy of the Merchant Regime focused too narrowly on canal burrowing and waterborne commerce and ignored the potential of railroads. Because canals operated seasonally, commercial activity in Cleveland was limited to the warm weather months. Editorialists lamented the departure of ambitious young men for railroad centers where they could secure employment and court business opportunities year round.[9]

Railroads became the Merchant Regime's next economic development policy fixation. Compared to other cities in the Old Northwest, Cleveland, as the newspaper editorialists rightly insisted, was a late entry into the rail era. Nevertheless, in the brief period between 1853 and 1861, the city attracted no less than six lines, rewarding Cleveland with the densest rail matrix in the Great Lakes region.[10] The rail density advantage was also responsible for Cleveland's emergence as a regional railroad repair center, a harbinger of the city's future in manufacturing.

Where orchestration of governmental decision making had been responsible for Cleveland's entry into the canal era, railroads were the creation of private enterprise. In the pre–Civil War era, railroad executives were primarily stock and bond drummers who indiscriminately sold their wares to localities susceptible to the drummers' ominous buy now or be left behind sales pitches.[11] Alfred Kelley and other Cleveland merchants, stung by critical newspaper editorials, were easily swayed by the beat of railroad company stock and bond drummers. The merchants organized local voluntary subscription campaigns to raise money to buy railroad stocks and bonds and persuaded the municipality to buy railroad stock and bond issues secured by the public purse. Kelley and other local merchants became directors of several of the railroads serving Cleveland during the 1850s.[12]

Besides successes in digging canals and laying rails, the economic development policy of the Merchant Regime added manufacturing to its priorities in the 1850s. As the editor of the Cleveland *Leader* put it, "A manufacturing town gives a man of means full scope to his ambition. Commerce alone cannot sustain us, as but few are benefited directly"; alternatively, "Manufacturing creates a demand for merchandise, mechanical labor, all the necessaries of life, and gives tone to all legitimate business in and around it."[13]

Advance into a manufacturing stage of development, however, took nearly two decades and stemmed in part from long-distance transportation connections. Servicing farmers and shipping their agricultural produce created ancillary manufacturing, including a cooperage industry and the small-scale manufacturing of agricultural tools. As weight was a significant factor in calculating shipping costs, a milling industry emerged to transform bulky grains into lighter weight flour. The water connections to the timber resources of the northern Great Lakes region made Cleveland a bulk break point for lumber shipments and allowed furniture manufacturing to flourish until, still driven by weight considerations, it moved west to sites even closer to bulky raw materials.[14]

Lumber bulk break point advantages also attracted a railroad repair industry to Cleveland because the city was a source of wooden rail ties. The railroad repair industry, in addition, stimulated local demand for the skeletal iron and steel products used for rails, bridges, structural beams, and pipe. This next step in economic development was made possible by the completion of a lattice work of canals and rail lines in Michigan and Wisconsin in the mid 1850s, which opened the iron regions to exploitation and shipment to Great Lakes cities. The earlier completion of the Ohio Canal system linked Cleveland to the coalfields of Western Pennsylvania and Southern Ohio. Rails in the 1850s traced the same paths.[15]

Capital formation was a handmaiden of economic development policy. Emerging manufacturing concerns required capital, and Alfred Kelley, elected in 1844 to the state senate, sponsored legislation organizing state banks in Ohio. This was an attempt to rationalize banking procedures and attract federal deposits as "pet banks." Indeed, Kelley's bill became the model for the legislation which became the federal Currency Act of 1863 and the National Banking Act of 1864, which identified Cleveland as one of sixteen regional banking centers.[16] The three pieces of banking legislation and the merchant bankers' eagerness to lend to local businesses created a capital density network sufficient to finance the early stages of the city's transition into manufacturing. This was an important achievement because it directed local banking activity into the primary circuit of capital, which was required for investment in industrial development.[17] Gains made from the sale of local real estate also found their way into the primary capital circuit. Cleveland's merchants owned land in the city and the surrounding agricultural region. Annexation of this outlying land turned merchants into real estate speculators. Profits from land sales were invested in the emerging manufacturing sector.

The Civil War also boosted Cleveland's manufacturing sector. Before the war, Cleveland's metals industry produced primarily for a local market, but wartime demand integrated Cleveland's metals manufacturers into a national market. Insatiable wartime demand for metals and metal products propelled Cleveland's manufacturing into the export side of the city's economy, where it joined and soon replaced agricultural goods transshipment, flour milling, and rail repair as the most dynamic industries in the export sector of the economy.[18]

Economic development policy not only adds new work to old work but also attempts to link the city to a defined market hinterland and to expand that hinterland. Alfred Kelley's early vision was of a hinterland encompassing the produce of farms in neighboring counties processed and transshipped from Cleveland. His critics regarded Kelley's vision as too narrow. Their hinterland included not merely adjacent farmland but a more expansive hinterland containing timber, oil, coal, and iron brought in from surrounding states by water and rail. The difference was considerable. Kelley's early vision of a hinterland shaped Cleveland as a merchandising, banking, and food processing entrepot, limited in potential by Ohio's declining fortunes as a grain producing region. The hinterland envisioned by Kelley's critics shaped Cleveland's future as a nationally important heavy manufacturing center. As the Merchant Regime economic development policy expanded, it forged long-distance transportation connections, which transformed Cleveland's export sector from raw materials processing to metals making and created a circuit of primary capital for investment in export sector enterprises.

As the city entered the 1870s, the Merchant Regime could look back on the fruits of fifty years of economic development policy, a vigorously pursued transportation policy that elevated Cleveland from an unpromising village settlement to a vigorous, bustling city entering a new age of industrial promise. Economic development policy also created an appetite for urban land to house the new enterprises and the nearly 93,000 people now living in the city. Urban land allocation presented an urgent need for an urban growth policy.

URBAN GROWTH POLICY, 1825–1878

Urban growth policy seeks to guide the process of land use allocation. Because land is a city's scarcest resource, land use allocation decisions form a crucial element in urban policy making. In the modern city, urban growth policy rests on attempts to impose rational controls on existing land uses. In contrast, urban growth policy in the nineteenth century sought formulas for adding land to the settled area. The most reliable formula was political: legal annexations of land to the municipality. Seldom, however, did the process of land use allocation and annexation proceed rationally or predictably.

In mid-nineteenth century Cleveland, push-pull factors dominated the allocation of land. The push factor in urban growth policy was supplied by land speculators seeking to profit from the city's expansion into vacant land at the fringes of settlement. Pull factor urban growth policy sought to bring residential areas within the city's corporate boundaries. But an even more compelling pull force was exerted by industrial districts mushrooming outside the city's political boundaries. Industrial districts were important to the city's economic development, and growth policy was used to bring these districts into the city proper and transform all, factory owner and home owner alike, into Cleveland taxpayers.[19]

Merchant era Cleveland was a walking city, for citizens traveled by foot, horse, carriage, and wagon and lived as close as possible to their places of business or employment. Competition for business and residential space was intense.

In the pedestrian city of the Merchant Regime, municipal annexation was the institutional means used to accommodate push and pull factor urban growth forces. The Merchant Regime annexed surrounding residential settlements, industrial suburbs, and rural townships. The growth policy of annexation was in full swing between 1829 and 1874, especially after 1836 when the state legislature gave Cleveland municipal status. During that half-century interval, the Merchant Regime, driven by both push and pull incentives, presided over the annexation of 27.5 square miles of land.[20]

The most important pull pressure annexation was Ohio City, a rival west bank village founded in 1818. (See figure 1.1.) Ohio City incorporated as a municipality in 1836, two days before Cleveland; but by the 1850s, Cleveland had a three to two population advantage over the west bank settlement, an edge credited to the east bank location of the canal terminus. Ohio City, however, was a serious commercial rival. Rivalry erupted into violence in 1836 when Ohio City residents blocked eastbound water traffic at Cleveland's new Columbus Street Bridge. Nevertheless, Cleveland grew more rapidly and in 1854 secured approval from the state legislature to submit an Ohio City annexation ordinance for voter approval. Both settlements approved the ordinance, though a dissident Ohio City minority complained loudly.

Chapter 1: Merchant Regime Urban Policy, 1825–1878   17

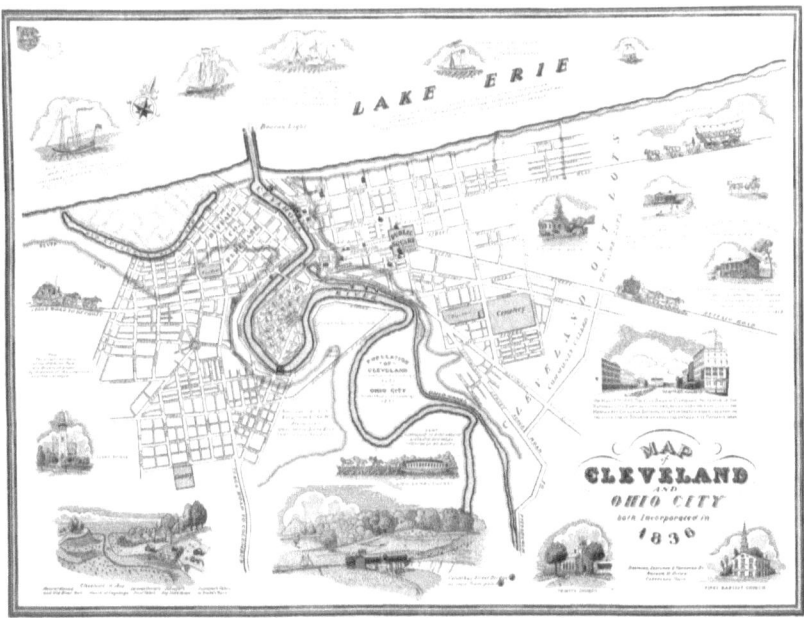

FIGURE 1.1 Cleveland and Ohio City, 1836 (Courtesy of The Western Reserve Historical Society, Cleveland, Ohio)

This pull factor annexation of Ohio City awarded Cleveland a 1.9 square mile tract of developed urban land, increasing Cleveland's land area by 36 percent and its population by a margin of 60 percent.[21] Ohio City boasted warehouses and mercantile establishments and a growing shipbuilding industry. The settlement's social dowry included 370 houses, 2400 school-age children, and three finished school buildings with three more under construction.[22]

Additional pull factor annexations in the 1860s rewarded Cleveland with territory and metals manufacturing in parts of Brooklyn Township bordering the west bank of the Cuyahoga River, and other annexations in the 1870s gave Cleveland title to the cross-river east bank settlement of Newburgh Township.[23] In that decade, moreover, push factors inspired the annexation of East Cleveland Village and portions of East Cleveland Township. East Cleveland Township was largely uninhabited, and it was the object of the attentions of real estate promoters who fancied it as a site for speculative residential development and pressured the Merchant Regime and an increasingly compliant city council to extend streets and utilities to this as well as other uninhabited areas within the city limits.[24]

The real estate industry was composed of large-scale land owners (many of them the policy making merchants), scores of small-scale speculators, and independent home builders. The real estate industry belongs to the local sector of the urban economy, and the capital needed to fund it is supplied by the secondary circuit (see endnote 17). The merchants were the largest players in the industry, and they invested profits from their land sales in the primary circuit capital funding manufacturing in the export sector. These major transfers of money created a capital-starved secondary circuit and real estate industry. Undercapitalized small-scale real estate operators and builders, accordingly, used push factor annexations to turn cheap farm land into more expensive urban real estate. A land allocation chain was thus established with links joining the large landholder merchant to the small-scale land speculator and the speculator to the builder. Merchant policy makers rejoiced in the profits and anticipated that the tax revenues from land development would pay for the added infrastructure and services to the annexed areas.[25]

Annexations forced the Merchant Regime to accept infrastructure building as a component of urban growth policy. On a topographical plane riven by hills, valleys, rivers, and creeks, bridges were essential to the movement of commerce and raw materials within the city. The Cuyahoga River was the most important obstacle to growth, and initially crossings were effected by ferry boats. A crude structure of logs laid on pontoon boats called the Center Street Bridge was constructed in 1800. The key engineering problem, then and later, was the necessity of having some form of drawbridge which could open to accommodate river traffic. The middle sections of the Center Street Bridge's chained logs and pontoon boat construction were designed to be decoupled to permit the passage of boats. A more permanent engineering solution was found in the 1830s when the wooden timber Columbus Street Bridge was built incorporating a draw section for river traffic. After the annexation of Ohio City in 1854, bridge building was enthusiastically endorsed by residents on both sides of the river. By the 1870s, four bridges spanned the river. These pioneering bridges were constructed from wooden timbers, but beginning in the 1870s the old bridges were rebuilt as iron truss structures, providing stimulus for Cleveland's evolving metals industry.[26]

Real estate speculators, for their part, were dependent on the construction of streets to their vacant land. Until the 1870s, the heyday of annexations, the merchant-dominated city council was judicious in responding to push factor infra-structure and service demands. During the early 1870s, the composition of the council altered, and the new membership, composed of small businessmen, tradesmen, and newcomers to the city, was

Chapter 1: Merchant Regime Urban Policy, 1825–1878

swayed by the buoyant growth projections of the land speculators. The council readily agreed to build streets to outlying areas and borrowed the money to do so. When the bubble burst in the Panic of 1873, the city council was left holding the bag.

Urban growth policy was a product of pull factors compelling the city to annex already developed areas and push factors impelling the city to annex vacant land. The policy was in both cases reactive and proceeded from no comprehensive plan, but it did accommodate urban growth into the early stages of the industrial era. The unintended consequence of a growth policy of annexation was the spiraling amounts of money spent for infrastructure and services. As long as growth continued in the export sector of the economy, the expense went unnoticed because land acquisitions and tax revenues kept pace with infrastructure and service demands. However, the Panic of 1873 dealt a serious if temporary blow to the export sector, and with it tax revenues earmarked for the regime's expansive urban growth policy came to a sudden halt. The Merchant Regime was blamed for the fiscal carnage that followed.[27]

SERVICE DISTRIBUTION POLICY

Housekeeping services in the mercantile city were—in a word—terrible. Urban housekeeping was an amenity, and amenities did not have the same priority status as economic development and urban growth as policy issues. In fifty years, Cleveland grew from a farm town to a city. Services perceived as amenities in a farm town became necessities in a city. But rural customs yielded slowly to urban institutions. Agricultural market towns resolved local problems through voluntary cooperative effort. Cities, by necessity, addressed problems by means of institutionalized bureaucratic structures. Economic development and urban growth issues were the first to give way to institutionalized solutions, and lower priority services such as police and fire protection and sanitation lagged. Some of the lag may be explained by the persistence of rural values, but shortages of tax revenues, reluctance of the merchant leadership to spend, and the lack of appropriate service delivery mechanisms are more persuasive explanations for Cleveland's delayed delivery of housekeeping services. When housekeeping services finally penetrated the Merchant Regime's consciousness as a policy issue, it was because lack of such services posed a threat to private property. Service distributive policy was reactive; the regime lurched from service crisis to service crisis.[28]

Police Protection

Voluntarism, failed attempts at crisis management, and lack of a service delivery mechanism were all evident in the halting progress toward municipal police protection. Police protection first emerged from a need to referee social relations and later to protect private property. When Cleveland became a village, the only full-time public employee was the village marshal. His energies were consumed by keeping the uneasy relations between Indians and whites from erupting into violence, a task in which the lawman achieved only marginal success.

In the 1820s and 1830s, assaults on persons and private property supplanted brawling with Indians as the preoccupation of local law enforcement. By the social benchmarks of the day, Indian baiting fell within the bounds of normative behavior, but assaults by whites on other whites and, worse, on their property were acts that could not be explained away as rational. Liberal consumption of intoxicants was seen as the primary causal motivator. Voluntary temperance societies and local ordinances attempted to place curbs on the sale and consumption of liquor. The marshal and his volunteer minions, known as the City Watch, were summoned when rowdyism triumphed over sobriety. To be safe rather than sorry, merchants hired nightwatchmen to look after their property during the hours of peak consumption.[29]

Despite these precautions, crime increased. In part, this was the unavoidable consequence of a city growing in size and social complexity; but, also, owing to the legislative successes of the temperance and other crusaders, there were now many more laws to be broken. Accordingly, in 1856 an independent municipal police court was created by the state legislature to relieve the overburdened part-time mayors who until now had doubled as police court judges. Courts, however, were a poor substitute for crime fighting. In 1866, prodded by the Ohio legislature's Metropolitan Police Act, Cleveland hired its first police force, composed of thirty-six uniformed officers, replacing the volunteers and nightwatchmen. Supervision was transferred from the town marshal to a Police Board whose members were appointed by the governor. In 1872, under revised legislation, control of the Police Board was awarded to the locality, and a new board composed of the mayor and four elected members was formed.[30] The board divided the city into seven police districts and staffed them from the seventy-man corps of officers. The city was nearly three-quarters of a century old before police protection became fully institutionalized.

Officer Michael Kick, killed during an attempted burglary, was the first fatality recorded by Cleveland's professional police force. Despite the insti-

Chapter 1: Merchant Regime Urban Policy, 1825–1878   21

tutionalization of police protection, Officer Kick and his fellows were hopelessly outnumbered. There was one police office for every 1,547 members of the population. European police-to-civilian ratios of 1:400 were more than three times better than local ratios, and this in cities with lower crime rates and an unarmed citizenry. Cleveland had only grudgingly turned to a professional police force. The tradition of voluntarism and moral suasion died hard. The size of the police force was restricted by the city's budget. The Merchant Regime had higher priority items on its policy agenda. It was only when crime threatened private property that the Merchant Regime took action.[31]

Fire Protection

Fires were a direct threat to private property. One city planner, recalling that planning as a profession did not emerge until the early twentieth century, offered the tongue-in-cheek explanation that nineteenth century cities did not need planners because they were leveled so frequently by fire.[32] The Great Chicago Fire of 1871 was not an isolated event. Cities built of wood and underserved by water reservoirs and fire fighters burned out of control with distressing regularity. Cleveland was not exempt from these larger trends. The fear of an out of control fire nagged at every resident and property owner.

The history of fire fighting as a distributive service in Cleveland parallels that of other cities. Fire fighting began as a volunteer effort in the 1820s and did not become a municipal responsibility until 1863, following an outbreak of serious fires in the 1850s, a decade when the town doubled its population. An impediment to professionalization was the great pride taken in the volunteer fire companies, squads which the city managed to keep abreast of fire fighting technology with timely purchases of new equipment. The great ethnic rivalries between the volunteer companies created a strong emotional incentive to maintain the status quo. But rivalries and turf conflicts frequently compromised sound fire fighting tactics, causing the Merchant Regime to concede that the city and its property holders would be better served by a professional fire department.

Cleveland City Council authorized the establishment of a fire department in 1863, and appointed James A. Craw chief engineer in charge of a force of fifty-three firemen. The next year, council approved a fire alarm telegraph system and approved funds for construction of a network of water mains. By the end of the Civil War, Cleveland firemen were supported by a network of 167 fire hydrants and 75 water reservoirs distributed about the city. In the early 1870s, the city employed 147 firemen, or about one fireman for every six hundred of the population.[33]

The ratio of firemen to the population was far better than the ratio of police to inhabitants. These numbers suggest that the Merchant Regime saw fire as a greater threat to their property than theft. The pressure on the Merchant Regime for better fire protection came not only from its own ranks but also from citizens whose nerves were frayed from the rash of fires in the 1850s and from the growing number of insurance underwriters in the city.[34] As the city entered the 1880s, police and fire protection rested in the hands of professional chiefs, and their governing boards were opened to public election. This completed the institutionalization of police and fire protection, but it also signaled that an important component of distribution policy making was in the hands of professional administrators and the broader public, meaning that demands for larger expenditures on these services would be more difficult for the Merchant Regime to resist.

Water Supply

The same water pipelines supplying the city's fire department also carried much needed fresh water to a city with a serious sanitation problem. All nineteenth century cities were warrens of filth and disease. Cleveland was no exception. Mortality rates rose with the increasing population and density of settlement. Size and density placed severe strains on the city's system of water supply.[35] Moreover, the two main sources of water—the Cuyahoga River and Lake Erie—reportedly were polluted as early as the 1850s. The Merchant Regime was obliged to view the water supply as one of the more crucial distributive policy issues.[36]

Water was needed by business and industry, the residents, and the fire department. Rural means of water supply and drainage were used by Clevelanders as late as the mid 1850s. Surface water was taken from ponds, streams, rivers, and the lake. Residential cisterns and wells were added as the city grew in size. A public well was dug at Public Square in the 1840s, and its limited production and distribution capacity was augmented by private companies serving residential areas. City streets served double duty as sewers and were patrolled by legions of hogs performing cleanup services. Mercantile era Cleveland was not merely untidy; it was a menace to public health.[37] Residents, the young most tragically, died in droves. Each year more people died than were born in Cleveland.[38]

In the 1850s the Merchant Regime, faced with public complaints and criticism from its own public health officials, acted to remedy the crisis. A measure was placed on the ballot in 1853, and voters approved a $400,000 expenditure for the construction of a water works. The water works supplied two distribution mains and 44 miles of pipe. Although the completed system supplied 38,000 gallons of water a day, it was not nearly enough. Residents converted to water-consuming indoor plumbing more rapidly than the city could construct a water supply system. Sewer drainage lagged even farther behind water supply. The first public sewer was built along Euclid Avenue in 1856. Others, including public and private sewers serving businesses, followed, but all emptied into the river or the lake.[39] In the 1860s, the city began building a unified water and sewerage system, and it appeared thereafter as an annual line item in the city budget.[40] By 1880, 125 miles of water pipe had been built with a capacity of 10 million gallons a day. The city now spent 11 percent of its budget on water and sewerage.[41] The benefits of this investment could be seen in the crude death rate (deaths per 1000 of the population), which dropped from 92 in 1860 to 35 in 1880. A parallel improvement was noted in the Vitality Index (a ratio of births to 100 deaths), which increased from 85 to 118 during the same years. The Vitality Index revealed the crossing of an important public health threshold: now more people were born than died in Cleveland.[42]

Once spurred to action by public protest and self-interest, the Merchant Regime institutionalized water supply and sewerage drainage systems. But the supply of water and sanitation continued to lag behind demand, and enforcement of existing sanitary standards was virtually nonexistent during the merchant era. Cisterns and residential wells and cesspools coexisted with the modern system, so a sanitation problem remained for succeeding regimes to grapple with in the waning decades of the century.

During the 1870s, the decade when the Merchant Regime lost its dominance over the policy making apparatus, service distribution emerged as the leading urban policy priority. During this depression-racked decade per capita municipal budgets actually declined, but service distribution expenditures rose by 52 percent.[43] A growing city required police and fire protection, a reliable supply of fresh water, and removal of waste. The Merchant Regime, however, refused to reorder its policy priorities and give appropriate rank to distributive services. It was a fateful choice.

WEALTH REDISTRIBUTION

Wealth redistributive policy in commercial era Cleveland centered on poverty, neglected children, and public education. Wealth redistribution emerged not as public policy full blown but rather as an extension of the merchants' private lives. The Merchant Regime at first shunned wealth redistribution as public policy. As devout yet well-off Protestants, the merchants were encumbered by an ethic of stewardship and service. Stewardship meant that the well-off had a responsibility for those less fortunate. And service meant voluntary participation in organizations dedicated to making life better for the less fortunate. Although public means of redistribution were initially resisted, the Merchant Regime learned that stewardship and service could be grafted on to public policy. In the interim, it groped for an institutional mechanism for policy implementation. Still, as Cleveland made its rapid advance into the industrial era, the growing disparities in wealth and social differentiation weakened and ultimately undermined the Merchant Regime's hold on wealth redistribution policy, opening the way for new approaches and new leadership.[44]

Poverty rates in the commercial city did not approach those of the industrial city. Although statistics are scarce and poverty line benchmarks nonexistent for the commercial era, one historian estimated that poverty afflicted only about one percent of the urban population, which, if accurate, meant that until the 1870s fewer than one thousand Clevelanders could be classified as poor.[45] Most contemporary commentary on the causes of poverty emphasized the family experience of sudden disaster, ill health, or injury to a bread winner. Low wages paid to farm workers were also part of the equation as rural to urban migrants entered the city in search of alternative work. Work on the farm and in the canal towns was seasonal, swelling the ranks of the needy during the cold weather months. Many lacked the money to buy or lease land and used the city as a holding area until their fortunes turned around.

Poverty, whatever its origins, became an issue during the policy making tenure of the Merchant Regime.[46] Rowdy boys who roamed the downtown streets in packs were the objects of much concerned commentary in newspapers and the reports of civic and religious organizations. The youngsters were occupied as neither students nor workers, and their idleness was a threat to the productive work ethic of the community. The boys' brash behavior and talents for petty crime roused the Merchant Regime to action.[47]

A solution to the problem of rowdy boys and perhaps to poverty as well was education. Education was simultaneously a wealth redistribution issue and a policy remedy. Thomas Jefferson's Northwest Ordinance established the principle of public education in Ohio, but the legislation offered little guidance on such service delivery issues as attendance, duration of the educational experience, or the content of the educational program. These were matters left to state and local initiative. Compulsory attendance might keep rowdy boys off the streets, but once off the streets and in school what should they (or anyone else) be taught, and until what age should young people be required to remain in school?[48]

The Poor

The values of the Merchant Regime and the institutional network it fashioned shaped the nature of redistributive policy. In rural America, where most of the merchant leaders formed their values, poverty was a matter to be addressed individually, family to family, neighbor to neighbor. In the city, even a city where the numbers of poor people did not exceed a thousand, the scale of poverty was much larger than anything imagined in a rural area. Moreover, poor people lived in their own residential quarters, out of sight and physically removed from the benevolent impulses of kindly neighbors. Poverty was initially dealt with by English-speaking Protestant churches, but as time passed, secular and public institutions also joined in the effort.[49] By the 1870s, the Merchant Regime's charity network was composed of individual-to-individual giving, the benevolence of churches, secular and sectarian charitable institutions, and the municipality. Cleveland's leading merchants gave individual to individual, were members of the key Protestant churches, served on the boards of charitable agencies, and were also the elected officials in the municipal government.[50]

Philosophically, however, the Merchant Regime's wealth redistribution policy was a patchwork of inconsistencies. The fundamental question (then as now) was: Why are people poor? The poverty of widows, orphans, the maimed, and the aged was easily explained, and they were fit into a class called the deserving (of assistance) poor. The able-bodied poor presented a more intractable problem. Was their poverty the result of personal failure or failure of the economic system? The leaders of the Merchant Regime suspected the former. If the problem, then, was personal failure, what type of personal failure produced this condition? Were the poor lazy and irresponsible? Were they not properly churched? Or were they merely people in the clutches of alcohol? Because the Merchant Regime was unclear and inconsistent about the causes of poverty, institutional remedies were inconsistent, controversial, and ineffective. The suspicion that personal failure caused poverty did, however, produce one constant in policy: the poor were not to be trusted.[51]

The benevolent work of Cleveland's churches was initially a simple extension of the neighbor-to-neighbor approach. Churches formed mutual aid societies to help their own, and when that effort proved inadequate to the size of the task at hand, the churches embraced the missionary approach of establishing institutional outposts in impoverished neighborhoods. The undergirding philosophy sustaining missionary outreach was that the poor were insufficiently churched. The neighborhood missionaries, accordingly, approached the poor with alms in one hand and a Bible in the other. By the 1870s, when the ranks of the poor included growing numbers of immigrant Catholics and free-thinkers, the Protestant missionary application of wealth redistribution policy was roundly resisted by client populations and was judged counter-productive even by some members of the Merchant Regime. Churchmen active in the emerging charity movement appealed to the merchant civic leadership to take action to broaden the base of fund raising and benevolent services.[52]

Yet the sectarian charitable agencies founded in answer to these pleas suffered the same fate when they proved unable to separate benevolence from missionary fervor or even raise sufficient monies to deliver services. The Martha Washington and Dorcas Society (1843) and the Society for the Relief of the Poor (1850) were early examples of sectarian charitable agencies. Fund raising was broadened, but clients were required to be subscribing Protestants and sabbath-keepers. Home visitations were introduced and, ironically, criticized not because they were invasions of privacy but rather because the home visitors were insufficiently insistent about the clients' commitment to Protestantism and sabbath-keeping.[53]

The maiden attempts of secular institutions at poverty abatement suffered in their own way from the perception of poverty as personal failure. The motives of agency clients were always suspect. The poor should not be trusted to manage cash money. Thus transfers of wealth from donors to recipients were made in-kind rather than cash. Even this failed to assuage the doubts of contributors and board members. Home visitations as a surveillance technique were also employed by secular agencies. Still, there were lingering doubts. The staff of secular and sectarian agencies agreed that their efforts were doomed because the private agencies were crippled for want of funding. Adequate funding, they argued, could come only from the city.[54]

In the meantime, local temperance crusaders found the root of poverty in the correlation between drinking and broken families, drinking and squandered income, and drinking and reduced employment opportunities. Between 1836 and the mid 1870s, dozens of temperance societies were organized in Cleveland, many of them the local branches of national organizations, and while they often fought bitterly over the tactical merits of moral suasion vs. political action, all temperance crusaders could agree that alcoholism was the personal failure at the core of society's ills. Local temperance societies used moral suasion as a technique to curb drinking among all classes but especially the poor. Moral suasion sustained the total abstinence approach to prohibition.

Political action temperance reform was a more moderate and more successful approach because it rested on regulation rather than abstention. Political action reformers were successful because like-minded people served on antebellum city councils and because ordinances regulating the hours and days when liquor could be sold was a moderate approach to political action. From the 1870s on, temperance leaders regularly appeared before city council as advocates of the more radical total abstinence remedy, but by then many saloonkeepers and their customers were members of that body. Temperance men and women were greeted politely by the council, but prohibition legislation remained in its own bottle safely corked in council committees. Frustrated in their efforts, temperance reformers joined benevolent and mutual aid society workers in the conclusion that the municipality would have to play a larger policy making role in poverty abatement.[55]

The municipality gradually assumed a larger role in redistributive policy. However, in the heyday of the Merchant Regime, municipal efforts at poverty abatement were similarly flawed by the pervasive view that poverty was symptomatic of personal failure. Reluctantly, the city created a poorhouse in 1836 but surrendered it to the township in 1838, pleading that the municipality lacked charter authority to levy taxes in support of the institution. In 1849, when charter authority was granted to the city, the municipality responded by creating a new poorhouse, known more formally as the City Infirmary. The City Infirmary housed three functional units: a hospital for the ailing poor, quarters for the insane, and a unit for the aged poor. The client population of the City Infirmary easily fit within the definition of deserving poor, and the Merchant Regime–dominated municipality was willing to allocate tax dollars for their upkeep. The City Infirmary building cost $20,000 to construct in the mid 1850s, and $13,000 was allotted for its operational costs in the 1870 municipal budget. The City Infirmary was an example of an "indoor relief" program; it served an important segment of the deserving poor.[56]

Outdoor relief was the approach taken with the undocumented poor, those ostensibly able-bodied people who were suspected of being poor by reason of personal failure. Work relief and aid-in-kind—but never cash transfer payments—were the bulwarks of the city's outdoor relief program. Five hundred dollars a year was spent on the municipality's outdoor relief program. The fiscal allocations of the municipality as a public institution implementing redistributive policy made clear distinctions between the deserving and the suspect poor. The amount of money allocated by city council amounted to an annual expenditure of about fifty cents a head for each poor person in the city. The hope that municipal involvement would bring adequate funds to aid the destitute proved unfounded.[57]

Rowdy Boys

The troublesome rowdy boys brought poverty and education as wealth redistribution policy issues into convergence. In 1855, a city council committee estimated that there were between two and three hundred such boys, about 3 percent of the population under 18 but fully one-third of the city's poor. One local newspaper, the *Daily True Democrat,* observed that "Our cities are nests of corruption for boys without parents, or with parents who cannot control them. But nothing is done for them. . . . Society pays dearly for its neglect, and as years roll on, and our population increases, it will pay dearer yet."[58] In 1847, when this editorial was written, the wave of midcentury migration had yet to crest. In its wake, the number of "rowdy and rascally boys" increased significantly, as the editor predicted.

In 1850s, when the rowdy boys problem was serious enough to engage the attention of the Merchant Regime, five agencies emerged to cope with the errant lads. The Merchant Regime initially tried to avoid paying dearly for the problem by ignoring it, but in the end, an institutionalized commitment was necessary. Two of the five agencies were church related institutions, two were joint government–church agencies, and one was wholly in the custody of the municipality. The Protestant Merchant Regime was incited to action by Bishop Amadeus Rappe, who established two Catholic mutual aid orphan asylums. The Protestants countered with the Cleveland Orphan Asylum (1852) and The Ragged School (1853) and lent support to the municipality's House of Correction (1857). The Cleveland Orphan Asylum and The Ragged School were not exclusive sectarian mutual aid societies but instead extended service to all rowdy boys regardless of conscience. They did, however, aim to teach Christian virtues. Both agencies, though drawing on the volunteer contributions of churchgoers, were chronically underfunded, prompting the city to adopt The Ragged School in 1857.[59]

The city changed the name of its new changeling from The Ragged School to the Industrial School, a gesture that offers a glimpse of the underlying philosophy of Merchant Regime redistributive policy. The name Ragged School conjured images of Charles Dickens's London. Cleveland was not London. Cleveland's merchants and religious leaders were not so orthodox in their Calvinism that they could accept the notion that these children were foreordained to doomed lives. The words rowdy and rascally were used to describe the boys. The boys were impish but not evil. Words such as hoodlum, thug, or incorrigible were seldom used as prefixes describing these children. Such language implied that the children were sociopaths, a term not yet invented. The rowdy boys seemed redeemable. Personal failure afflicted adults, but a child cared for by an institution acting *in loco parentis* could be put on the right track toward a self-sustaining adulthood. While the Merchant Regime was reluctant to pay for this, it yielded to the moral imperative by building a childcare network of private, quasi-public, and public institutions.

HERALDS OF REGIME SUCCESSION

The Merchant Regime was reluctant to support service distribution and wealth redistribution policies. Services cost money that the regime increasingly did not have, and wealth redistribution was clouded in moral ambiguity. The expansionistic urban growth policy of the regime not only created pressure for service distribution and wealth redistribution, but it also added thousands of new voting residents and a new institutional base that would form the twin forces upending the Merchant Regime.

A Segmented Urban Geography

The growing segmentation of urban society was an important herald of regime succession. Segmentation allowed for the emergence of neighborhood institutions that became constituencies for new directions in urban policy, and this of course worked against the continuation of the Merchant Regime's policy making consensus.[60]

The demographic paradox of early industrial Cleveland was that even as the population nearly doubled every decade, it nevertheless became segmented by place of residence and by the rise of segmented parochial institutions. Neighborhoods were segregated by race, national origin, and occupation. Residential segregation meant social isolation and a growing tendency of each segment in the society to construct its own institutional base. From this base the apparently isolated constituencies drew away from the policy making network of the Merchant Regime.

Merchant Regime urban growth policy transformed Cleveland into two cities, one composed of long-term native born residents and the other composed of the foreign born and the recently arrived native born. In 1870, the foreign born population amounted to 42 percent of the city's 92,829 total. The foreign born were found in each of the city's fifteen wards, but many of the more assimilated foreign arrived during the earlier Irish and German migration of the 1850s. The most recently arrived, the eastern European immigrants, clustered in wards 12 and 14, wards housing the southeast and southwest side industrial districts. Native born Clevelanders lived in close-in wards surrounding the central business district. A silk stocking district was taking shape along Euclid Avenue on the city's east side. Lower status native born Clevelanders, however, were more likely to live on the city's west side than on the east side. Native born, rich and poor, tended to be affiliated with Cleveland's older commercial era businesses, and the newcomers with industrial era businesses.[61]

Occupational grouping yields an even more finely grained pattern of residential segmentation. Entrepreneurs and professionals clustered around their places of business. The growing trend toward the separation of residence and place of work could be seen in the growth of Euclid Avenue silk stocking Ward 15, which was significantly distant from the Flats-area business district and was the place where the new millionaires were building their houses. Clerical workers lived in west side wards close to the central business district. Skilled workers concentrated in just five of the city's fifteen wards. Four of these were outer-ring wards. Two of the outer-ring wards bordered the new industrial districts, two bordered the newly emergent high-income district, and the one inner-ring ward was in the city's old commercial era core. Semi-skilled workers lived in wards bordering the new industrial districts, while unskilled workers were found in a ring of wards encircling the west side beginning near the port of Cleveland and in a second east side ring of wards conforming to the location of the new southeast side manufacturing districts.[62]

These patterns of segmented living reveal an urban physical structure in transition from a classical commercial era configuration to an industrial configuration.[63] In the commercial city, the well-off classes lived closest to the central business district. The preponderance of proprietors, professionals, and clericals lived in these close-in wards. These least well-off in the commercial city—here represented by skilled, semi-skilled, and unskilled workers—lived in the outermost districts of the city. The fact that some proprietors, professionals, and clericals were moving away from the central business district reveals a new industrial configuration of urban space. The physical structure of the city is evidence of Cleveland's industrial era segmentation.

Institutional Heralds of Regime Succession

Cleveland's institutions mirrored the segmentation of society. Institutional segmentation in the late 1870s and early 1880s realigned policy making constituencies and ushered in the Populist Regime and the segmented urban policy associated with it. The institutional metamorphosis worked in three directions. First, merchants holding elective offices in the municipality and school board were replaced by newcomers to the city. Second, the bureaucracies in the policy making network of private, quasi-public, and public institutions gradually came under the sway of the new professionals, elements initially friendly to the Merchant Regime. Third, a new institutional network appeared, mirroring the residential and occupational segmentation of early industrial society in Cleveland. From these institutional bases a new policy making regime would form.

A vital institutional link in the Merchant Regime's policy making network was the municipal government. The municipal charter, which dated from the 1850s, was outmoded twenty years later when the population reached 92,000. The charter limited the mayor to part-time duties. The part-time nature of the position perhaps caused the merchants to not take the position as seriously as they might have. In the late 1870s, the old boy network of caretaker merchant-mayors lost control of the office to a new breed of recently arrived small businessmen, mayors who took their lead from city council. The Merchant Regime responded to this challenge with futile attempts at charter reform. Charter reform backfired when mayors elected in the 1890s under the new charters turned out to be professional politicians with a power base in the new neighborhood institutional network.[64]

The municipal charter dating from the 1850s gave Cleveland a "weak mayor" system of government. Under the weak mayor charter, the executive is essentially a figurehead and the most important powers are reserved for the city council. In the wake of the fiscal crisis triggered by the Panic of 1873, the Merchant Regime lost its dominance in city council to a coalition of small businessmen and professional politicians, the group that coalesced as the Populist Regime. Its emphasis was on improving services, containing urban growth policy, fiscal restraint, and patronage politics in the municipal bureaucracy. By 1878, the merchants had lost their council majority and control over the mayor's office.[65]

At the outset of the Merchant Regime a municipal bureaucracy barely existed, but as service distribution policy assumed a higher priority status, bureaucratic means of policy implementation became imperative. The

Merchant Regime steadily lost control of the expanding bureaucracy. The water and sanitation bureaucracy was controlled by professionals and clerks who communicated directly with their constituencies and who pressured decision makers to spend more money on water and sanitation. The claims of the water and sanitary professionals were difficult to rebut because they were experts and the merchant decision makers were amateurs. The police and fire departments were headed by professionals, but the ethnic favorites of city councilmen formed the rank and file in both departments. In neither instance was the Merchant Regime able to dominate the safety forces.[66]

The public school system presented a similar problem in the late 1870s. Elections during that critical decade changed the composition of the school board from merchants to neighborhood shopkeepers and ordinary citizens, as well as a scattering of the new breed of full-time politicians. The superintendents hired by these newly constituted school boards mouthed the conventional New England Common School pieties but administered the public school system in ways quite baffling to the merchants. The schoolmen introduced the professional ideal to the administration of the system. By 1880, merchants had neither a majority on the school board nor the ability to impose their values on the hireling professional schoolmen.[67]

The private, quasi-public, and public bureaucracies charged with wealth redistribution policy also slipped from the grasp of the Merchant Regime. Here, as above, the professional ideal was the culprit. Because the merchants, and increasingly, entrepreneurs, provided the money to sustain the private and quasi-public network of redistributive agencies, the philanthropic policies of the Merchant Regime died a slower death. The hallmarks of Merchant Regime philanthropy were proselytism and victim blaming. The redistributive service professionals employed in Merchant Regime agencies walked a fine line between tolerating Bible thumping proselytizing and home surveillance and pushing their own agenda for greater commitments of public money and impartial investigations of the social origins of poverty.

Rival religious groups, ethnic mutual aid societies, and neighborhood organizations also emerged to challenge the institutional dominance of the Merchant Regime's redistributive policy network. Public redistributive policy institutions came under the sway of city council and professionals. Under the politicians patronage became a redistributive policy. And public-sector civil service professionals and patronage-rewarded clerks were inclined to dispense with the client means tests so essential to the merchants.[68]

In all, by the early 1880s, the Merchant Regime had lost its grip on the policy making institutional network and was replaced by a new political generation, working class newcomers to the city and professionals. The economic development and urban growth policies of the Merchant Regime unwittingly created a segmented society, and these segments in the late 1870s and early 1880s came to wrest control of the merchants' institutional base from them and launch a policy making regime of their own.

CONCLUSION

For a period of nearly fifty years, a pivotal span bracketed by commercial and industrial revolutions, the Merchant Regime made urban policy in Cleveland. Policy making was a halting yet incremental process that eventually yielded a policy making whole. The issue that clearly generated the most enthusiasm among the merchant policy makers and achieved their highest policy priority was economic development. Economic development policy was also the Merchant Regime's most unequivocal success. It integrated Cleveland into a national transportation network of waterways and rails and made the city's transition into the industrial era possible. The regime's second priority was urban growth policy. Marketplace land use allocation decisions were given a tremendous boost by the regime's urban growth policy of municipal annexation. Urban, rather than rural, land use choices were richly rewarded by the annexation scheme. Annexations not only enlarged the city geographically and demographically, they also added tax revenues and capital which could be diverted into the primary capital circuit funding industrial development. Annexations created demand for infrastructure and distributive services.

The Merchant Regime displayed less enthusiasm and achieved less success in service distribution policy, but gains were made. Bridges, streets, and harbor facilities were built, and at the end of the era, Cleveland had police and fire protection and was committed to solving its water sanitation problem. A clear-cut wealth redistribution policy was blurred by lack of agreement on worthy clients and the causes of poverty, and by an elusive institutional delivery system. It was the Merchant Regime's least successful policy area.

Each of the four policies required institutional delivery vehicles, especially a cooperative municipal government. Because the merchants were full-time businessmen and part-time public officials, the municipality, chartered in 1836, served as an institutional partner in implementing economic development and urban growth policies. The municipality, however, was wholly responsible for building infrastructure and delivering services. As the population grew and became more heterogeneous and increasingly achieved representation in government, the municipality won some measure of independence from the merchants in wealth redistribution policy. The most impressive institutional network—and the model for succeeding regimes—was created to deliver the least successful of the Merchant Regime policies—wealth redistribution. It was a network of public and private agencies that labored in vain to find a common philosophy of charity from which a coherent wealth redistribution policy might flow. The institutional approach, the policy making coalition of private and public organizations, however, would be the wave of the future in urban policy making in Cleveland.

The decline of the Merchant Regime was caused by the unforeseen consequences of its policies. Economic development and urban growth policies made possible an industrial economy and ushered in a heterogeneous industrial society whose members inhabited a greatly enlarged urban geography. Cleveland's newcomer population grew disenchanted with the apparently self-serving urban policy priorities of the Merchant Regime and with the fiscal ruin the merchant–public officials brought to the municipality in the years following the Panic of 1873.

Part Two
The Populist Regime, 1878–1895

2

IDEALS AND POLICY MAKING INSTITUTIONS

The Merchant Regime's failure in the 1870s to change unpopular policy priorities opened the way for the Populist Regime and a new era in urban policy making. The Populist Regime was a pliant weave of middle and working class elements, the policy making emissary of the assertive new segments in the evolving system of social stratification. Populist elements overran old policy making organizations and founded aggressive new organizations. From this institutional setting, the new policy making regime emerged, and for a period of eighteen years it addressed the policy concerns and priorities of the more pluralist society of the late nineteenth century. The Populist Regime, the only regime to rely heavily on the formal mechanisms of government, did what the Merchant Regime refused to do: it slashed municipal budgets for economic development and urban growth and steered policy toward distributive services and redistribution of wealth. This chapter recounts the regime's internecine clash of values and the emergence of a new network of policy making institutions.

AN UNEASY MARRIAGE: PROFESSIONAL AND WORKING CLASS IDEALS

From the beginning the Populist Regime was a regime partitioned by inimical ideals: the universalist professional ideal of middle class professionals, managers, and clerks,[1] and the more parochial working class ideal of native born and foreign born newcomers.[2] These incompatible ideals set the regime ideologically at odds with itself. At the outset, both ideals served a common purpose: residents of Cleveland should be served fairly and impartially by local governmental institutions. Consensus, at the beginning, was achieved on policy priorities. Since Merchant Regime economic development policy satisfied business infrastructure demands, money now could be directed to other policy priorities. And all Populist Regime factions agreed that urban growth policy had been mismanaged by the self-serving merchants and deserved a lower priority status. Most significantly, the new regime censured the merchants' low priority service distribution and wealth redistribution policies as pinch penny and so self-serving that they failed fairly and impartially to serve all constituencies in the city. In the early years of the regime, the twin motivating ideals were more cohesive than divisive.

The glue of the middle class professional ideal was its definition of policy making as an impartial and representative process. The professional ideal drew on the newly current assumption that the industrial environment rather than personal failure bred clients for service distribution and wealth redistribution. Distributive services and wealth redistribution could be delivered efficiently and impartially if management was in the hands of professionals and if more money could be allocated for these policies.

These expressions of professional goals, taken at surface value, also mirrored the aspirations of the working class.[3] But the working class ideal, in contrast to the middle class professional ideal, was a stew of both modern and traditional elements,[4] the latter of which eventually proved incompatible with the modernist professional ideal. However, as long as the modernist element governed workplace relationships and the traditionalist element applied to the neighborhood, the divisions within the working class ideal could be reconciled.[5]

The modernism of the working class ideal followed from the divisions of the workplace into skilled, semi-skilled, unskilled, and idle workers. Workplace challenges were met by labor unions and labor-oriented political organizations and parties. From these organizations came an apparently modern agenda calling for wage and hour regulations; guidelines for the labor of women and children; health, safety, and sanitary standards for the workplace; and some visionary discussion of the proper relationship between government, business, labor, and the citizen, especially the empowerment of workers in local, state, and federal politics. These economic and political agendas gave the working class the appearance of being one of the most progressive elements in American society. This agenda, when it appeared on the printed page rather more so than when it was hand lettered on placards, appealed to the fair-mindedness of middle class professionals.[6]

Less understandable and less susceptible to integration with the professional ideal was the strong traditional component of the working class ideal. Traditionalism in the working class ideal stemmed from the social

Chapter 2: Ideals and Policy Making Institutions   39

divisions of the working class, those of national origin, race, sex, and religion. What the first working class generation had in common was their overwhelmingly rural origins. Many were former agricultural workers with traditional rural values, and rural values buttressed the traditional component of the working class ideal.[7]

Working class traditionalism rested on home, family, church, and neighborhood. These institutions offered continuity and stability in a modernizing world. The workers, American and European alike, migrated from so-called mechanistic societies in which the values of home, family, church, and neighborhood define human behavior in fixed categories grounded in tradition and custom, not in reason, law, contract, or behavioral science. Tradition gave the working class fixed standards and goals and set limits on human aspiration.

The professional ideal, however, had no such sense of limits. It was a boundless ideal buoyed by notions of rationality, choice, change, and limitless potential. The working class ideal dismissed these notions as fantasy, as values and aspirations that, even if true, certainly did not apply to working class people. This was the source of the split between professionals and the working class factions in the Populist Regime, the fault line that ultimately divided the Populist Regime.[8]

A TYPOLOGY OF POLICY SETTING ORGANIZATIONS

The populist era was a transitional period in Cleveland's institutional history. The emerging system of social stratification and the parallel cultural ideals were accommodated, albeit uneasily, by the evolving organizational structure of the early industrial era. New taxonomies of organization emerged which gave expression to the traditional merchant ideal and the modern entrepreneurial and professional ideals as well as the partitioned working class ideal. The resulting organizational network was a patchwork of all four ideals. Several of the modern organizations played awkward host to the regime's rival ideals.

Business Organizations

The business organizations of the industrial era not only transformed the local economy and tied it to the emerging national industrial economy, but they also were the incubators of the entrepreneurial, professional, and working class ideals dominant in the age of industry.

The buoyant merchant ideal was an outgrowth of the countinghouse, the institutional backbone of the Merchant Regime. As a business organization, it played a middleman's role in an economy that transshipped goods from city to regional hinterland and back. Countinghouses were small wholesale jobbing operations owned by individuals, families, or partnerships. Alfred Kelley's was typical: an owner-operated business employing clerks and a small contingent of unskilled laborers to perform loading dock mule work. At one remove were local banks. Banks financed the countinghouses and were keenly interested in the same policy issues as their customers. Countinghouse owners and bankers doubled as the mayors and city councilmen and wed themselves to urban policy driven by transportation infrastructure and boosterism.[9] Boosterism drove countinghouse owners to vigorously support an economic development policy of long-distance transportation connections to link their town, the imaginary new Athens, to an only dimly perceived larger commercial world.

The industrial era transformed the export sector of Cleveland's economy and brought with it new forms of business organization and the new values that would undergird policy making. The first industrial era business organizations, those producing nondurable goods, differed only slightly in ownership, management, and operations from the countinghouse. The key difference was that the nondurable goods manufacturer hired more labor than the countinghouse. But its markets were also local and regional and its interest in policy making was primary in a good regional system of roads.[10]

Large-scale durable goods production gave birth to very different forms of export sector business organization. From the 1870s to the turn of the century, durable goods manufacturing organizations evolved from local family owned businesses, to partnerships, to local corporations, to multi-locational corporations. These new business organizations were founded by visionary, risk-taking entrepreneurs. As these organizations grew, they required sophisticated managerial competencies to solve complex production and distribution problems, compelling founding entrepreneurs to hire professional managers, technicians, and white collar clerks to attend to the details of daily management. These businesses soon evolved into military-like command and control organizations managed by bureaucratic hierarchies. These organizations employed a highly segmented labor force of white and blue collar workers, assigning to each worker a specific task and a specific supervisor. From top to bottom, from middle class white collar manager to working class blue collar laborer, these corporate employees created the professional and working class values of the new entrants in the evolving industrial era system of social stratification.[11]

A modern corporate culture emerged. The late nineteenth century business organization was an incubator for the conflicting ideals of its employees: entrepreneurial, professional, and working class. Ultimately, the professional ideal of managed change triumphed.[12] Professional managers and white collar clerks pioneered imaginative and effective new bureaucratic management techniques for business organizations, techniques which in turn were transferred to bureaucratic units within the municipal government and charitable agencies. The traditional values of the working class, held in check by the industrial corporation, took root in municipal government.[13]

Small businesses, of course, continued to exist in Cleveland, and they typified businesses in the local sector of the economy. In the industrial era, small business owners no longer saw themselves as provincial countinghouse merchants but instead performed as entrepreneurs who, with some hard work and luck, might emerge as the next Rockefellers, Hannas, or Mathers. These men, retailers, building contractors, and small-scale real estate operators, had a large stake in urban growth policy, and these local sector entrepreneurs aggressively lobbied city council to make their voices heard. Local sector businessmen were gamblers who believed in the idea of urban growth at any cost. In the name of growth, these small business entrepreneurs made insistent demands on the municipality on behalf of publicly funded urban growth schemes intended to extend the boundaries of settlement.[14]

After the speculative bubble in urban land burst following the Panic of 1873, for which local growth policy enthusiasts were justly blamed, the Populist Regime held real estate operators and utilities companies at bay until the mid 1880s, when the regime relented and sanctioned privatized urban growth schemes anchored by franchise agreements. These small task driven businesses were not only impatient with the municipality's cumbersome bureaucratic procedures, but they also resented the working class patronage network at city hall.

The Populist Regime made policy when values were in transition from traditional to modern. It was a regime conflicted by merchant, entrepreneurial, professional, and working class values systems. Modern values were manifest in the many types of Cleveland business organizations that the Populist Regime tried and largely failed to bring under its policy making umbrella. But the traditional values of the Populist Regime originated in the neighborhoods.

Neighborhood Colonies and Neighborhood Organizations

Neighborhood colonies supplied the traditional element in the Populist Regime. Within heterogeneous cities are homogeneous colonies or neighborhoods peopled by individuals of similar rankings in the class, status, and power hierarchy. People within these colonies have institutional allegiances, such as membership in a church, and create organizations, such as ethnic social clubs and political ward organizations, and use both to advance their commonly held goals.[15] The geographical layout of the neighborhood colonies was ordered by the newly emerging streetcar system. Colonies formed around the radial streetcar lines like stepping stones in a series of pathways running east and west from the central business and industrial districts, the classic hub and spoke configuration of American cities. Each colony formed its own organizational base from which to influence urban policy.[16]

Neighborhood colonies had political ward organizations, ethnic or American social clubs, churches, saloons, worker organizations, charitable agencies or branches of citywide charitable agencies, and in some cases foreign language newspapers. These organizations were the vessels of the working class ideal represented by city councilmen who were the point men for the working class ideal, the champions of the urban policy priorities of particular neighborhood organizations. But the highly parochial rhetoric of each colony obscured the fact that working class colonies demanded citywide urban policies that were service and neighborhood oriented. From the working class colonies came much of the political pressure to reorder urban policy priorities, trading economic development and urban growth for a greater emphasis on service distribution and wealth redistributions.[17]

Each of Cleveland's working class colonies was a mosaic of policy shaping organizations. The ward clubs, ethnic organizations, churches, and saloons that made up the policy making institutional base of the neighborhoods were anything but professional and bureaucratic. These organizations had one leader, however brief his tenure, and many impatient, combative followers who placed priority on neighborhood service distribution services and wealth redistribution patronage rewards.[18]

The Municipal Government

The institution from which key urban policies ultimately flowed was the municipal government. Organizationally, municipal government was both structurally flawed and ideologically conflicted, externally between the opposing claims of the regime's constituencies and internally by the tension between professional and working class ideals. Nevertheless, the Populist Regime relied more heavily on the formal structure of government than any subsequent urban regime.

The Populist Regime spanned the administrations of nine mayors (1879–1900) who served under two city charters (1852 and 1892). Cleveland's municipal charter of 1852 was a "weak mayor" system of government that gave the city's chief executive officer few policy making or administrative powers. The mayor's duties were limited to presiding over city council meetings, compiling the annual reports of the city's departments, and making policy recommendations to city council in the annual address.

The 1852 city charter awarded real administrative authority to an unwieldy network of elective and appointive supervisory boards, commissions, and committees. Those who served on them were a band of unpaid elected officials, citizen appointees, councilmen, and career public servants, appointed variously by the mayor, the council, local judges, county commissioners, and the governor. Administratively, the boards, commissions, and committees were accountable to no one. They were required only to present an annual report to the mayor, which he in turn submitted to the city council.[19]

Budget making and taxation were the responsibility of city council. In annual addresses to the city council, mayors attempted to set policy priorities with budget and tax rate recommendations. Although the mayor's policy guidelines and budgetary and revenue advice were sometimes heeded, the city council was more than capable of frustrating mayoral pretensions to leadership with independent action. Neither the mayor, nor the city council, nor the boards, commissions, and committees were legally accountable for the monies spent by the municipality.[20]

Because accountability was lax, fiscal abuses and outright incompetence were frequent and frustrating. Mayoral pleas to council for support on charter reform were ignored, as were other attempts to reform the system. In 1873 Mayor Charles A. Otis argued that a measure of administrative accountability from the boards, commissions, and committees could be achieved if the members' services were paid for rather than volunteered. "Gratuitous service," Otis warned, "is expensive."[21] His successor, Nathan Perry Payne, rejected the idea of paid commission members, claiming that "It should be a source of great pride to every citizen of Cleveland that her best men are glad to serve on her various boards and commissions without pecuniary compensation."[22]

A few years later, the Populist Regime removed Cleveland's "best men" from the various boards, commissions, and committees. Cleveland's first Populist mayor, R. R. Herrick, explained this situation by saying that the city government was obligated to be representative of the city's various neighborhood colonies and their "peculiar ideas."[23] Viewing this rationalization from four years' distance and considerable experience as a city councilman, Mayor John H. "Honest John" Farley[24] disclosed that the lack of mayoral power and failed oversight by the appointed boards resulted in a situation in which the city council was besieged at budget time by utility company lobbyists and by city departments packed with patronage appointees.[25]

By the late 1880s, mayoral impotence was the object of gallows humor. Mayor George W. Gardner likened the mayor to "a ship's figurehead, except that he is animate."[26] In 1888, Mayor Brenton D. Babcock took leave of office, "Being still of the opinion that numerous recommendations and voluminous matter in the annual message will be little favored and as little heeded by your body (the city council), that your patience may not be wearied nor you be permitted to lapse in slumbers of forgetfulness, I shall claim your attention for a few minutes only while performing my last official act and bidding you a final adieu."[27]

Mayor Babcock noted that city council was not the only obstacle: "There is but little opportunity for the nominal chief executive to render valuable service to the general public" because "nearly every executive department of the city government is practically independent...."[28] During the scandal-plagued Gardner administration (1885–86, 1889–1891), the habitually absent City Treasurer Thomas Axworthy at last turned up in Canada sporting a bankroll of $500,000, money he had "borrowed" from the city treasury. Even after a year of angry finger pointing, the combatants failed to untangle Axworthy's bureaucratic lines of accountability.[29]

The bureaucracy was not only independent of the mayor and city council; it was also conflicted by incompatible class ideals. Administrative departments grew only by grudging accretions during the Merchant Regime, but the Populists gleefully added employees to pay off political obligations and dispense city services. Experts in accounting, engineering, and public health were added to the city's payroll at the same time as deserving friends of city councilmen were hired as clerks and laborers. The experts were guided by the professional ideals and the patronage employees were guided by the working class populist ideal.[30]

Some administrative departments were segregated by ideal, but when a mingling of the conflicting ideals took place within a single key department, friction was inevitable. In the police department, for example, a hierarchy of professional officers supervised the work of beat-walking patronage employees. The police department was administered through a paramilitary line and staff system of command and accountability. It was independent of the mayor and virtually independent of the Police Commission. The department policy and procedures manual provided a job description for each position in the organizational hierarchy, detailing responsibilities and lines of authority and accountability. The chain of command ran from the police superintendent to captains, lieutenants, detectives, sergeants, and patrolmen. Higher ranking line officers were aided by staff assistants. The higher ranking line officers and staff assistants were professionals, while most sergeants and virtually all patrolmen were patronage appointees.[31]

The bureaucratization of public safety exasperated populist Mayor John H. Farley because it sacrificed neighborhood service delivery at the altar of managerial apparatus. Sergeants, he complained, were too preoccupied supervising patrolmen to arrest a disorderly drunk. "We also have detectives, too proud and too capable for drunks and disorderlies" and lieutenants "who keep watch over empty station houses."[32] Farley defined a captain as a man of a rank so "unfortunate that it deprives the public of his services" and charged that the superintendent and assistant superintendents were men whose ambitions and rank exempted them from making arrests. Farley added that the hierarchy, the job descriptions, the detailed responsibilities, and the lines of authority and accountability created some policemen "splendid in their contempt for other grades, jealous of the rest of the force and of each other."[33]

Farley's plea was for replacing the cumbersome managerial apparatus with neighborhood patrolmen free to arrest criminals, corral the disorderly, and make the neighborhoods safe for decent citizens. Honest John Farley's plea went unheeded. The working class ideal of Mayor Farley assumed delivery of neighborhood services with a minimum of bureaucratic fuss. He blamed bureaucracy for elevating some men above others without apparent reason and for obscuring the mission of the police and other departments in a jumble of rules, policies, and procedures.[34]

Charter reform was at last embraced as the antidote to the weak mayor system. A new "Federal" charter, awarded by the state legislature in 1891, was enthusiastically supported by businessmen and professionals who trumpeted the new charter as the stake in the heart of Cleveland's mounting legacy of bad government. The Federal charter, so labeled because it was grounded in the principle of separation of executive, legislative, and judicial functions, created a strong mayor system. The mayor was at last empowered to appoint his own cabinet of municipal department heads (subject to the approval of city council). Businesslike management accountability was expected to follow.³⁵

It did not. The Federal charter served, among other things, to reorder the power relationships among Cleveland populist politicians. Until the advent of the Federal charter, leadership in both political parties was dominated by Cleveland city councilmen. The parties, then as now, were devoid of principle and were too myopic and self-serving to see policy making whole. Party leaders were immersed in the remunerative particulars of distributive policy, patronage, franchise awards to utilities, and municipal service contracts to their friends in the neighborhoods. The party rank and file, composed of subaltern city councilmen and precinct committeemen, seldom challenged the leadership because they were divided against each other by ward and neighborhood turf wars.

But the appointive power granted to the mayor by the Federal charter vaulted the municipal chief executive to center stage in the fractious environment of local party politics. From 1892 forward, the mayor of Cleveland was a force to be reckoned with in party councils. Populist mayor Robert E. McKisson seized upon the advantages bestowed upon the mayoral office by the charter and built a powerful patronage network among workers at City Hall. In this he was aided by Harry "Czar" Bernstein, a city councilman and neighborhood boss whose power in party councils was decidedly second rank to the mayor. But even a powerful political "boss" under the Federal charter could not improve the operations of Cleveland's municipal government.³⁶ The strong mayor system made the mayor "stronger" and subdued but did not tame city council.

A major aspect in both the 1852 and 1892 city charters, and a major factor in the longevity of the Populist Regime, was the that the charters facilitated the proliferation of wards. In 1860, Cleveland's 43,417 residents lived in eleven wards. In 1890, Cleveland's 261,353 residents lived in forty-three wards. The increase in the number of wards may be viewed simply as a consequence of a sixfold population increase, but more pointedly, the proliferation of wards was a direct result of the Merchant Regime's growth policy of annexation, for each annexed settled territory became a new city ward. The increase in the number of city councilmen coupled with the weak mayor charter meant that the city council would be the body most responsible for making urban policy during much of the Populist Regime. The voices of the neighborhoods were never more clearly heard than during the Populist Regime. The strong mayor Federal charter might have entirely silenced the voices of the neighborhoods but for the proliferation of wards. The policy preferences of the neighborhoods continued to be heard in Cleveland City Council until a series of lawsuits and charter reforms in the first decade of the twentieth century attempted to introduce nonpartisan elections, at-large representation, and a reduction in the number of wards from forty-two to twenty-six.[37]

The organizational base and the sustaining value system of Populist Regime Cleveland were in a state of transition. Business organizations were making the transition from commercial era countinghouses to industrial era corporations, but the process was not yet complete. An ideal appropriate to the function of the industrial era business had yet to evolve. Which of the three contending ideals—entrepreneurial, professional, or working class—was the right ideal for guiding the industrial business organization into the new century? The municipal government, the institutional offspring of the merchant ideal, was wholly inadequate as a policy making vehicle for the industrial city. The municipal government was structurally flawed, but it was also split by the incompatible professional and working class ideals. The professional ideal of middle class managers seeped into the municipality from the industrial corporations. The traditional element of the working class ideal entered from the neighborhood organizations that elected the city councilmen, who in effect ran the city and set policy priorities. During the Populist Regime attempts at reforming existing organizations and reconciling ideals proved futile, so the regime made do with the institutional base it had. Nevertheless, the Populist Regime was able to reorder policy priorities even if operational consistency was elusive.

3

ECONOMIC DEVELOPMENT AND URBAN GROWTH DEVALUED

Continued economic development seemed certain to Populist Regime decision makers, even if they were uncertain about the direction it would take. As a result, much of the energy of the Populist Regime was given over to managing the unforeseen distributive and redistributive consequences of the Merchant Regime urban growth policy of annexation. What followed was a rapid reordering of priorities. Just how rapid the reordering was can be seen in the municipal budget.

THE MUNICIPAL BUDGET AS A GUIDE TO POLICY CHANGE

Deep Throat, Bob Woodward's unidentified nocturnal informant, advised the young reporter "to follow the money" to the end of the Watergate mystery. By following the money, we track the passing of the Merchant Regime but also the sudden shift in policy priorities made by the emergent Populist Regime.

The money in this case was legitimately in the Cleveland municipal budget. The municipal budget, however, was a tattered laundry list of two dozen or more line items perversely arranged in alphabetical order. When the line items are rearranged under more useful taxonomies corresponding to the four areas of urban policy, trends announcing a realignment of policy priorities are evident. For our purposes, the budget taxonomies are Economic Development and Urban Growth, Service Distribution, Wealth Redistribution, and Interest. The 1870 and the 1880 budgets can now be compared in terms of total expenditures and in terms of the new taxonomies (table 3.1). Comparison discloses a shift in regime policy priorities.[1]

TABLE 3.1
Municipal budgets, 1870 and 1880 (values in $1,000)

Budget Category	1870	Percentage of Budget	1880	Percentage of Budget	Percentage Increase
Development and Growth	279.5	43.2	295.5	22.9	>5.7
Distribution	176.2	27.2	461.4	35.9	>167.8
Redistribution	14.0	2.0	39.0	3.0	>178.6
Interest	101.5	15.6	402.0	31.3	>296.0
Total	571.2		1,200		>110.0
Per Capita Expenditures	$6.97		$8.00		>14.8
Per Capita Debt	$26.93		$62.05		>130.4

Source: See Methodological Note 1.

The Merchant Regime practiced a tightfisted fiscal policy in 1870. The $6.97 per capita spending figure was among the lowest rates in the country. When compared to such places as New York, Philadelphia, or Boston, the per capita debt carried by the city pales to insignificance. The merchants took considerable pride in their vigilance over the public purse.

The budget also clearly spells out the policy priorities of the Merchant Regime. In 1870, the Merchant Regime spent money primarily on Economic Development and Urban Growth, some 43 percent of the budget. Service Distribution—the money spent on such services as police and fire protection and water supply—was a distant second line priority, amounting to only 27 percent of the budget, even after two decades of public pressure to improve these services.

The 1880 budget, by contrast, displays a stunning reversal of urban policy priorities. Economic Development and Urban Growth declined from 43 percent of the 1870 budget to just 23 percent of the 1880 budget. Service Distribution increased from 27 percent to 36 percent. The dollar increases are even more imposing. Economic Development and Urban Growth spending increased by only $16,000 during the decade; but the dollars spent on Service Distribution swelled by $285,200, a 162 percent increase over 1870. The per capita budget increased only 14.7 percent during the decade, underscoring the radical reordering of the line item policy priorities from Economic Development and Urban Growth to the new emphasis on Service Distribution.

Not all the new spending could be met from current revenues. Debt also increased. Money spent on debt service increased fourfold over the decade, and per capita debt increased 130 percent from $26.93 to $62.05. Some of this borrowed money went to finance the water system, which supported the fire department and sanitation. The remainder financed such urban growth infrastructure projects as bridges, street extensions, paving, and lighting. The money trail led to a new array of policy priorities.

ECONOMIC DEVELOPMENT POLICY

The commercial era economy was nearly a relic when the Populist Regime took power in the late 1870s, but the new industrial order still had not come into full flower. Manufacturing was the wave of the future, a trend that had been evident since the 1850s, but manufacturing itself was at a crossroads. Would Cleveland be a manufacturing center of durable or nondurable goods? Populist Regime economic development policy was inhibited by this uncertainty. An economic development policy in support of a nondurable goods manufacturing sector was quite different from an economic development policy supporting durable goods manufacturing. As the industrial era unfolded, it became apparent that durable and nondurable goods would be produced on altogether different organizational scales. Nondurable goods manufacturing organizations proved substantially smaller in scale than the giant organizations manufacturing durables.

Small-scale organizations producing nondurable goods are usually locally owned. Organizations manufacturing durable goods evolved into corporations owned by anonymous stockholders and directed from corporate headquarters by professional managers. The policy making implication of these two very different forms of business organization is that in cities producing nondurable goods economic development policy is locally controlled because the owners live locally and their capital is immobile. Multilocational corporations, in contrast, ordinarily represent mobile capital and out-of-town headquarters decision making. Economic development policy, accordingly, is no longer local; it is made at corporate headquarters. This transition in the business organization was taking place during the Populist Regime.[2]

Whatever the future might hold for the city's economy, the incoming Populist Regime assumed policy making authority in the midst of a fiscal crisis and believed that the merchants had devoted entirely too much energy and treasure to economic development policy. The casual observer could see that the economic development policies of the Merchant Regime transformed Cleveland's export sector from commerce to industry. Entrepreneurial activity, an important indicator of adding new work to old work in the export sector, seemed robust, and the city's capital resources were employed in investments encouraging forward and backward linkages from existing industries.³

These achievements won Cleveland stature as a national manufacturing center. Still, the type of manufacturing city Cleveland would become remained murky during the entire Populist Regime.⁴ The censuses of 1860, 1870, 1880, and 1890 reported that Cleveland's economy was split between more than a dozen varieties each of durable and nondurable goods manufacturers. Nondurable goods manufacturing was represented in the food products industry, an example of Cleveland's ability to turn its agricultural hinterland to industry. Regionally available lumber and mineral resources provided the base upon which Cleveland's earliest durable goods industries were built. Lumber from the upper Great Lakes supplied the city's cooperage, sash and door, broom and brush, furniture, and paper industries. Ore and coal imports sustained the primary metals and fabricated metal products industries. The Civil War stimulated both durable and nondurable goods export sector manufacturing activity, and Merchant Regime economic development policy advanced both forms in the decades following the war.⁵

Durable vs. Nondurable Goods

Durable and nondurable goods manufacturing, however, were quite different types of export sector activity. Specialization in one or the other export sector activity would bind the city to very different economic futures.⁶ Each made very different public policy demands, particularly for infrastructure. Durable goods industries made heavy infrastructure demands, while nondurable goods industries made only modest demands on the treasury for infrastructure.⁷

Which industrial activity was the wave of the future? Which was more valuable to the city? To understand the importance of these questions to local policy makers some sense must be made of nineteenth century business statistics, especially those describing the export sector of the local economy. The export sector of the economy is important because it stimulates local factors of production and spins off a wide range of service activities. Economists call this the multiplier effect, an economic phenomenon measured by a statistic called value added.

Value added measures the local multiplier effect of a given industry, the difference, in short, between materials costs paid by the local manufacturer at the outset and the price received when the finished product is sold. Value added dollars flow to local factors of production, and local trend watchers followed these statistics very carefully. A derivative business statistic, value

TABLE 3.2
VAPE for durable and nondurable goods by decade: The United States and Cleveland, 1860–1920.

Category	1860	1870	1880	1890	1900	1910	1920
U.S. Durables	761	637	680	851	960	1,042	1,285
Cleveland Durables	845	778	854	967	1,362	1,614	2,251
U.S. Nondurables	504	606	717	1,051	1,204	1,282	1,442
Cleveland Nondurables	747	658	628	1,205	1,154	1,217	1,488

Source: See Methodological Note 5.

added per employee (VAPE), is a shorthand method for making comparisons of the multiplier effect of various industries. VAPE is calculated by dividing value added in an industry by the number of employees in the same industry. If VAPE is to be a meaningful barometer of the local importance of an industry, VAPE for the local industry must be higher than the VAPE of the same industry nationally. Table 3.2 shows VAPE for durable and nondurable goods, comparing Cleveland in both categories to the country.

The Declining Fortunes of Nondurable Goods Manufacturing

Durable and nondurable goods VAPE figures reveal some disparate patterns. The disparities between durable and nondurable goods figures reveal the reasons behind the uncertainty of economic development policy early in the Populist Regime and cast light on the path that the city's economic development policy eventually followed. Cleveland durable and nondurable goods VAPE ratios reveal complex patterns of local development and local multiplier effects. The nondurable goods VAPE ratio shows Cleveland at best at par with national nondurable VAPE and generally, with each passing decade, lower than national trends for nondurables, meaning that the local multiplier effect of value added in nondurables was weak and sinking fast. Durable goods VAPE reveals a significantly different pattern. After two decades of uncertainty, local durable goods VAPE skyrocketed above national averages and sealed the economic development future of Cleveland. This significant trend did not become obvious until the decade of the 1890s, just as the Populist Regime was ending.

Chapter 3: Economic Development and Urban Growth Devalued   53

In 1860, however, Cleveland's undeniable industrial specialty was nondurable goods manufacturing. Table 3.2 shows that VAPE in 1860 was fifty points higher than the national average, indicating a high degree of local specialization and a strong local multiplier effect. The majority of the city's manufacturing workers were employed in nondurable goods industries. During the next twenty years, however, value added per employee declined steadily in nondurable goods industries. More ominous was Cleveland's position relative to urban nondurable goods competitors. By 1880, VAPE declined from fifty points above to twelve points below the national average. The city's competitive advantage in nondurable goods production evaporated in the brief period of two decades. Cleveland's first nondurable goods high VAPE manufacturing enterprises—liquors, tobacco products, bread and bakery, and meat slaughtering—were linked to nearby agricultural production. As the urbanization of the nation advanced, food products manufacturing proved to be as ubiquitous as agriculture itself, and Cleveland during the decade of the 1870s lost its initial competitive advantage in the food products industry.

The city gained a respite in nondurable goods production during the 1880s when John D. Rockefeller headquartered his oil refining business in Cleveland. In that decade Cleveland became the nation's oil refining capital and built impressive forward linkages to chemicals and other allied industries. Initial advantage in the oil refining industry proved to be short-lived when Rockefeller, pressured by marketing and distribution considerations and the legal implications of the Sherman Anti-Trust Act, decentralized his refining operations to other cities in other states. Crude oil does not have to be refined near the wellhead if cheap transportation can be arranged to bring it closer to final markets. This Rockefeller was able to do with his own pipelines and preferential agreements with rail shippers. His competitors in time followed suit and the nation's oil refining capacity quickly decentralized from Cleveland to final market locations.[8] The result was that Cleveland's nondurable goods VAPE ratios slipped well below the nation's during the decade of the 1890s. By the turn of the century, Cleveland's earliest and most promising high VAPE nondurable goods industries were almost nonexistent.

Durable Goods: An Uncertain Beginning

As nondurable goods manufacturing declined, durable goods manufacturing made only halting advances (see table 3.2). Businesses initiated by imported timber gave Cleveland its first high VAPE durable goods manu-

TABLE 3.3
Employees in durable vs. nondurable goods industries by decade, 1860–1920

Category	1860	1870	1880	1890	1900	1910	1920
Durables	1,135	2,509	7,682	14,899	22,086	32,662	50,260
Nondurables	1,285	1,834	3,176	6,863	9,762	18,285	25,457

Source: See Methodological Note 5.

facturing activity in lumber products in the middle decades of the century. Yet in 1890, the lumber products industry was dead. The reasons were just the reverse of those causing the parallel decline in the city's oil refining industry. Neither resource—oil or timber—is ubiquitous, but the weight and value of the final product combine in such unique ways as to encourage the lumber products industry to locate as close as practicable to sources of raw materials, whereas oil refining locates near final markets. The timber states beckoned the lumber products industry, and Cleveland soon could not compete with factories located close by timber resources.[9]

Table 3.3 shows that in 1860 slightly more workers were employed in nondurable than in durable goods industries; however, a decade later it was apparent the employment advantage was shifting in favor of durable goods metals industries. Railroad repair in the 1850s and the Civil War in the 1860s provided the initial momentum for the metals industry in Cleveland. Metals making was the first durable goods metals industry, and in the next decades metals making spawned related metals fabricating and finished metals products industries.[10] A breakthrough occurred in the 1870s when employment in durable goods industries permanently shifted to a more than a two-to-one advantage over employment in nondurable goods industries. It seemed that Cleveland's economic development future was in durable goods manufacturing.

That future, however, was difficult to foresee during the two decades the Populist Regime was in power because, even though employment figures looked promising, the all important VAPE in durable goods manufacturing did not become commanding until the 1890s when the Populist Regime was slipping from power. Although the durable to nondurable goods employment figures looked impressive to readers of the 1880 census, these same tables informed readers that value added per employee grew laggardly and would continue to do so during the next decade when VAPE actually declined. These were the economic tea leaves populist policy makers considered.

Chapter 3: Economic Development and Urban Growth Devalued   55

The Policy Impact of Ambiguous Economic Development Trends

Uncertainty over the course of economic development was reflected in the municipal budget. In the heyday of the Merchant Regime, municipal spending for economic development reached a high of 13 percent. During the Populist Regime, this percentage tumbled to less than 5 percent of the budget.[11] The declines in municipal spending were a reflection of three things. First, because it had other policy priorities, the Populist Regime was less willing to spend on economic development. Second, the public policy needs of durable goods and nondurable goods industries are quite different, and decision makers, for reasons explained above, were uncertain about which policy course to follow. Third, the Cleveland economy apparently was in the grip of the growth pole effect (discussed below), an enigmatic business phenomenon that puzzled and divided populist policy makers.

A Populist Regime article of faith was that businessmen should make business decisions not necessarily because businessmen are divinely ordained to do so but because there are boundaries and limits to what government ought to do on behalf of any supplicant. Business rhetoric dovetailed with populist policy and provided the regime with a convenient rationale for not spending on economic development. Businessmen tirelessly lectured populist public officials about the need for businessmen to make business decisions without interference from public authorities. The rhetoric of business was decidedly anti-government and, by implication, anti-populist. Businessmen preached a doctrine of market-driven decision making. Epiphanies on labor relations conjured similar images. Workers should not organize; the workplace relationship was individual to individual, owner to worker, each party bargaining from the high moral high ground of fairness and equity. Governments should not tamper with these inviolable relationships. Government attempts to tax business enterprise were likewise defamed as confiscatory and parasitical. Money so taken was money not invested in improved plant or higher wages for labor. The Populist Regime responded to the surface message rather than the deeper theological content of business rhetoric.[12] If business needed money spent on such infrastructure requirements as river dredging and harbor improvement, then perhaps the money spent should come from their pockets and not those of the taxpayers. Municipal budgets reflected the attitude.[13]

Even so, when the Populist Regime did allocate public money for economic development, policy makers were confused about the needs of business. As noted above, the regime's bewilderment was a product of the uncertainty over Cleveland's future in durable or nondurable goods production. Each course had unique public policy implications. Nondurable goods were manufactured from locally and regionally available raw materials and finished products (oil excepted) and were sold locally and regionally. In the food products industry, for example, raw materials came by road from the surrounding agricultural hinterland. These perishable commodities journeyed by highway directly to processing plants, bypassing wharves and warehouses. The production turnaround time was relatively short, after which the finished food product was retailed in the city or sold back to customers in the countryside. The public policy priority of the agricultural products industry was a reliable regional system of roads.[14] Road construction and maintenance were the responsibility of the county and the state, not the municipality.

Similar infrastructure prerequisites prevailed in the lumber products industry. Although timber came by water from the distant north woods of Michigan, lumber products manufacturers preferred not to keep expensive, bulky inventories on hand. The turnaround time for a finished lumber product was, as in the food industry, relatively short. The lake and the river were important for raw materials sourcing, but wharves and warehouses were not. Finished lumber products were sold in the same markets as food products. The public policy requirements of both industries were similar: a reliable system of roads.[15]

Oil was a very different industry. But in terms of publicly financed infrastructure needs, the oil industry was self-sufficient. During the brief period in the 1880s when Cleveland was an oil refining boomtown, John D. Rockefeller made precious few demands on the municipal purse because he supplied his own infrastructure. Rockefeller brought his crude oil from the Pennsylvania wellhead to Cleveland refineries in pipelines he built, and he shipped his finished product by rail to final markets under exacting contractual arrangements he personally negotiated with the companies. He was a businessman that a populist policy maker could admire.[16]

In brief, nondurable goods industries had minimal infrastructure requirements. If Cleveland's business future was in nondurable goods, as seemed probable at the outset of the Populist Regime, then the municipality was not obligated to spend large sums of money in its support.

Durable goods manufacturing in primary metals was an altogether different matter. Metals making operations consumed southern Ohio coal by the carload and kept the Great Lakes dotted with ore boats during the open water months. If metals making was to be a twelve month a year enterprise, the huge inventories of coal and ore would have to be stored locally. Lakeside docking and unloading facilities were needed and so too was a river

TABLE 3.4
VAPE for primary metals vs. metals fabricating by decade, 1860–1920

Category	1860	1870	1880	1890	1900	1910	1920
Primary Metals	1,267	885	892	883	1,876	1,230	1,145
Fabricated Metals	822	802	745	803	982	1,183	1,324

Source: See Methodological Note 5.

dredged deep enough to accommodate lakegoing ore vessels. The Merchant Regime made liberal investments in these facilities. The Populist Regime spurned them.[17]

An odd coupling of business and politics helps explain the Populist Regime's reluctance to spend money on economic development. Although primary metals industries were important to Cleveland during the Populist Regime, the value added dollars generated were small relative to demands on the public purse. In primary metals industries, VAPE was stagnant during the years the Populist Regime was making economic development policy (table 3.4).

In 1880, barely into the Populist Regime's tenure, VAPE in the metals fabricating component of the metals industry experienced an increase that the Populist Regime took to be permanent. Metals fabricating proved to be permanent, but the advantage in VAPE did not. Primary metals making made an enduring comeback late in the 1890s. Populist Regime policy makers anticipated stagnant VAPE in primary metals and growing long term VAPE in metals fabrication.

The assumption was critical for economic development policy making. Metals fabricating operations are not dependent on bulky waterborne imports of raw materials. Metals fabricating operations, therefore, did not require river dredging, hydraulic bridges, wharves, docks, and breakwaters. The products consumed and produced by metals fabricating plants entered and left the city by rail. If the city's future was in metals fabricating rather than metals making, then the expensive infrastructure investments necessary to sustain a metals making industry were not necessary. The populists did not see that the two industries were linked.

The Populist Regime concluded that the necessary infrastructure investments in support of a now stagnant metals making industry had been completed in the 1870s by the Merchant Regime and decided that a new round of investment in metals making infrastructure was a foolish waste of taxpayer dollars. In 1878, Populist Regime Mayor Rensselaer Russell Herrick declared in his inaugural address that "nothing so effectively strangles manufacturing and all business enterprises as a high rate of taxation."[18] This statement established the fiscal boundaries of Populist Regime urban policy. Budgets would be cut and tax rates would be lower. As good as his word, the Herrick administration implored a receptive city council to reduce budgets and lower taxation, cutting in half the annual budget for economic development schemes. Succeeding administrations won even greater reductions in the economic development budget.

When the Populist Regime reached midpassage, mayors John H. Farley and George Gardner served notice on their fellow populists in city council that retrenchment in economic development policy had gone far enough. Farley warned that the "river must be dredged to accommodate the needs of factories that have moved up river."[19] His warnings fell on deaf ears, and in 1884 the city council cut economic development spending still more. In 1886, Mayor Gardner sounded a new call of alarm. He told the council that "We have suffered loss by reason of our failure to keep pace with other Lake Erie ports in the matter of improvements, thereby losing trade that naturally belongs here."[20] Competing lake cities—Lorain, Elyria, Ashtabula, Conneaut, and Erie—captured large shares of the city's coal and ore import trade because Cleveland failed to keep pace with river and harbor improvements.[21]

When former Merchant Regime mayor W. G. Rose was elected to another tour of duty in 1891, under the terms of the new anti-populist Federalist municipal charter, he delivered an obituary for Populist Regime economic development policy. A throwback to the bygone days of Merchant Regime economic development policy, Mayor Rose castigated the city council and the railroad companies for failure to dredge the river to the city limits and to build docks and wharves on the river and lake banks. The railroads he blamed for not building unloading facilities for ore and coal. When city council rationalized its failure to act on lakefront improvements because of the legal uncertainty over who owned the lakefront land, the city or the railroads, Rose challenged the legislators to take the railroads into court to resolve the land title issue. In the meantime, he ordered the city council to soldier on with river dredging and harbor improvements east of Erie Street (E. 9th). "The future prosperity and greatness of the city," he warned, "largely depend upon the firm maintenance of a broad policy with respect to our harbors and approaches thereto."[22]

Rose's inaugural address put more pressure on city council by defining the infrastructure situation as an emergency, but City Council refused to be pressured or intimidated either by Rose, Mayor Blee (in 1893), or Mayor

Chapter 3: Economic Development and Urban Growth Devalued   59

McKisson (in 1895).[23] Council failed to act for a number of reasons. After the strong mayor charter reform of 1892, the responsibility for bringing suit against the railroads belonged to the law director, not the city council.[24] Various mayoral administrations dragged their feet on the confrontation, and even after suit was brought, the legal battles with the railroads dragged on inconclusively for three decades. Though the mayor's office passed from populist control in the mid 1890s, the populists lingering in city council had no interest in spending on economic development. The council was reluctant to tax all businesses and all residents to support the interests of one business, the metals making industry. The low VAPE data reported early in the 1890s reinforced the view that the metals making industry was stagnant or dying and not worth the infrastructure investment (though, as noted, the patient made a dramatic recovery later in the decade—see table 3.3).

The six mayors from Payne to McKisson buried city council in data showing that rival lake ports were importing more iron and coal than Cleveland. In fact, the data from Elyria, Ashtabula, Conneaut, and Erie could be read in three ways: (1) as evidence of Cleveland's impending economic doom, as the mayors claimed; or (2) that this was the "growth pole effect," an inevitable trend in Cleveland's economic evolution and was therefore no cause for alarm; or (3) that these cities, especially the three east of Cleveland, were in fact the lake ports of Pittsburgh, a rival metals making city which consumed at least as much iron ore as Cleveland. Mayors Payne, Farley, Gardner, Rose, Blee, and McKisson followed the economic doom interpretation of these data and used it to bludgeon city council into spending more money on infrastructure for the metals making industry. When the council refused, the mayors were despondent.

The second interpretation was the "growth pole effect," economic jargon not in use then but an occurrence common in Cleveland's nineteenth century business history.[25] In the early stages of economic development an urban center favored by strong transportation connections, such as Cleveland's to agriculture, timber, and oil, will, like a magnet or growth pole, attract all manner of productive elements, raw materials, labor, entrepreneurial talent, and capital. New businesses and new industries form quickly and indiscriminately. Backward and forward linkages between businesses readily form in like magnetic fashion. Then something happens: a threshold is reached, and the magnet reverses its poles and spins off to other venues the very businesses that brought the city its early prosperity. Historically, the reverse growth pole effect propelled such nondurable goods industries as food products and oil refining from Cleveland to other centers, leaving such forward linkage or spin-off industries as chemicals

60   Part Two: The Populist Regime, 1878–1895

behind. Spin-off industries, such as chemicals, remain and spin off businesses of their own, such as paints and varnishes, which together keep the export sector of the local economy developing.[26]

It was reasonable for populist policy makers to assume that the same process could happen in the metals making industry. Metals making had already spun off high VAPE industries in metals processing (rolled steel) and metals fabrication (rails, wire, screws, and nuts and bolts). The growth pole effect, it appeared, was now discarding the metals making industry from Cleveland to rival lake cities where ore and coal could be brought in by water and rail more conveniently and at a lower cost. If it was natural and inevitable for the metals making industry to leave Cleveland, then it made little sense to lavish money on the infrastructure needs of a departing industry.

The mayors and other alarmists refused to acknowledge that the eastern Lake Erie cities recording more iron shipments than Cleveland were, in fact, the lake ports of Pittsburgh, which, despite its distance from the lake, trumped Cleveland in primary metals production.

If Cleveland was losing its base in metals making, the infrastructure needs of the emerging industries in metals processing and metals fabrication were for land for factory sites and land for inner belt rail connections rather than expensive river dredging and dock, wharf, and warehouse construction. Land for factory sites served by rails fell under the rubric of urban growth policy.

AN URBAN GROWTH POLICY OF RETRENCHMENT

The high-priority status of Merchant Regime urban growth policy was dealt a serious blow by the Populist Regime budgetary meat ax just as growth policy was growing more complex and more vital to the quality of life led by Clevelanders. The Populist Regime slashed urban growth policy budgets because the Merchant Regime's growth policy of indiscriminate annexations placed severe demands on the incoming Populist Regime for distributive services to the newly annexed areas.[27]

The Consequences of Merchant Regime Growth Policy

Hidden in the Merchant Regime's urban growth policy of push and pull factor annexations were a variety of buried costs and suspect practices. Push factor annexations gave the city vacant land that would not be brought into use for years. Pull factor annexations brought in factories that, after the Panic of 1873, were laying off rather than hiring workers. Both forms of annexed territory demanded and received municipal outlays for distributive services, streets, paving, water, sewer, gas, and electricity. In its haste to bring the land into the municipality, the city paid far too much for these improvements, which now connected the city to vacant land and shuttered factories. Municipal budgets soared during the depression that followed the Panic and so too did the city's bonded indebtedness.[28] When the Populist Regime assumed policy making authority, the day of urban growth policy fiscal reckoning was at hand.

The day of reckoning was highlighted by acrimonious, finger pointing debates within the municipal government. Hapless mayors were charged by incoming Populist councilmen with lax administration, while the remaining Merchant city councilmen were libeled as obtusely compliant if not corrupt.[29] The corruption charge stemmed from the fact that many members of the Merchant Regime were not simply merchants; they were also owners of the land on which the city was built. Eager to increase the value of their holdings via annexation and equally eager to shift the cost of the utilities serving the land from themselves to the city, the merchant estate holder/public officials had dipped liberally into the municipal purse for public improvements and shared culpability for the increasing budgets and bonded indebtedness the city found itself with late in the 1870s. Smaller holders of real estate, following the lead of the merchants, also reaped a share of the bounty. Small building contractors and upstart real estate operators devised highly imaginative schemes for converting taxpayer money to operating capital.[30]

The excesses of Merchant Regime growth policy can be graphed in tax and municipal budget increases, debt accumulation, and annual operating deficits. Between 1871 and 1876, taxes increased 60 percent, ensuring the political unpopularity necessary to unseat the Merchant Regime. The municipal budget more than doubled, and the lion's share of the monies flowed into growth-related schemes. Because expenditures grew at a steeper pace than revenues, deficits became chronic during the years of excess, peaking at 40 percent of the budget in 1876. Deficits and capital expenditures both were financed with bond issues. The city's bonded debt increased more than twofold between 1871 and 1876. The Panic of 1873 wreaked additional fiscal havoc on the municipality by lowering property valuations, thereby contracting the flow of revenue needed for operations and debt service.[31]

In 1873, a full year before the Panic was felt locally, Mayor Charles A. Otis issued an early warning of the fiscal chaos ahead. Although he did not think that Cleveland carried too heavy a load of capital debt, Mayor Otis was concerned that the city's operating deficits, amounting to $200,000 annually, placed the entire system of municipal finance in jeopardy by adding senselessly to the city's burden of debt. The deficits demonstrated an absence of fiscal restraint, and the bond issues floated to fund them seemed to him acts of political cowardice or criminal irresponsibility. These deficits, illegal under the municipal code, represented over 40 percent of the operating budget.

Four years later, at the very bottom of the local depression, the fiscal crisis became the problem of Mayor Nathan Perry Payne, a member of a New England family with substantial holdings in Cuyahoga County real estate. Payne moved quickly but belatedly to establish a sinking fund to meet interest payments on the old debt, but his administration also added 35 percent to the deficit and $1.8 million to the total debt. Just to meet interest payments on the debt required a tax rate of 8 mills, two-thirds of the total millage the city could legally levy for all purposes.[32] Payne's successor, William Grey Rose, a real estate developer and subdivider in private life, touted massive election-year budget cuts, mostly in services, a strategy that further alienated the service conscious populist constituency and paved the way for the election of the first Populist Regime mayor, Rensselaer Russell Herrick.[33]

Mayor Herrick and the council elected with him in 1877 assumed office early in 1878 with a two-year mandate to take drastic action to remedy the fiscal crisis. Concentrating mainly on urban growth line items, Herrick slashed 28 percent from the budget, eliminated the deficit, reduced the debt by one million dollars, and cut taxes by 26 percent. In the 1879 and 1880 fiscal years, Herrick was aided by the local economy's recovery from the Panic of 1873, which rewarded the treasury with a sharp increase in property tax valuations.[34]

The small contractors and real estate operators doing business in the vacant land adjacent to the city were smaller players in the political drama of the 1870s, but they inflicted considerable fiscal damage of their own and came in for a fair share of the blame for the city's fiscal woes. In early 1873, Merchant Regime Mayor Charles A. Otis, while loath to criticize his social peers, the merchant–real estate speculators, had no qualms about exposing the villainies of small-scale real estate speculators.[35] In the 1870s, some 18.4 square miles, or 11,748 acres, were annexed to the city. Small-scale real estate operators, who supplied much of the political support for annexations, rushed in to buy small parcels of vacant land within the annexed territory, virtually worthless as development property because it lacked utilities and streets. The capital-starved small-scale real estate operator lobbied friendly city councilmen for streets and utilities. City council, pressured by both large- and small-scale speculators, was more than agreeable, since many members of that body were also in the real estate business or had side lines as building contractors.[36]

More subtle forms of small real estate operator mischief surfaced. When recalcitrant property owners blocked a street right of way to a speculator's land, council was prevailed upon to use its power of eminent domain to buy the impediment property. Once done, the real estate operator bought the property from the city, frequently eluding payment for as long as two years. The city not only improved the value of the speculator's property with publicly funded improvements, it also played banker by unintentionally extending credit to the fleet footed speculators. While these practices caused tax rates to go up for all taxpayers, parcels of land along the right of way leading to the speculator's land were especially hard hit because special tax assessments were levied to help defray the cost of improvements. In the aftermath of the Panic of 1873, many of these entailed property holders defaulted on tax payments and lost their property. Default of payment cases rose from 76 in 1872 to 208 in 1877.[37]

Mayors of this period not only railed against the financial consequences of land speculation, they also called attention to the urban design implications of land speculation: "Land is being platted in the suburbs almost weekly," noted Mayor Otis, "often in small parcels not exceeding a few acres, and each laid out with no reference to any others, but simply with a view of making the most money out of it. Short crooked streets run at all points of the compass and there is no regularity, no uniformity."[38]

Bringing the fiscal crisis under control meant a radical change in urban growth policy, beginning with the budget. The early Populist Regime administrations slashed budgets, deficits, debt, and taxes. To avoid a reprise of the urban growth folly, annexations were brought to a halt (the city annexed 12,000 acres of land during the 1870s, but only 98 acres were annexed during the eighteen years of the Populist Regime). Merchant Regime annexations actually lowered the population densities of a rapidly growing city from 12.1 to 8.9 people per acre. The Populist Regime stranglehold on annexations drove densities up to 17.4 people per acre, a 19 percent increase.[39]

Instead of annexation, Populist Regime policy focused on delivering services to those settling the annexed space. During the Populist Regime, Cleveland grew by nearly two hundred thousand people, a fact itself suggesting that the Populist Regime should make transportation, utilities, and other services its highest priority. But given the fiscal realities, the municipality had to find means other than taxes and debt to provide transportation and utilities.

Cleveland was rocked by the fiscal crisis just as massive capital expenditures were needed for streets, street paving, commuter rail transit, gas, and light. With 40 percent of the city's budget going to debt service alone, massive capital expenditures seemed out of the question. Gas, electricity, and commuter transportation were not only expensive; they also represented sophisticated technologies beyond the competence of the municipal bureaucracy. Moreover, taxpayer support for these sophisticated and expensive services was on the wane.

4

THE REALIGNMENT OF POLICY PRIORITIES

*T*he Populist Regime steered urban policy priorities away from economic development and urban growth toward service distribution and wealth redistribution. The reordering of policy priorities was prompted by the fiscal crisis and the service demands of a population that nearly doubled each decade the Populist Regime was in power. The extravagant land annexations of Merchant Regime growth policy committed the Populist Regime to make such services as streets and paving, sidewalks, street railways, and utilities high-priority concerns. Because the Populist Regime claimed much of its support from an expanding constituency of working class Clevelanders, a constituency rocked by recessions in the mid 1870s and mid 1890s, wealth redistribution became an unavoidable component of urban policy. More traditional services—police and fire protection, sanitation, and education—received greater attention and became more efficient and consumer oriented.

Steering urban policy through dangerous political and bureaucratic shoals, the Populist Regime took the helm of policy making in the midst of the worst fiscal crisis yet faced by the city. Construction of a utilities network and commuter transportation confronted the regime with capital and management intensive technologies.[1] Competent delivery of sophisticated and even ordinary services compelled the regime to staff many units within the municipal bureaucracy with professionals, while wealth redistribution claims pressured the regime to pad the municipal bureaucracy with working class patronage appointments and political favorites. These conflicting claims of professional and working class ideals could not all be met, and in the end the Populist Regime divided against itself, paving the way for the emergence of a new coalition of policy makers as the city approached the twentieth century.

The regime succumbed to a late nineteenth century politics of divide and ruin, culminating in the coalition-shattering mayoralty of Robert E. McKisson (1895–1899). Although the election of Populist Regime Mayor Robert E. McKisson in 1895 signalled the apparent triumph of the working class value system, the corruption of the McKisson administration created a crisis of ideals within the administration which in the end drove professionals from the ranks of the Populist Regime. When a new coalition of corporate and disaffected professionals formed, it brought the McKisson administration down and with it the Populist era in policy making. The clash of ideals arose in the context of the Populist Regime's attempts to provide low-cost, efficient services.[2]

SERVICE DISTRIBUTION: THE LURE OF FRANCHISING

The service demands necessitated by population growth and an expansive urban geography came at a time when the municipality was reeling under a crushing burden of debt.[3] The new service demands also came at a time when energy and transportation technologies were becoming unwieldy both in terms of cost and management.

Franchising offered an escape from this tangle of cost, technology, and management. Contracts with private companies for street lighting, street construction and repair, and for community transportation enabled the regime to meet constituent service expectations and shift management responsibility from the municipality to private providers. Franchising freed the regime from the burden of raising capital and wrestling with the fiscal and management challenges of changing technologies in utilities and transit. But franchising also proved to be a hazardous policy choice because franchises awarded to private companies led to mergers and monopoly power in the delivery of crucial services. By the close of the regime, the monopolists were acting against the interests of the consumer and were major contributors to the corruption of local politics.

A new era in urban services began on the night of April 29, 1879, when the inventor Charles F. Brush's arc light miraculously brought daylight to Public Square.[4] The year Brush cast his spell at Public Square, the municipality was entirely dependent on gas lighting, a technology Brush's invention made instantly obsolete. Thereafter, cities rushed to install Brush arc lights, and hastily formed electric companies raced to bid for lucrative franchise contracts to provide electricity. Cleveland, the home of the inventor, could do no less.[5]

Franchising, whether for gas or electricity, was the city's only option because the municipal charter did not allow the city to own utilities. The charter defined the city as just another customer, no different from a business or residence, and customers, including the city, supplied the fixtures and the company provided the gas (or light) for a fee. The gas light company franchises set the standard for all utilities providers. In each industry, there were, after a few years of consolidations and mergers, few competitors, so that by 1879 the East Ohio Gas Company, owned by Rockefeller interests, enjoyed a monopoly position, and within a decade of Brush's invention the local electrical industry was also a monopoly.[6] The service monopoly was an unintended consequence of franchising. Franchise grants placed too much power in the hands of a single company for too long a period of time.[7] Franchises brought company ownership and management into an unholy alliance with the political leadership. While franchising allowed for tidy municipal ledgers, the long-term victims of franchising were the very consumers the Populist Regime vowed to protect.[8]

Street Railways

Commuter transportation followed suit. Although Cleveland's population doubled nearly every decade in the nineteenth century, the aggressive annexation policies of the Merchant Regime added even more territory. Annexation resulted in a low-density settlement which presented Populist Regime policy makers with journey-to-work as an urban service issue. The spread of job sites and residences out from the downtown necessitated some form of mass transportation. In the 1890s, the technology of electricity was transferred to conveyance and created the electric streetcar industry, a capital and technology intensive industry, the sort of industry which made the cost conscious Populist Regime wary and eager to regulate.[9]

Regulation of public transit was not a new phenomenon. The city charter allowed the municipality to regulate public conveyance, and in 1852 a Merchant Regime city council passed an ordinance "regulating Cabs, Hackney Carriages, and Drays."[10] Remarkably comprehensive for its time, the ordinance set terms and hours of service, rates, and licensure requirements for drivers.[11]

In 1861, moreover, the state legislature passed "An Act to Provide for and Regulate the Street Railroad Companies,"[12] an updating of an old law giving municipalities the same regulatory powers over street railways that they had earlier taken with cabs, hackneys, and drays. This state statute allowed municipal regulation of street railways under franchise grants but not municipal ownership.[13]

The Populists issued franchise grants to both horse and electric lines, and the terms, at least outwardly, did little to ease the conditions under which the street railway companies did business. Between 1863 and 1887, the city of Cleveland issued franchise grants to fifteen street railway companies. Most were issued by the city council in the 1870s, during the heyday of the Merchant Regime annexation policy and the years when the city was reeling from the fiscal crisis.[14] In Cleveland, each franchise grant was a carbon copy of the first, the grant awarded to the St. Clair Street Railway on June 9, 1863.[15]

This initial ordinance required operators to post performance bonds, build, maintain and repair track in accordance with specifications set by the city, establish a fixed schedule, and train drivers and other personnel. Operators also had to pay car license fees to the city, provide the city each year with a list of company stockholders, and commit to the five-cent fare for the 25-year duration of the grant. The 25-year franchise grant, however, was a 25-year monopoly on service along a specified route. Reopener clauses allowed companies to petition for service extensions along the same route, an opportunity made feasible by Merchant Regime annexations.

The contractual ban on raising fares to meet changing business realities pressured the companies to seek revenue raising alternatives, for upward pressures in operating costs, capital requirements, or new technologies could put the companies in a cash flow bind. An obvious and well-used option was to increase revenues at the expense of labor. Franchise grants freed companies to unilaterally reduce hours, cut wages, or terminate employees altogether. The franchise grants permitted the companies to work their employees twelve hours a day, six days a week, at a time when the municipality's own employees were working a nine-hour, six-day week.[16] But the frequently exploited layoffs and wage and hour reductions set in motion a self-defeating cycle of disgruntled employees delivering unreliable service to angry riders.[17]

A far less disruptive option for increasing revenues was extension of the service area, an option allowable under the reopener clause in the franchise grant.[18] The service area extension reopener allowed a street railway company to expand its route to increase ridership and thereby meet unanticipated cost increases through the fare box. However, before any fare box revenues could accrue, the company had to make a sizable capital investment in track and sometimes rolling stock in the new service area. The service extension precedent was set during the 1880s, when the Populist Regime was firmly entrenched in city council.[19] The Broadway and Brooklyn Street Railway Company, under the aggressive ownership of Joseph Stanley, repeatedly resorted to the extension of service strategy. A compliant city council agreed, and other companies quickly followed suit with their own requests for service extension reopeners.[20]

Some revenue enhancing opportunities did exist outside the terms of the franchise grant, however. Real estate owned by the company along its routes could be sold. Street railway companies generally lacked the capital necessary to become real estate developers, a business tactic that might have guaranteed the parent transit company a reliable flow of rental revenue. But local taxation of vacant but platted land dampened enthusiasm for the practice.[21]

In the end, extension of service was the only practical way cash-starved street railway companies could increase revenues. Aggressive street railway companies survived the 1880s by extending their routes, while rival companies timidly playing pat hands went bankrupt. The fate of smaller companies was sealed by lack of nerve and the five-cent fare, which left them unwilling or unable to pay for the capital intensive technologies of the 1890s.[22]

The Streetcar Merger Wave

Most of the franchise grants awarded in the late 1860s and early 1870s expired between 1897 and 1905. A new round of franchise grant negotiations offered the possibility of increased fares and profits. This prospect fueled the merger mania of the 1890s. The 1890s was the decade of the electric streetcar, but conversion to an electric transit system required capital investments of daunting proportions, and mergers became the rainmaking divination needed to make electric streetcars affordable and companies profitable. Mergers reduced the number of competing companies and gave the merged company an expanded service area without an expensive investment in capital equipment. The magic of mergers was that they could be effected without cash. Merging companies engaged in a courting ritual in which watered stocks were exchanged for junk bonds and the newly wed company received in exchange an expanded service area and the capital equipment necessary to serve it. The revenue generated by the sheer volume of merged ridership serviced the bonds in the few years remaining on the franchise grant and provided the capital necessary to make the conversion to electricity.[23]

In 1889 more than a dozen street railway companies served Cleveland. In 1897 only two remained, the Big Con(solidated) and the Little Con (solidated). Next, Big Con and Little Con raced to electrify the remainder of their lines and jockey for monopoly position in 1897, the first year of the franchise renewal window of opportunity.[24] After the battle, in 1901, the two became one, the ConCon charging seven cents a ride.

The Franchise Renewal War

It appeared that the task of negotiating the streetcar franchise grant renewals would fall to populist Mayor Robert E. "Corky Bob" McKisson and his city solicitor. The new Federal city charter of 1892 gave the mayor full executive powers, including the authority to conduct contract negotiations with city service providers, subject to the approval of city council.[25] In 1897, McKisson, a Republican, was serving the final year of his first term as mayor of Cleveland. Re-election loomed and McKisson, wet finger pointed expectantly skyward, was uncertain which way the political winds were blowing on the franchise renewal issue. Publicly, he postured as the populist champion of transit riders, but privately the mayor was known to be friendly to the companies, particularly the "Little Con" of Marcus A. Hanna. McKisson leaned toward the transit magnate because Hanna was both county chairman of McKisson's political party and the newly appointed Republican U.S. Senator from Ohio. Hanna himself, however, muddied the political waters of franchise renewal by having legislation introduced in the state legislature allowing municipalities to extend street railway franchises to periods of fifty and eighty years. These controversial bills were still pending in the state legislature when councilmen friendly to the companies introduced in Cleveland City Council a franchise renewal law called the Reynolds Ordinance.[26]

The timing of the Reynolds Ordinance, the political ambitions of the mayor, and Hanna's machinations in the state legislature prompted a group of young Republican professionals, led by lawyer Frederic C. Howe and his law associates, James and Harry Garfield, to break ranks with the Populist Regime. In 1895, during McKisson's first run for mayor, they founded the Municipal Association, a good-government organization staffed by professionals and funded by local export sector entrepreneurs, a key group whose political activism was now beginning to stir. The Municipal Association rapidly became anti-McKisson and anti-populist.[27]

The Municipal Association in 1897 issued an elaborate public broadside condemning franchising, the franchise renewal process in general, and the Reynolds Ordinance in particular. Its author, Frederic C. Howe,[28] noted that as the land area of the city expanded, business and employment opportunities had confined themselves to a few centrally located quarters and that residential land occupancy fanned out from these enclaves to diverse and increasingly remote precincts. The streetcar system, the consequence of the mergers and consolidations of the 1890s, knit all together, weaving in the process a contrasting fabric of rider dependency and street railway company monopoly. "It may be laid down as an economic law as fixed as that of gravitation," Howe wrote, "that wherever combination is possible . . . competition is impossible. The history of all our cities has shown this, whether it be in the gas, electric lighting, or street railway business. Rates in all monopolies will be set by whatever the market will bear."[29]

The companies' ritualistic reply to such public criticism was that fares charged and dividends paid were based on the book value of the company. Howe dismissed these assertions as nonsense. The book value of Cleveland street railway companies, he claimed, was built, layer by layer, upon decades of watered stock certificates. Howe claimed that "franchise value indicated by watered stock is a social product, the result of the growth of population and its congestion into a business center."[30] Classical political economists counseled that a social product is subject either to public regulation or public ownership. Howe, taking a more conservative approach, opted for public regulation; but the Reynolds Ordinance in his view failed as a regulatory measure because it did not adequately protect the public interest.

The particulars of the Reynolds Ordinance, as Howe noted, did not deviate significantly from earlier franchise grants. It provided for a 25-year extension of the franchise (in contrast to the 50- to 80-year extensions Hanna was seeking from the state legislature), repeal of all other franchise grants (meaning closure on the franchise issue in the first year of the window of opportunity), a continuation of the five-cent fare (six tickets for a quarter), universal transfers, and an annual payment to the city of 2 percent of gross receipts in place of the existing annual flat rate $200,000 paving tax.[31]

Howe contended that the Reynolds Ordinance neither adequately compensated the city for the value of the grant nor offered adequate value for riders. Howe also objected to the 25-year duration of the franchise grant and contended that an even longer grant, such as the 50- or 80-year term advocated by Hanna, was positively corrupt. Long-term grants without reopener clauses worked against the interests of the municipality and the public, for the transit industry was too unpredictable technologically. In the span of just a dozen years the lines had changed from horse drawn trolleys to electric streetcars and the number of operations declined from twelve to two. What would the next twelve years of a proposed twenty-five bring? Without contract reopeners, the city was at the mercy of external forces it could not control.

Howe's suspicion, however, was that the long-term economic prospects of the industry were far more predictable and these also worked against the interests of the municipality and riders.[32] Howe described street railways as an industry of "increasing returns." Initially, a street railway company must invest heavily in capital equipment. Each year following the initial investment, costs subside and profits increase even when ridership remains stable. The initial capital investment in electrical technology had already been made by the Big Con and Little Con, and both, in Howe's estimate, were poised on the threshold of an era of increasing returns. The Reynolds Ordinance set the companies' payment to the city at a flat rate of 2 percent of gross receipts, and fares were set for the duration at five cents. The political arithmetic of Howe's increasing returns argument suggested that the municipality should receive a proportionately higher rate of gross receipts and that fares should go down. Without reopener clauses, neither event would occur.[33]

Finally, Howe argued that the decade-long wave of mergers and consolidations in the street railway industry resulted in an integrated transit system made even more attractive by a universal transfer policy. An integrated system oiled by a universal transfer policy would have more riders. Increasing returns and increasing ridership promised large profits for the street railway monopolies.[34]

The companies rebutted Howe's arithmetic with accounting schemes which inflated book value to minimize profits, overlong amortization and depreciation schedules, and claims that profit rested in the per-unit ride and not in the volume of ridership. The sum and substance of the companies' position was that the business would be same in twenty-five years as it was in 1897.[35]

To buttress his case, Howe compared the Reynolds Ordinance to franchise grants awarded by New York, Detroit, St. Louis, Milwaukee, Indianapolis, and Toronto. Franchise grant reopener clauses were common to all. In addition, companies in these cities were obligated to open their books to independent auditors, which was central to the success of the gross receipts method of payment to the city. In these cities, payment scales were progressive and were pegged to increases in audited gross receipts or, alternatively, to five-year time intervals. Gross receipts payments ranged in scale from a low of 2 to a high of 15 percent. Universal free transfers were the norm and fares ranged from three to four cents. No one charged five cents. Even with these liberal terms, critics in the sister cities accused transit companies of gouging the public. What, then, could be said of

Cleveland?[36]

Howe's detailed analysis, grounded in arcana of statistics, classical economic theory, accounting, and contract law, had surprising popular appeal, a local milestone in public acceptance of the professional ideal. Newspapers and voters rallied to Howe's side, and a chastened city council meekly voted down the Reynolds Ordinance. Mayor Robert E. McKisson, now quite certain of the direction of the political winds, denounced the greedy, monopolistic street railway company owners and charged Howe and the Municipal Association with complicity because they would regulate the transit industry. McKisson manfully declared for municipal ownership of the street railway system, knowing full well that municipal ownership would require a change in the city charter, a difficult task.[37]

In 1898, McKisson launched a one-man political crusade against the chief villain in the piece, Marcus A. Hanna. McKisson, the knight errant of Cleveland populism, ran against Hanna for chairman of the county Republican party and challenged the aging tycoon again in the state legislature when he sought election as United States Senator. McKisson narrowly lost both contests, but McKisson announced that he would seek re-election for a third term as Mayor of Cleveland.

Unfortunately for McKisson, his style of populist mayoral politics had made him many political enemies, including the young professionals who founded the Municipal Association. During the McKisson administration, professionals at last split from the populist regime. The Municipal Association, fresh from its street railway franchise grant victory, made the defeat of McKisson its highest priority for 1899.[38] Early in the race, the good-government group published Bulletin No. 11, a campaign broadside which devoted forty-six of its forty-eight pages to an indictment of McKisson and only two pages to praise of his Democratic opponent, former mayor John H. Farley (1883–1885). Bulletin No. 11 made it clear that Farley's most laudatory attribute was his pledge if elected not to seek re-election, an utterance witnessed by several persons the publication identified by name.

Meanwhile, Hanna secretly made a $20,000 contribution to Farley's campaign. Both Farley and his supporters later acknowledged that Hanna's money was the margin of difference in Farley's victory over McKisson.[39] The quid pro quo surrounding the $20,000 contribution did not become clear until February 5, 1901, when Hanna's Little Con submitted a franchise renewal proposal to the city council, which was formally introduced two weeks later as Ordinance #31483. Mayor Farley immediately endorsed the proposed ordinance, which was a better franchise proposal than the Reynolds Ordinance of 1897.[40] But it still fell far short of the franchise grant minima set by Frederic C. Howe and the Municipal Association in

1897. The Municipal Association, the Cleveland Chamber of Commerce, the newspapers, and mayoral candidate Tom L. Johnson all opposed Hanna's ordinance, and a wary City Council quickly tabled it.[41]

SERVICE DISTRIBUTION: CONTRACTING

The Populist Regime encountered other trouble as the nineteenth century waned, including complaints about the practice of contracting for services,[42] a way of delivering services without burdening the municipal budget with additional employees and fixed costs. Contracting as a money saving device was initially applauded by all ranks of the citizenry, but by the 1890s, professionals critical of abuses in franchising grew equally contemptuous of corrupt and wasteful service contracts.[43] Mayor Herrick's claim that Cleveland had more miles of streets and alleys than any other city its size perhaps exaggerated the facts but not the pressures on services caused by excessive annexation and fiscal mismanagement.[44] Clevelanders grew uncompromising in their demands for paved streets and sidewalks, water pipes, and sewer lines, but they were equally insistent on the low-cost delivery of these services.

Abuses of street and sidewalk paving contracts first raised concerns about the contracting system. Paving lagged far behind street construction. At a time when the nation's ten largest cities had achieved 50 percent levels of street paving, only 15 percent of Cleveland's 462 miles of streets and alleys were paved.[45] This statistic launched a street and sidewalk paving mania in the 1890s. Street and sidewalk paving monies and contracts were routed through city councilmen to the wards. With only two years between elections, councilmen, eager to please constituents in the most visible manner possible, let sidewalk contracts at a fervid pace.[46]

M. F. Bramley, just one of many contractors, was awarded $774,395.88 in paving contracts between 1897 and 1899. Today one can walk the sidewalks of Cleveland wards and read, imprinted in the concrete, the names of Bramley and the other favored paving contractors, names mirroring the ethnic identities of those living in the wards when the sidewalks were paved.

Professionals jumping ship from the Populist Regime to the Municipal Association scrutinized municipal budgets with sharp pencils and found much to arouse their ire.[47] Paving contracts were only the tip of the iceberg. Reformers discovered a widespread pattern of contractor-rigged bids and kickbacks to councilmen in addition to overpayments by city agencies to suppliers of such essential commodities as coal.[48] Contracting in garbage removal and disposal also fell under the skeptical eye of disaffected professionals. Garbage was a singular problem in nineteenth century cities. Streets in the nation's cities were uniformly foul and malodorous. Individual citizens, who annually parted with nearly five hundred pounds of garbage each, contributed their share to the growing urban public health problem. Cleveland, additionally, was home to an equine population estimated at 20,000, each of which made a daily deposit of twenty pounds of manure and twenty gallons of urine on the city's streets while slaughter houses, factories, steel mills, and other businesses made their own unique contributions to the deteriorating urban environment.[49]

In the 1880s and 1890s these realities fell under the scrutiny of public health officers, sanitarians, engineers, and a public grown intolerant of the aesthetic and medical menace posed by the reeking and dangerous mounds of human and animal refuse. Contracting for what was now clearly a vital urban service seemed not merely corrupt but foolhardy and irresponsible. A tug of war ensued. Contracting, the Municipal Association reform leaders pointed out, rewarded contractors with monopoly positions from which they gouged a longsuffering citizenry. Cleveland paid $2.83 a ton to contractors for garbage collection, a figure 15 percent higher than the national average, and for garbage disposal $1.04 a ton, a rate 40 percent higher than other urban Americans paid. Populist defenders of the contracting system replied that there were no guarantees that the municipality could deliver the service for any less money than the contractors. Capital investment in equipment, the addition of scores of new permanent employees to the city payroll, and the acquisition of disposal sites were not insignificant costs.

The Populist Regime found no political resolution of this key policy issue until early in the new century because professional opinion was divided. Expanding medical knowledge and rapidly changing waste management technologies combined to divide health professionals, sanitarians, and civil engineers over the issue of "the one best system" of waste removal and disposal.[50] In the last year of his administration, Mayor Robert E. McKisson's frustrated Board of Control proffered a uniquely populist solution to the problem. It passed a resolution offering to contract with any citizen willing to take responsibility for street cleaning on his block,[51] a symbol of the policy making bankruptcy of the late Populist Regime.

THE MUNICIPAL BUREAUCRACY

Franchising and contracting not only angered the public but also divided the Populist Regime against itself, a conflict quite evident in the municipal bureaucracy. Administrative incompetence was the residue of the conflicting ideals dogging the municipal bureaucracy. The Populist Regime hired professionals to run such departments as water and sewer, police and fire, and public education. But in each instance the Populists compromised professionalism by liberally sprinkling the attending bureaucracies with their political supporters and petitioners able to make convincing redistributive claims on the regime. Mixing the two groups heightened tensions between the ideals of the professionals and working class elements within the municipal bureaucracy.[52]

Mayor McKisson ignited a firestorm of protest when he summarily fired a health department physician for his refusal to kickback 5 percent of his salary to the mayor's reelection campaign. Municipal Association professionals rushed to Dr. Campbell's defense and to the defense of men much lower in the bureaucracy such as William C. Bevan, a modest engine cleaner at the Division Street Pumping Station, who resigned in protest over the same political demands made on Dr. Campbell.[53] Yet other city employees, imbued with the working class ideal and politically or financially indebted to the administration, saw in the entreaties of the mayor's bagmen the reciprocity their situation required. They paid up and remained contentedly on the job. The tension between professional and working class ideals erupted into public view during the McKisson administration, but the conflict had long simmered beneath the bureaucratic surface.

Mayor John Farley in his first term complained about the conflict between the managerialism of the professionals and neighborhood demands for police protection. Police department personnel, as Farley rightly observed, were divided between a small managerial cadre of professional officers and a significantly larger number of beat walking cops, working class patronage appointees selected from ethnically favored groups. The two levels of police operatives differed in their interpretations of law enforcement, the former seeking universal enforcement and the latter a more elastic application of codes and ordinances.[54]

Precinct beat cops were working class ethnic patronage appointees, the Irish most commonly, and working class policemen were concerned about keeping the neighborhood streets free from murderers, thieves, and disturbers of the peace. What took place behind the closed doors of the saloon, brothel, and gambling house concerned them far less. Corrupt bargains were often struck between the beat cop and the owners of these establishments, and appeals to councilmen to regulate the liquor trade in saloons and shutter brothels and gaming houses were routinely ignored.[55] Beat patrolmen, city councilmen, and saloon owners were products of the

Chapter 4: The Realignment of Policy Priorities 77

same culture and sometimes were members of the same families. They understood that in working class culture the saloon was an integral part of the male routine because it offered respite from the drudgeries and responsibilities of work and family. The saloon was a social club, a convivial center where information about job openings could be exchanged, and a forum for political opinion and activism.[56] In 1898, the Municipal Association complained that 600 saloons had tallied up 15,000 Sunday law violations. Rather than concede that the Sunday Law was unenforceable because it ran counter to working class culture, the Municipal Association charged the police department and city council with corruption, cupidity, and complicity.[57]

THE PUBLIC SCHOOL SYSTEM

The Cleveland Public School System offers another example of bureaucratic conflict. Here, the conflict was between the governing boards and school administrators, the emerging class of professional schoolmen who challenged boards to take ever more modernist measures in the delivery of educational services. School boards, on the other hand, vainly fought to press their values upon the school system. In the 1870s, years before the populists achieved a majority position on the expanding school board, conflict in educational philosophy and pedagogical direction surfaced between the merchant board majority and the professional staff headed by the superintendent. With an expanding and increasingly unmanageable board, the professional schoolmen who ran the system played the old merchant and rising populist board factions against each other. When the smoke cleared, the schoolmen had overhauled the public school system.

The dominant schoolman was Superintendent Andrew Rickoff (1868–1882), who pushed through far reaching management and pedagogical reforms. Rickoff's most important achievement was a graded school system, one through 12, which he created within the primary and secondary taxonomies allowable under state law. The graded system allowed Rickoff to reduce the student/teacher ratio from 78 to 57 to 1. The merchants objected on pedagogical grounds when Rickoff jettisoned the common school system, but when the bills came in for the new buildings and the additional teachers and administrators required in a 57 to 1 student teacher ratio, the argument came round to dollars and cents. Rickoff, however, was an able schoolman/politician. When he enforced the hitherto ignored compulsory attendance laws, created an in-house normal school to train teachers from populist backgrounds, and instituted German language instruction, a manual training school, evening classes, and a school for incorrigibles, he not only won the support of populist members of the board of education, he also crafted a populist public education agenda.[58]

In 1882, the merchants remaining on the board of education were able to muster enough votes to depose Andrew Rickoff and replace him with his leading critic, Burke A. Hinsdale, a Protestant minister and President of Hiram College. Hinsdale won the merchants' affection because he very vocally opposed the graded school system, Rickoff's populist leaning public education agenda, and the costs of both. The merchants, now smarting from the realization that their fiscal excesses had cost them the control of the city government, were bent on retaining control of the school board. Hinsdale, facing stiff opposition from the school board's populist minority, was unable to scuttle Rickoff's educational reforms but did manage to contain escalating costs. However, by 1885 there were twenty-five seats on the school board, and the municipal elections that year gave the overwhelming majority of them to populist candidates. Hinsdale was summarily fired and replaced by Lewis Day, the first superintendent hired by a school board dominated by a populist majority.[59]

The Day administration (1886–1891) reflected the strengths and weaknesses of populist policy making. During Day's administration, the number of city wards increased from twenty-five to forty-two and the number of board members increased accordingly. The merchant element on the board, now a small minority, remained vocal, supported by the Republican Party and key elements of the press. As the city's immigrant Catholic population increased, nativism and anti-Catholic sentiment became a divisive element in board politics. The merchant element became increasingly more anti-Catholic in its educational policy orientation. As an isolated minority, the anti-Catholicism of the Protestant merchant board members might have been contained, but with the continuing addition of wards and board members, the expanding populist majority itself frayed along social class, foreign born/native born, ethnic, and Protestant/Catholic lines. Superintendent Day, hired by the newly elected populist board majority, soon found that the consensus that hired him evaporated over policy direction.[60]

Diverse and antagonistic subcultures, heralding the arrival of modern industrial America, were represented on Cleveland's school board during the 1880s, each with its own educational agenda. Day, a man who lacked Rickoff's political skills, resorted to appeasement tactics. Throwing a bone to the Protestant New England merchant element, still fuming over the sacking of Hinsdale, Day declared his opposition to vocational education. Meanwhile, he assembled a group of businessmen with New England credentials to privately fund a vocational school, which in time was annexed to the public system as the Manual Training School. Day retained the populist programs initiated by Rickoff and added popular evening programs which served nearly two thousand adult immigrants in 1887 alone, but these efforts failed to dampen the sectarian bickering and ethnic animosity. While 32,000 students were enrolled in the public school system, nearly 26,000 were enrolled in parochial schools, and Catholic Bishop Richard Gilmour, an ardent and vocal opponent of public schools, counseled his flock to reject taxes in support of them. Father Smythe, pastor at St. Malachi's Catholic Church, was elected to the Cleveland School Board and was a constant irritant to the superintendent and a constant reminder of the new urban demography.[61]

Day's appeasement tactics did not stop at the schoolhouse door. Day exploited the hiring needs of a growing educational network to reward favored supporters with jobs in the school system. Building contracts, supplies, and textbook orders were similarly let to the favored. Day hoped to use patronage to build a network of support for his populist education policies. These efforts backfired, for they stimulated opposition to populist dominance of the school system.

In 1891, a coalition of traditionalists and increasingly disaffected professionals won a new charter for the city of Cleveland, known as the Federal plan, that included a structural reform contrivance that laid waste to the populist school board. By reducing the school board in size to just seven members, five of whom were elected at large and two from geographical districts roughly conforming to the east and west sides, the new charter deprived the populists of their dominant weight in numbers, though they were not swept entirely off the board of education. The first board elected under the Federal charter contained three merchants, a Euclid Avenue lawyer, a clerk, and a tailor.[62]

Another anti-populist structural element was the imaginative executive function created by the charter. The executive was the director of schools, elected at-large. The director, in turn, appointed the superintendent of schools, who was the de facto chief administrative officer. Because the superintendent was the employee of the director of schools, he was shielded from board oversight and interference. H. Q. Sargent, a merchant, was elected director of the schools in 1892, and he in turn appointed Andrew Draper to the post of superintendent of the Cleveland Public Schools.[63]

With the populists at bay and merchant culture poised to shape education policy once again, a period of reaction seemed sure to follow. Draper pledged an end to the rule of the "uneducated and unthinking classes" and promised to lead the public schools into a new era of educating students in "good citizenship, the protection of property, and the preservation of the state."[64] The apparent end of populist rule did not end the debate over education policy, however. It only marked the beginning of a new round of policy debate fought by new contestants. The decade-long conflict between populist and merchant elements masked the issue that triggered the conflict to begin with, the growing centrality of the professional ideal within the school system itself.

WEALTH REDISTRIBUTION

The corrupt practices of Superintendent Day's administration were described above as appeasement tactics, but patronage and favoritism in franchise awards and service and building contracts were also part of a larger pattern of political behavior that was symptomatic of the entire Populist Regime. By the time the populists assumed control of policy making, economic development, urban growth, and distributive services were accepted as the legitimate concerns of public institutions. Wealth redistribution, in contrast, was not. Redistributive policy was the ward of the private charity system over which the populists never won control. Instead, to effect a needed redistributive policy, the populists resorted to devious means of manipulating the public purse.

The private redistributive system was institutionally in flux and philosophically in conflict through the length of the regime. Private sectarian charity organizations were being challenged by a new network of private nonsectarian agencies. Even within sectarian agencies, tensions arose between sectarian boards and professional staff. Traditional charity philosophies were challenged by new charity philosophies. What all, old and new, had in common was an almost Calvinist obsession with victimization and blame. Who or what was to blame for poverty? Some blamed the victim for his condition. Others blamed society. Ironically, consensus was achieved on funding. Dollars spent on charity were to be redistributed from the funds of private benefactors in preference to public dollars wrested from taxpayers.[65]

Populist redistributive policy was built on an institutionalized system of indoor and outdoor relief, reciprocal arrangements with franchisers and contractors, and the public payroll. The system of indoor relief was inherited from the Merchant Regime. It included such institutions as the city infirmary, The Ragged School, and the workhouse. The clients of these institutions stirred little controversy, because the clients of these institu-

Chapter 4: The Realignment of Policy Priorities   81

tions were "deserving." Under the Merchant Regime the monies spent went up and down in response to the vicissitudes of the local economy.[66] Until the mid 1880s redistributive spending was kept low by the populists, but from then on amounts were increased to a range of $200,000–$250,000 annually. Although the Federal charter of 1891 introduced a new accounting system and merged these functions under the Department of Charities and Corrections, the amounts of money spent did not change significantly.[67]

The 1891 budget taxonomies eliminated outdoor relief entirely. Outdoor relief had been for the able-bodied clients who were given day work in exchange for in-kind payments. It was a cumbersome program to administer because it required disbursement to clients of chits and script which in turn were exchanged in stores whose owners in turn had to present these to the city treasurer for cash reimbursement. More to the point was the controversy sparked over whether the clients were in fact deserving and, if so, whether the private system of benevolence should tend to them rather than the municipality.[68]

Instead the populists spurned outdoor relief (except in times of grave economic distress) in favor of steering the able-bodied needy toward jobs on the public payroll or to franchisers and contractors obliged to reciprocate for their favored status. The padded payrolls of franchisers and contractors escaped critical notice, but the swelling of the public payroll did not.

During the twenty-year Populist Regime, the municipal payroll expanded sixfold (from 700 employees to nearly 4,500). The raw numbers were most staggering during the last decade of the regime when 1,000 employees grew to 4,500, and critics of the regime were quick to charge the populists with payroll padding. The apparent improvidence of the populists was actually in line with national trends. Until the decade of the 1890s, Cleveland lagged far behind the national ratio of public employees to the general population. In 1880, when the national ratio was 1 to 195, Cleveland's was 1 to 230, and when the national ratio dropped to 1:129 in 1890, Cleveland's actually increased to 1:252, mirroring the fiscal prudence of the early Populist Regime. The late Populist Regime, notably the administrations of mayors McKisson and Farley, brought the municipality up to par. In 1900, as the Populist Regime entered its final year, both Cleveland's and the national average were at 1 to 85. Nearly 3,500 employees were added during the decade of the 1890s.[69]

As the city's services expanded, legions of professionals and paraprofessionals were hired in heath care, engineering, management, and accounting departments. Large numbers of white collar support staff positions were also opened. But many employees, especially the unskilled, were added for redistributive rather than distributive purposes. Civil service laws failed to arrest these accretions to the public payroll because the regulations affected only police and fire department hiring. Even in the affected departments, civil service restrictions were routinely finessed by skillful bureaucrats and ignored by elected officials.[70]

The Populist Regime created a democratic political culture in Cleveland and opened the system of governance to popular participation for the first time. The democratic political culture of the Populist Regime originated in the working class ideal. The Corporate Regime came next with its stress on the language of professionalism, order, and efficiency, and subordinated and trivialized the democratic political culture of the populists.

By the close of the Populist Regime, however, both political parties were infused with the working class democratic ideal but were also home to other competing value systems, making the two parties broadly inclusionary. Late in the Populist era, the Cuyahoga County Republican Party was chaired by businessman Marcus A. Hanna. Hanna appealed to the new and old rich residing in silk stocking wards; but the Republican Party was also the party of such young professionals as the Garfield brothers (sons of the slain president) and lawyer Frederick C. Howe and professional politicians such as populist mayor Robert E. McKisson and the notorious ward boss Harry "Czar" Bernstein. The Democratic Party was the party of two time populist mayor John H. "Honest John" Farley and entrepreneur reformer Tom L. Johnson. Both men were wise in the ways of working class and ethnic ward politics. Corporate Regime spokesmen denounced both parties as corrupt, incompetent, and bankrupt ideologically. Dominated by business entrepreneurs, their managerial subalterns, and professionals, the incoming Corporate Regime used structural political reform from without and command and control organizational strategies from within to purge the populists' policy making governance system of its democratic political culture.

Part Three
The Corporate Regime, 1895–1919

5

IDEALS, INSTITUTIONS, AND POLICIES

*A*fter the long era of populist policy making, the Corporate Regime formed new policy making institutions and radically altered policy priorities. One of the elements contributing to the demise of the Populist Regime was the clash of incompatible ideals, working class and professional. The ideal of the professionals moved with them into the Corporate Regime, there to be in contest with two renderings of the entrepreneurial ideal. Entrepreneurs were driven by an ethos of individualism. For the professionals individualism was irrelevant; the means and ends of policy were collective.[1]

ENTREPRENEURS AND PROFESSIONALS

Entrepreneurs saw themselves as individuals, saw the beneficiaries of their policies as individuals, and saw individuals as responsible for righting the wrongs of society. They also believed that individual goals and outcomes could only be achieved when channeled through organizations.[2]

Professionalism, conversely, rested in collectivism, both the subject and object of the professional ideal. For professionals, an organization was a collectivity managed by a collectivity to benefit a collectivity. To professionals, then, the organization was both ends and means.[3]

TWO RENDERINGS OF THE ENTREPRENEURIAL IDEAL

The entrepreneurial ideal motivated Samuel Mather, the iron monger Chamber of Commerce president, and the entrepreneur turned politician

Tom L. Johnson. In an 1895 speech before the Cleveland Chamber of Commerce, Samuel Mather pointed to English municipal reformer Joseph Chamberlain as the archetype of the entrepreneur as civic activist, a role model for the would-be Cleveland entrepreneur as activist. Mather praised Chamberlain for his willingness to trade his flourishing business career as a screw manufacturer for public service in Birmingham, which he parlayed into the leadership of the British Liberal Party.[4]

Tom L. Johnson, a member of Mather's audience, was also impressed by the leadership role played by entrepreneurs in the English municipal reform movement, but for intellectual sustenance, Johnson drew more directly on the social reform doctrines of the quixotic American reformer Henry George, though the ripple effect of Georgeist doctrines spread also to England.[5] The value of Chamberlain's municipal reform movement and the ideas of Henry George to Cleveland's entrepreneurial reformers is found in the distinctions drawn between active (good) and passive (bad) capital. These distinctions sustained Corporate Regime policies in tax reform, economic development, urban growth, service distribution, and wealth redistribution.

The treatment of monopoly capital divided the entrepreneurs. All agreed that monopoly capital was bad capital, but Tom L. Johnson and his allies wanted to replace monopoly capital ownership of transit and utilities with public ownership, while the entrepreneurial faction represented by Samuel Mather and the Cleveland Chamber of Commerce wanted to regulate and tax the franchisers. The stage was set for a split between the entrepreneurs.[6]

THE INSTITUTIONAL SETTING

The Cleveland Chamber of Commerce

Policy initiatives in the Corporate Regime were the near monopoly of the Cleveland Chamber of Commerce, but the task of policy implementation was dispersed through a mélange of private and public institutions, especially the municipality and the board of education, two suspect public institutions. The Cleveland Chamber of Commerce was also the keystone organization in the Corporate Regime's institutional network, and it was here also that the triangular stresses between the two renderings of entrepreneurial ideal and the professional ideal first appeared. In 1893, however, the issue was not reconciling incongruent ideals but the more pressing matter of organizational renovation.

Created in 1893, the Cleveland Chamber of Commerce borrowed from the chamber of commerce movement in neighboring cities. They demonstrated that businessmen's organizations infused with a new sense of purpose and a more effective organizational structure could play a greater role in the city's business development and shape the larger course of urban policy. This prospect inspired a newly policy-sensitive corporate community in Cleveland to reform the Board of Trade. Cleveland, like other growing cities, spawned dozens of businessmen's trade associations, each isolated from the other. The new chamber of commerce movement federated these separate businessmen's entities under one organizational umbrella. So structured, the information services offered by the chamber enabled each businessman to see the local economy whole and in relationship to regional and national business trends. The federated setting also enabled chamber members from diverse business backgrounds to appreciate the nexus between business and public policy making.[7] Ryerson Ritchie, a local man with a broad business vision and considerable organizational talents, was retained to mold the old network of business organizations into a modern chamber of commerce. Ritchie brought to the enterprise the skills and values of the professional manager, and he created in the Cleveland Chamber of Commerce an organization structurally and operationally the mirror of the modern business corporation.[8]

Ryerson Ritchie's first task was to assemble a board of directors. It was composed of highly visible entrepreneurs whose reputations and fortunes had been made in durable goods manufacturing. A president elected for a one-year term was the chief executive officer, and he reported to the board. Reporting to the chamber's president were several subsidiary boards corresponding to the functional sectors of the local economy: minerals, shipping, manufacturing, retailing, banking, wholesaling, and construction. The business sector boards supplied business information and economic development policy recommendations to a civic board that was primarily responsible for shaping the larger contours of urban policy. In addition, the civic board supervised several ad hoc committees chartered at various times to study specific policy issues, including city and regional parks, civic beautification, pubic education, the charity system, housing, the criminal justice system, and more.[9]

Initially, the policy research civic committees were chaired by entrepreneurs. As the Corporate Regime entered midpassage, however, entrepreneurs were replaced by corporate managers and professionals in law, medicine, architecture, engineering, education, and religion. This succession stemmed from differences in values between entrepreneurs and professionals. Under entrepreneurial direction, chamber civic committee policy recommendations were individualistic, highly dramatic, and accompanied by recommendations for private-sector or quasi-public institutions to implement policy. Managers and professionals, driven by a collectivist managerial ethos, wanted to standardize policy and make implementation the responsibility of public bodies. But public institutions were captive of the populist political culture. Therefore, Corporate Regime professionals, from the outset, campaigned for structural reforms aimed at purging populism from the formal system of governance.[10] Above the daily tumult of democratic political culture, chamber policy making committees dispassionately evaluated the city's economic development, urban growth, service distribution, and wealth redistribution needs and made policy to serve these ends. With an annual calendar of meeting times, agendas, schedules, and a generous supply of money from the parent organization to hire professional staff, conduct surveys, and publicize results, the chamber's policy committees were businesslike, efficient, hard working, and highly effective. Ryerson Ritchie's organizational reforms gave the chamber an operational structure, even though the formal structure of the organization was at first eclipsed by the charismatic leadership of Cleveland's entrepreneurs.[11]

Early in the process of forming the Chamber of Commerce, entrepreneur Samuel Mather delivered an after dinner address in 1895 that defined the civic responsibilities of the entrepreneur and set out the goals of the chamber of commerce.[12] Getting down to basics, Mather bluntly told the assembled businessmen that Mayor McKisson and ward politicians were not responsible for McKissonism. "Gentlemen, the fault seems entirely ours. Government will not be as good as we deserve until we are willing to take the time and the pains to make it better."[13] For that purpose, Mather advised his fellow entrepreneurs to take time out from money making and turn their energies to making the city better.[14]

Samuel Mather's dinner speech admonishment bore immediate fruit. Businessmen rushed to serve on chamber committees, including street railway and steel magnate Tom L. Johnson, who, in the spirit of Mather's talk, entered politics and eventually became mayor of Cleveland. Johnson and the business community represented by Samuel Mather and the Cleveland Chamber of Commerce are often depicted as implacable foes, but the two had far more in common than the food and sparkling wine shared that night in 1895.

The Municipal Association

More than launching political careers, the Cleveland Chamber of Commerce initiated an institutional overhaul of the city's policy making apparatus. One of the most enduring new organizations was the Municipal Association. In 1895 the chamber lent its support to the group of young anti-McKisson professionals who founded the Municipal Association, which became the voice of the policy concerns of Corporate Regime professionals. The immediate object of the Municipal Association was the reform of government.[15] In the long term, Municipal Association professionals believed policy would have to be implemented by institutions visible to the public and institutions in which the public could place its confidence, which meant structurally sound institutions not too much under the influence of mass democracy.[16]

The first targets of Municipal Association criticism were machine politicians, corrupt municipal bureaucrats, monopoly franchisers, and, at times, Mayor Johnson. Even though Johnson and Municipal Association professionals endorsed many of the same reforms, the essential difference was that Johnson professed affection for mass democracy, while the Municipal Association would place restraints on it.[17]

For this reason, the Municipal Association tinkered with structural reforms in the municipal government. After initially supporting the strong mayor system, the Municipal Association backed the franchisers' efforts to weaken the mayor during the Johnson administration, only to endorse home rule and strong mayor charters thereafter. Exasperated at repeated failures to satisfactorily improve the performance of the executive function, the Municipal Association (by now the Civic League) in 1919 touted yet another panacea, the city manager system of government buttressed by nonpartisan elections and reductions in the size of the city council and school board as means to blunt the effects of mass democracy.

As civic architecture each of these structural reforms was flawed, inevitably falling short of an ideal design of public governance. Frustrated Corporate Regime professionals therefore tirelessly returned to the drawing boards in search of the perfect new form, only to be frustrated by the political tradesmen who sabotaged their work. But in the twilight of the regime, the collectivist municipal functions the professionals sought were far closer to realization than they could see.[18]

TAX REFORM

Chamber of Commerce professionals regarded institution building as a necessary prerequisite to policy making. But the entrepreneurs who guided the Cleveland Chamber of Commerce in its infancy were deeply preoccupied with what they saw as the parasitic relationship between various forms of capital and taxation. The policy course they chose for Cleveland would cost large sums of someone's money, and taxes would have to pay for it.[19] But who should pay most? To sort out the issue of tax burden, the Chamber of Commerce entrepreneurs borrowed the good capital–bad capital distinctions from Chamberlain and the Liberal Party.[20]

Good capital was active capital, that is, the money the entrepreneurs invested in the export sector of the economy, related real estate, and personal property. Active capital was good capital not simply because it was beneficial to its holders but also for the goods it produced and the thousands of jobs it created. Active capital was taxed more heavily than other forms of wealth. Against this there were three forms of bad capital: (1) inactive capital, which was money invested in land, especially land held vacant against future gain by speculators, (2) monopoly capital, which most conspicuously included the assets of traction and utilities companies holding franchises awarded by the municipality, and (3) passive capital, the income from investments.[21]

The entrepreneurial reformers schemed to transfer the tax burden from active capital to the three forms of bad capital. State and local tax revenues rested heavily on the property tax. However, property was so broadly defined by law that it failed to make distinctions crucial to the entrepreneurs, as between real property and personal property, the latter including the assets of individuals and corporations. The personal and corporate property tax exposed such assets as furnishings, machinery, inventories, and cash, certificates, bonds, and stocks deposited in banks to the tax collector and perfidious public officials. Real property was inactive (bad) capital. Personal property was active (good) capital, and it was the bulwark upon which the prosperity of the city depended. To reduce the multiplier effect of this hoard of active capital through confiscatory taxation was in the long run economically and socially damaging to all.[22] Even before the Cleveland Chamber of Commerce made public its formal lamentation of this state of affairs, entrepreneurs comported unilaterally to evade the personal property tax. Their tax avoidance artifices were well noted by embattled mayor Robert E. McKisson, who very loudly complained that the personal property tax collected annually amounted only to a minuscule fraction of the money on deposit in local banks.

Tom L. Johnson, the entrepreneurial reformer who was elected Cleveland's mayor in 1901, came to the defense of good capital by launching a vigorous tax reform crusade. While campaigning for election, Johnson founded his "Tax School," and for the first two years of his administration it attempted to educate the public on the need for tax reform. The Tax

School, echoing the thunder from the Chamber of Commerce, focused on the inequities of the property tax and on the tax favoritism shown monopoly capital represented by the franchisers. Tax reform became a staple of Cleveland politics, and in 1911, two years after Johnson was defeated in his final election, a Tax Commission was elected and the Johnson tax philosophy was carried forward by the commission's chairman, Frederic C. Howe.[23]

Johnson held that high taxes on vacant real estate would bring land into the market sooner and thereby achieve its highest and best use. Moreover, high taxes on land already in use (in place of taxes on structures built on the land) would force land already in the market into higher and better uses.[24] Johnson's attack on inactive capital was misinterpreted in the popular press as an attack on property generally. Many of Johnson's white collar and working class supporters, however, rallied to his side precisely because they thought he was making a more generalized attack on property, although Johnson never proposed to lay heavier taxes on active capital.[25]

Real estate interests, of course, criticized the higher land tax proposed by Johnson. To Johnson's claim that a higher real estate tax on vacant and underused land would force land into higher and better uses, real estate interests replied that high real estate taxes would have just the opposite effect. High real estate taxes would force vacant land into the market too soon and into expedient rather than higher and better uses. Similarly, high real estate taxes on developed land would encourage owners either to abandon real holdings in marginal sites or alternatively put them to short-term inferior uses. Higher taxes on land, occupied or vacant, would have just the opposite consequence of higher and better uses.[26]

Tom L. Johnson, oblivious to real estate industry criticisms, next launched a parallel crusade to tax monopoly capital. Monopolies held by utilities and streetcar franchisers were easy targets, unpopular with both respectable people and the masses. Franchisers were given long-term service monopolies by the city in return for which the monopolists paid trifling sums in taxes. Johnson believed that monopoly capital had been given a privilege which franchisers exploited to price gouge consumers and dodge taxes. Abuse of privilege was the most frequently bandied term in the Johnson vocabulary of entrepreneurial reform.[27] Chamber of Commerce entrepreneurial reformers saw nothing inherently wrong with Johnson's reasoning. As a form of bad capital, monopoly capital merited severe taxation. The Chamber soon learned, however, that Johnson's zeal for heavy taxation of monopoly capital was only a stop-gap remedy. His ideal solution lay in municipal ownership of these services.[28]

Johnson's attacks on inactive and monopoly capital prompted the chamber to formulate its own tax reform initiative, a strategy also calculated to shift the burden of taxation from good capital to bad capital, that is, from active to inactive, monopoly, and passive capital. The strategy was only partially successful. Johnson's rhetoric, and the popular response to it, made taxation a polarizing issue. Commercial real estate interests and traction and utility companies were not without their own political resources and tax avoidance strategies. Moreover, the chamber's passion for taxing passive capital waned with the advance of time and the realization that passive capital represented the assets of entrepreneurial widows and heirs. The tax burden, thanks to the parallel efforts of the chamber, the Tax School, and the Tax Commission, was in the end shifted to real property, but the large commercial land interests, in turn, used their political resources to shift the burden of the real estate tax from large holders of realty to small home owners, who expressed their displeasure at the ballot box by killing many worthwhile civic projects on election day.[29]

ECONOMIC DEVELOPMENT AND THE MULTILOCATIONAL CORPORATION

One of the more curious ironies in the history of urban policy making is the low priority status the Corporate Regime assigned economic development policy. Once in control of the policy making apparatus, the men who built Cleveland's industries practiced an economic development policy of benign neglect. A low-priority economic development policy was a misshapen response to the changing organizational realities of turn of the century industrial enterprises. American business organizations were evolving into larger and more impersonal forms, organizational changes that had a very personal and largely remunerative impact on the business lives of individual entrepreneurs and professionals; but as a civic decision making group, the men who built Cleveland's industrial era economy failed to see the impact the evolving business organization had on the making of economic development policy.

Early in the Corporate Regime, key local manufacturing businesses changed from locally owned entrepreneurial enterprises into multilocational national corporations during a merger mania that erupted in the 1890s and peaked in the years before World War I. Mergers were effected by financiers resident in the nation's financial centers, and mergers caused ownership to pass from highly visible local entrepreneurs, their families, and partners to anonymous nonresident stockholders and boards.

The multilocational corporation was important for both its sum and its parts. The multilocational corporation located its headquarters operation in large urban centers, preferably a major capital market, and strategically placed its parts—the branch plant and distribution centers—in key urban markets. Management of the multilocational firm passed from local entrepreneurs to a new class of professional managers. Professional managers transformed the merged business entities into a unitary multilocational corporation managed by means of a military style command and control organizational hierarchy. From offices in high-rise corporate headquarters buildings, executives and their staffs issued directives for implementation by subordinate line officers in branch plants and distribution centers.

In the new organizational hierarchy, Cleveland's key businesses became branch plant operations of and distribution centers for multilocational corporations. Corporate headquarters decision makers, far more than local policy makers, directed the course of Cleveland's economic development. Corporate location policy—the decisions about where to locate its parts—had a far greater long-term impact on Cleveland's economic development than did the economic development policy of the Corporate Regime. In this new organizational environment, local policy makers did not control Cleveland's economic destiny, although several decades passed before the impact of this new business paradigm was felt or even acknowledged locally.[30]

The Corporate Regime was unconcerned and unaware that economic development policy was no longer in its hands. In the earlier Merchant and Populist eras, by contrast, businessmen depended on the various favors and services local government could provide. Local public officials gladly acted as lobbyists for Cleveland businesses in the state legislature; more importantly, local public officials secured local funding for and supervised the construction of business related infrastructure. But the political needs of the national multilocational corporation transcended the authority and influence of local public officials and ex-officio policy makers. Multilocational corporations in metals, chemicals, electrical, and automobile industries, the largest employers in Cleveland, did business in several states, and their political needs in an era of expanding government regulation were federal rather than state or local. There was little that even the most compliant of local public officials could do to advance the political agenda of a multilocational corporation. Corporate Regime leaders continued to push the old economic development agenda of local infrastructure improvements as though nothing had changed.[31]

The corporate merger movement had an enervating effect on the lives of the entrepreneurial class. Cleveland's entrepreneurs, once the holders and vigorous defenders of active capital, became the holders of passive capital as they exchanged ownership and management in their firms for cash and stocks in the new multilocational corporate enterprises. Removed from the active management of the firms they founded, their business energies were directed toward managing paper assets, stocks, bonds, and deeds. With their bankers and lawyers, the entrepreneurs preoccupied themselves with estate management, family trusts, real estate trusts, and leaseholds. These defensive investment strategies signaled that the entrepreneurs were unwilling to convert their money into active capital for investment in new local business enterprises.[32]

The apparent strength of Cleveland's economy contributed to the Corporate Regime's disinterest in economic development policy. This was an outgrowth of resolutely optimistic readings of the economic tea leaves, renderings which led policy makers to a false sense of security. Between 1895 and 1919, the years the Corporate Regime dominated local policy making, Cleveland's population increased from 320,000 to 796,000.[33] A two and a half fold population increase was the sort of idle statistic that Cleveland Chamber of Commerce annual report writers seized upon as irrefutable evidence of the city's prosperity. Even so, more probing looks into the demographic nooks and crannies sustained the enthusiasm of local boosters. In-migration and a comparatively high urban birth rate more than tripled the number of males in working age cohorts, but the number of jobs created rose fourfold, even drawing women into the labor force in substantial numbers, notably in the growing low-wage needle trades industries. Only in the World War I decade, when an 85,000 increase in the male working age cohort was offset by an 85,000 job increase in the war-driven manufacturing sector, did working age population growth even threaten to challenge the pace of job creation.[34] Chamber of Commerce boosters saw in Cleveland's economy a business Eden that needed little tending, but they erred in doing so.

The essence of economic development is adding new work to old work in the export sector of a city's economy; thus, a sound economic development policy is a predetermined plan to add new work to old work in that sector. Satisfied that the economy was fundamentally sound, the Corporate Regime did little that was premeditated to add new work to old work. The core of Cleveland's export sector economy was manufacturing.[35] When the Corporate Regime assumed policy making dominance in the mid 1890s, over 40 percent of Cleveland's labor force was employed in manufacturing, a proportion that increased to 50 percent in 1920. Reports published by an entrepreneur-dominated Chamber of Commerce proudly brandished this statistic, and it drew prolonged applause from an audience long accustomed to taking economic development for granted. But jobs added in the manufacturing sector only masqueraded as economic development policy. New work was not being added to old work. The added jobs were only an expansion of old work.[36]

The Corporate Regime deduced false conclusions from misread statistics. The reality was that manufacturing in Cleveland was heavily concentrated in the metals industry. Just three industries—primary metals, fabricated metals, and industrial and commercial machinery—accounted for 40 percent of all manufacturing jobs in 1890 and over 50 percent by 1920. Between 1890 and 1910, sixteen thousand jobs were added in these three industries, and in the single decade between 1910 and 1920, twenty-six thousand jobs were added in the three core metals industries.[37] These were the very industries that were being merged into national multilocational metals corporations managed from out-of-town headquarters operations. Cleveland factories employing as many as 40 percent of all workers in the manufacturing sector became branch plant operations of multilocational corporations. In these industries so vital to the city's economic destiny, Cleveland surrendered control over its economic development policy.[38]

Early in the Corporate Regime, the electrical apparatus industry actually did add new work to old work, and late in the regime the automobile industry added new jobs to the local economy at a staggering rate, some fourteen thousand in the 1910–1920 decade alone. The appearance of both of these industries was encouraging because they not only gave Cleveland new work but they also bestowed upon the city "initial advantage," the rapid growth deriving from an early start in an industry which gives the pioneering city an initial and sometimes permanent advantage over all urban competitors.[39] In the electrical industry, Cleveland acquired its initial advantage when Charles F. Brush invented the arc light in 1879 and founded the Brush Electric Company in 1880 to manufacture his invention. But initial advantage in the electrical industry was squandered when Brush sold his business interests to the Thomas Houston Electric Company in 1889, which two years later merged into the General Electric Company. What had been Brush Electric became a branch plant operation of the General Electric Company. Jobs at the company expanded but the decisions to add new work to old work in Cleveland were made in the New York office tower housing General Electric's corporate headquarters, not in downtown Cleveland.[40]

Westinghouse was another electrical company founded in Cleveland. George Westinghouse had already invented a railroad air brake, which he manufactured in Cleveland. In the early 1890s, when municipal demand for electrical power and apparatus offered a shorter route to riches, the entrepreneurial George Westinghouse diversified his air brake manufacturing operations to include electrical power and apparatus and added scores of new jobs at his factory. In the late 1890s, however, Westinghouse merged his holdings into a larger multilocational corporate entity, and the corporate headquarters building bearing the Westinghouse standard was built in Pittsburgh. Cleveland remained an important branch plant operation in the Westinghouse corporate family, but the city's designation as an important branch plant operation was made in Pittsburgh. Cleveland's initial advantage in the highly promising electrical industry washed away in the merger movement.[41]

The automobile industry provides a gloss on this familiar merger story. In the early 1900s, Cleveland rivaled Detroit as the center of the emerging automobile industry. Several Cleveland inventors built automobiles equaling in technological virtuosity those crafted in Detroit. The inventors not only manufactured them locally but allied Cleveland enterprises quickly converted existing manufacturing facilities to the production of automobile parts and accessories. Cleveland's initial advantage seemed assured. But after 1910, nearly all of these companies merged into larger multilocational automobile corporations headquartered in Detroit. Clevelanders applauded the Ford Motor Company's decision in 1914 to build a large assembly plant in Cleveland, a factory designed to employ hundreds of workers. Despite its size, it was never more than a branch plant operation of the Detroit headquartered company.[42]

By 1920, nearly 22,000 workers were employed in the automobile industry, nearly all of them employees of Detroit-headquartered multilocational corporations. The auto industry was a classic but misleading example of initial advantage and adding new work to old work. The 1899 Census of Manufacturers did not even list automobiles in its taxonomy of manufacturers. Two decades later, automobile and related manufacturing was one of the nation's largest employers, and Cleveland was one of the industry's most important production centers. What the 1919 Census of Manufacturers did not explain, however, was that Cleveland's status as an important automobile manufacturing center was a determination made in Detroit, not Cleveland.[43]

Cleveland was not master of its own economic development destiny in the five crucial industries that formed the core of the export sector of the local economy. These five industries—primary metals, fabricated metals, industrial machinery, electrical apparatus, and automobiles—employed one of every four workers in Cleveland's entire labor force. Policy decisions about the fate of these key industries and 25 percent of Cleveland's total work force were in fact made in corporate headquarters office buildings in New York, Chicago, Pittsburgh, and Detroit.⁴⁴

A Policy of Benign Neglect

The entrepreneurs, the men who in the nineteenth century laid the foundations for the export sector of Cleveland's economy, dominated the Chamber of Commerce until 1913; moreover, an entrepreneur was mayor of the city from 1901 to 1909, and a corporation lawyer served as mayor from 1912 to 1916. What all had in common was an inability to understand the relationship between the important changes taking place in the relationship between the modernizing business organization and economic development policy. The Chamber was the Corporate Regime's primary vehicle for municipal reform. It debated the issue of land use controls, improved the delivery of distributive services, and redistributed the community's wealth from haves to have-nots. But it neglected economic development policy.

This ordering of the regime's policy priorities did not happen without internal debate. In the federated setting of the Chamber of Commerce, leaders of the Wholesale Merchants Board and the Retail Merchants Board challenged the industrial entrepreneurs' urban policy priorities. Wholesale and retail merchants argued that the Chamber of Commerce should make economic development rather than civic betterment its highest policy priority. Although the protests of the wholesalers and retailers appeared self-serving and their concept of economic development skewed toward businesses with regional rather than national markets, wholesale and retail merchants sensed that Cleveland's economic development should not be left to fate.⁴⁵

Entrepreneurs, however, dismissed the wholesalers and retailers as narrow-minded, self-interested bumpkins attempting to preserve the remnants of an older, out-moded commercial era economy at the expense of civic betterment.⁴⁶ This rejection did the wholesalers and retailers a disservice. They understood the importance of the export sector of the industrial era economy and of course their relationship to it, though they could only sense but not fully articulate the fear that playing a pat hand in economic development policy would in time lead the city's economy in a direction opposite of the one intended.

Savings and loan banker Jeremiah J. Sullivan did considerable business with wholesale and retail merchants, and he was one of their spokesmen in chamber debates on policy priorities. Yet when elected president of the chamber in 1903, Sullivan recanted his earlier position and proclaimed that the civic work of the chamber was and should be the primary goal of the organization.[47] Ryerson Ritchie, the man who reorganized the chamber in 1893, agreed and said so publicly when invited back to address the organization on the occasion of the twentieth anniversary of the reform effort. "I was speaking today to a gentleman," Ritchie told the assembled members, "who some years ago openly criticized the Chamber for dabbling in public affairs. I asked him what he now thought of it. He said: 'It is the best institution we have in Cleveland today.'"[48] And entrepreneur Ambrose Swasey, the chamber president following Sullivan, said in 1905 that "Commercial and industrial success are merely the foundations for the higher development of our city. We strive for something nobler than that."[49]

Despite the high-minded rhetoric, economic reality, from time to time, did intrude on the chamber's dream of a city upon a hill. Between the election of Swasey and the reappearance of Ryerson Ritchie, specific concerns were voiced about two related issues: the lack of investment capital available in Cleveland and the need to attract new industries.[50] Measured by such conventional yardsticks as individual wealth, bank deposits per capita, assets of local banks, value of plant, production, and value added, Cleveland ranked high among the nation's urban centers in capital density. The issue was less the presence or absence of capital than it was the flow of capital into tributary circuits.

Capital flows through an economy in three tributary circuits, primary, secondary, and tertiary. Primary circuit capital is invested in raw materials, manufacturing equipment, labor, and transport vehicles. Primary circuit capital is what was earlier defined as active capital. Cleveland's active capital, generated by entrepreneurs and commercial banks, built the primary capital circuit during the early phases of the industrial revolution, and the primary circuit consequently fueled the development of the export sector of Cleveland's economy. Primary circuit capital was locally controlled until the advent of the merger movement. The merger movement transferred control of the primary circuit from local entrepreneurs and commercial banks to multilocational corporations and investment banking houses, neither of which, to belabor the point, was headquartered in Cleveland.

Cleveland entrepreneurs who sold their assets in the primary circuit either became passive investors in the primary circuit or reinvested their gains as inactive capital in the secondary capital circuit. Secondary circuit capital is money invested in undeveloped land and the "built environment" of industrial, commercial, and retail buildings, housing, and public works projects. The secondary capital circuit during the Corporate Regime, in contrast to the departing primary circuit, was purely local in character.

Chapter 5: Ideals, Institutions, and Policies

Many entrepreneurs, having sold their active capital assets in the primary circuit, became passive investors in the secondary capital circuit, resulting in a flood of capital flowing into this circuit. Commercial banks joined savings and loan institutions and a diverse and aggressive local real estate industry as active capital participants in the secondary circuit. All elements in the burgeoning secondary capital circuit, passive and active, placed considerable pressure on local government to invest in public works projects emphasizing street and utilities expansion and a correspondingly expansive urban growth policy. These developments were evidence of the volatile and oscillating relationship between primary and secondary circuits of capital. During the Corporate Regime the oscillations between the circuits of capital were driven by the merger movement, the consequence of which was a primary circuit largely controlled by out-of-towners and an overheated secondary circuit locally controlled.

The tertiary capital circuit is represented by investments in education and culture. Considerable public capital was invested in the Cleveland Public School System, and private capital was raised from working class parishioners to fund the sizable parochial school network. The entrepreneurs weighed in with heavy tertiary capital investments in Western Reserve University, the Case Institute, and a host of other University Circle cultural and educational institutions, investments which were also a manifestation of the flow of capital out of the primary circuit. When dissident members of the Cleveland Chamber of Commerce complained of a shortage of capital locally they lamented a shortage of primary circuit capital, not fully appreciating that the oscillations between the three capital circuits had resulted in a massive transfer of capital from the primary circuit to local secondary and tertiary capital circuits. The loss of the primary circuit, however, was not irretrievable. Countervailing measures could have been taken.

The chamber regularly dispatched delegations of Clevelanders to visit sister organizations in other cities and report on their progress. Long accustomed to having these delegations report back to the parent body that the Cleveland Chamber of Commerce was vastly more enlightened and progressive than similar bodies in other cities, the chamber was startled when a 1909 delegation of members visited several of Cleveland's industrial rivals and reported to a stunned audience that chambers of commerce in other cities aggressively pursued new industries and placed economic development over civic betterment as their highest priority. Chambers of commerce in rival industrial cities commissioned highly sophisticated economic base studies of their towns, studies which followed the principle of adding new work to old work with a carefully calibrated economic development plan calculated to add new but related industries to the manufacturing base already established. These same chambers aggressively recruited compatible out-of-town industries and made primary circuit capital available to them as well as to promising local enterprises. Under the sponsorship of local chambers, economic development partnerships were forged between local capitalists and commercial banks to provide these promising businesses with primary circuit capital, demonstrating that a local primary capital circuit could be revived even in the face of the merger movement overtaking older, established industries.[51]

These revelations caught the Cleveland Chamber of Commerce flat-footed, and the organization was momentarily gripped in panic. The chamber hastily formed an Industrial Development Committee, which, two years later, issued a preliminary report identifying potential industries that would add new work to old work. Cleveland, the report observed, was a metals making town. The city's metals making factories exported their product in an unfinished state to other cities where it was turned into finished metals products. The obvious related industry and the object of any economic development plan, the report concluded, should be the addition of local finished metals products industries to Cleveland's existing manufacturing base in metals making. These observations, the Industrial Development Committee cautioned, were merely preliminary. The whole matter required more detailed study, tracking transportation flows in and out of the city, identifying potential sites, assessing the availability of capital, and developing a public relations plan to sell the advantages of the city to out-of-town finished goods enterprisers. The Industrial Development Committee promised a detailed study and economic development plan posthaste. Despite repeated promises over the next two years, the economic development study and plan never materialized.[52]

Debates over the several components of the committee's preliminary report did take place, but the outcome was foreordained when the entrepreneurs refused to fund a primary capital circuit. The entrepreneurs insisted that Cleveland's merits as an ideal location for manufacturing were self-evident, and once potential finished metals products enterprisers were so informed, their decision to locate in Cleveland would not require such artificial inducements as a pool of privately raised primary circuit capital. The entrepreneurs said that economic development policy had only two prerequisites: (1) a promotional campaign touting Cleveland's locational advantages with potential manufacturers as its target and (2) renewed efforts to maintain and improve the city's transportation, harbor, and wharf infrastructure.[53]

This narrowly focused economic development strategy cost Cleveland opportunities to share in the automobile, aircraft, and motion picture industries, among others. More aggressive cities such as Detroit, Pittsburgh, Chicago, and Los Angeles, cities on the travel itinerary of the Chamber's Industrial Development Committee, were more aggressive and won these industries and more. The economic development policy of the Corporate Regime remained what economic development policy had always been: plodding demands on the municipality for river and harbor improvements, more dock and wharf space, and redundant studies of the industrial site potential of a lakefront still controlled by railroad companies with out-of-town headquarters. The Corporate Regime's economic development policy was frozen in time, and, even though the trend drew scant local notice, rival cities soon outpaced Cleveland as manufacturing centers.[54]

In the 1970s and after, Cleveland lost manufacturing jobs at an alarming rate. Shuttered factories and steel mills littered the landscape. The seeds of these departures were sown in the first two decades of the century when key Cleveland businesses were merged into larger multilocational corporate entities, many of which later were merged into multinational enterprises or were simply looted and left as empty casings in the battle of leveraged buyouts. As long as Cleveland retained its locational advantages relative to domestic and international markets for metals products and the city's labor force was competitive by international standards, the city retained its attraction as a site for branch plant operations; but when these business prerequisites changed in the 1970s, Cleveland lost its appeal. Cold-hearted accountants and strategic planners in corporate headquarters cities made decisions to move their branch plant operations elsewhere.

6

URBAN GROWTH POLICY I
Land Use Controls at the Periphery

The controlled use of land was the centerpiece of Corporate Regime policy making. In the mid 1890s, Cleveland continued to suffer the ill effects of the Merchant Regime's laissez faire growth policy. The Populist Regime's counterattack aimed at limiting the geographical boundaries of the city and dampening the demands of an expanding urban growth constituency in favor of providing distributive services to a population already living within the city's fixed boundaries. The Corporate Regime, in contrast, charted imaginative new directions in urban growth policy, policies linked to specific projects designed to achieve the elusive goal of land use controls. The imagination was supplied by the entrepreneurial wing of the Corporate Regime, which dominated the first two decades of its urban growth policy making. Late in the regime, leadership in growth policy was taken over by the regime's professionals, who picked up the missing pieces, filled in the details, and steered the city toward comprehensive public land use controls.

In the 1890s, many of the newly rich and recently leisured entrepreneurs toured the wonders of urban Europe, and, returning home, declared Cleveland an affront to their lately acquired sense of urban aesthetics. To them, the legacy of Cleveland's untrammeled growth was land put to dubious uses, a repetitious gridiron street layout, and a hideous monotony in the design of residential and commercial buildings. Dramatic, well-designed civic land use projects in Cleveland, such as those so admirably on display in London, Paris, and Berlin, the entrepreneurs hoped, might have an availing effect on private developers.

This false premise of good design by example gave way to a second phase of Corporate Regime urban growth policy, a phase dominated by the regime's professionals. Professionals, late in the regime, decided that the entrepreneurial land use projects were too costly and good urban design by architectural suasion had limited utility. Missing in Cleveland was an orderly, comprehensive set of land use controls, a set of rules that would not simply inspire good design but more importantly sustain the higher goal of urban efficiency, a quality visitors to the city said was notably absent. Professionals equated good design and urban efficiency with city master planning and regulatory zoning. The Corporate Regime effected both policies, and Cleveland looked far different in 1919 than it had in the mid 1890s.

The entrepreneurs' urban growth policy is a living artifact and remains on display in four grand civic land use projects: the municipal and regional park systems, the downtown civic center, and a cultural and educational satellite city (University Circle). Each bore the earmarks of the entrepreneurial ideal. They were bold, dramatic, innovative, highly capital intensive, and they captured the public imagination in ways that nothing else could. Implementation of these projects was perilous and lengthy, but the experience of project implementation created opportunities for the institutionalization of professional expertise in design and management, which culminated in further accretions of professionalism in urban growth policy.[1]

PARKS AS URBAN GROWTH POLICY:
Structure, Scale, and Function

Structure

The Corporate Regime built one park system, the Cleveland Park System, in the 1890s and started another, the Cleveland Metropolitan Park System, begun in 1917. Both illustrate the Corporate Regime's emphasis on land use controls as the centerpiece of urban growth policy and both raised the corollary issues of structure, scale, and function in park building. Park planning enthusiasm coincided with the transition from the Populist Regime to the Corporate Regime. The overriding structural goal of the Corporate Regime was not only park building but also administrative and fiscal control over them. But structural uncertainty slowed the development of a Cleveland park system, a casualty of the long running battle over municipal charter reform. Between 1865 and 1905, administrative responsibility for the city's parks changed hands no less than seven times. With administrative responsibility revolving on an average of every six years, continuity was a major stumbling block in the forging of a coherent long-term parks and recreation policy.[2]

In 1865 responsibility for parks rested in the hands of the city council, but a new weak mayor city charter in 1871 awarded the parks to an independent Board of Park Commissioners composed of appointed public officials. A decade later, state legislation mandated the appointment of new five-man municipal park boards composed exclusively of citizens who presumably had greater independence of both the city council and the mayor.[3]

The strong mayor Federal charter of 1891 reversed the philosophy of citizen control and independence of political influence, but the structural independence of the parks system was largely retained in yet another five-man commission, appointed in 1892, and composed also of private citizens but with the mayor and city council president acting in ex-officio capacities.[4]

Populists and professionals, in pursuit of separate but parallel agendas, opposed the 1892 structure, arguing instead for a park system as an executive department reporting directly to the mayor. The two groups were also concerned about where the parks should be built and what purpose they would serve. A compromise of sorts was reached when the Board of Parks Commissioners was given a limited seven-year life span, at which time the system would become an executive department.

Lawyers John A. Smith and John A. Zangerle, representing the Park Board Reorganization Association, a citizens' home rule charter reform organization, brought suit against the Board of Park Commissioners in 1899, convinced that the seemingly irrelevant urban perimeter scale of park planning was the fault of the independent park commission. In 1900, before the courts ruled, the seven-year charter of the board expired, and the park system became an executive department under the direction of a park superintendent, an appointee of the mayor.[5] But in 1902, the Ohio Supreme Court nullified Cleveland's 1891 Federal charter, and the new weak-mayor city charter restored the independent Board of Parks Commissioners. This lasted only until 1905, when the courts amended the 1902 decision and allowed the transfer of the park system to an executive department.[6]

Opposition to mayoral control finally dissipated when Mayor Tom L. Johnson appointed William A. Stinchcomb director of the parks system. Stinchcomb was a career public servant who had served in the city's engineering department since 1895. While not a university trained engineer, Stinchcomb's professional expertise and personal integrity were such that he won the confidence of middle class professionals who did business with him in the city's engineering department and did the same in the 1890s when he served as the Board of Park Commissioners' in-house expert assigned to work with outside design consultants to develop a municipal park plan.[7]

Throughout this long-running, tedious see-saw structural conflict, the entrepreneurs stood behind the idea of independent park boards because such boards lay beyond the contaminating grasp of partisan politicians. Professionals, late-comers to the park movement, concluded that bureaucratic expertise, more so than structural independence, was the antidote to the meddling of politicians; therefore, they promoted the park system as part of the executive function of government, so long as the parks' directorship was in the hands of a professional. Both structural goals were at last joined in the Cleveland Metropolitan Park District, created in 1917.[8]

By 1917 urban sprawl leapfrogged the Cleveland Parks System and threatened to engulf Cleveland's newly developing suburbs. A second, suburban ring of parks might halt urban sprawl, but a regional park system brought about yet another round of conflict over administrative structure. The spread of settlement beyond the city limits into the outlying rural reaches of Cuyahoga County outpaced the development of governing institutions. The geography of political institutions was place specific, but the city's physical geography was now regional in scale, transcending the traditional political boundaries of the village, township, municipality, and county. How would a regional park system be governed?[9]

William A. Stinchcomb searched for an answer. While serving as city engineer and during his Johnson administration tenure as superintendent of city parks, Stinchcomb became a forceful advocate of regional park planning. Comprehensive park systems, designed by professionals and administered by dedicated public servants, not only served as land use controls but were visible proof of government's ability to serve the public. During dozens of impressive appearances before the several Cleveland Chamber of Commerce committees devoted to land use matters, Stinchcomb built a circle of allies among the young professionals serving the Corporate Regime. In the judgment of Stinchcomb and his allies in the city building professions, structure, planning, and professional management should be the scaffolding of an urban growth policy of land use control.[10]

In 1905 Stinchcomb enlisted the support of his chamber allies to lobby the state legislature for a county park system, taking care to avoid political controversy by limiting the parks' function to the preservation of nature. These efforts came to no avail. In 1911, Stinchcomb and his supporters in the chamber, joined by the Cuyahoga County delegation to the state legislature, at last achieved their goal when the legislature amended the state constitution to allow counties to create park districts for the express purpose of resource preservation.[11]

The legislation mandated administration by a four-man board of county park commissioners. The four were appointed by a probate judge in 1912.[12] Later in 1912, Stinchcomb was elected county engineer and in this capacity was able to supply professional management to the county park commissioners. Stinchcomb knew well the bureaucratic powers that staff could wield, but his hands were tied from the beginning because the state enabling legislation did not allow the Board of Park Commissioners to spend public money. The fiscal powers of the board were limited to accepting private donations in either cash or land.[13]

Remedial legislation followed in 1915 which allowed county commissioners to appropriate money for park purposes, condemn property, and put park bond issues on the ballot, a measure which eased the fiscal burden but only temporarily. In 1916, shortly after the county commissioners appropriated money to commission a plan for a county-wide park system, the Ohio State Supreme Court ruled in a related jurisdictional matter that all county officials must be elected. An injunction suit restraining the Cuyahoga County Board of Park Commissioners from any further operations immediately followed.[14]

But William A. Stinchcomb and his Chamber of Commerce allies found a way out of the political morass. They took heart in the evolution of the park planning movement in Boston. In the 1890s, Boston park planners found a way to escape the structural restraints imposed by political boundaries and the binding ties of state constitutions. Their discovery was the regional special purpose district, which allowed Boston's park planners to deal with a metropolitan problem on a metropolitan scale. The special purpose district concept was not new—public schools had been special purpose districts for decades—but the idea of building and managing a park system as a special purpose district was novel.[15] In 1917, Stinchcomb, Chamber of Commerce lawyers and architects, and the county legislative delegation, drawing on the Boston model, drafted the legislation that would make possible the Cleveland Metropolitan Park District.[16]

The legislation granted the Cleveland Metropolitan Park District regional authority to plan and build parks. Chiefly, the district functioned in Cuyahoga County, but it had the legal authority to acquire contiguous land in adjacent counties when necessary. The special purpose district was governed by a three-person board of park commissioners appointed by the senior county probate judge. The board was empowered to levy taxes and issue bonds and acquire land by purchase or eminent domain. The board could hire staff to plan and manage the park system. The first Metropolitan Park District Board appointed was composed of Louis A. Moses, Henry M. Farnsworth, and William Diehl. They promptly hired William A. Stinchcomb as parks engineer. Here, at last, was the political institution that could address regional recreational needs on a regional scale.[17] The special purpose district fulfilled the two major structural goals of the Corporate Regime. It satisfied the now fading entrepreneurial faction because the Cleveland Metropolitan Park District had an appointed board independent of partisan politics and had financial independence as well. The Stinchcomb appointment satisfied professionals because the management of the park district was in the hands of a competent public servant.[18]

The two park systems, the Cleveland Park System and the Cleveland Metropolitan Park District, provided a solid structure of governance from which an urban growth policy grounded in land use controls could be launched. A system of parks provided the means to demonstrate that land use controls could serve a public purpose. Just as the development of an institutional structure proceeded through a series of false starts and assorted setbacks, so too did the scale of intervention pose dilemmas, debate, and reevaluation before the regime cultivated a comprehensive recreational strategy to serve the two park systems.

Scale: Where and Why

The city and regional park systems' structure of governance was a milestone achievement for the Corporate Regime. Scale was the next issue of importance in establishing an urban growth policy of land use controls. Scale is a dual-purpose locational term meaning *where* in urban space the parks should be built, and what objectives the dual park systems were created to achieve—the *why* issue raised above. The where of park planning was the urban periphery rather than the densely settled urban core. The choice of where made both the Cleveland and Metropolitan park districts the objects of considerable internal debate and outside criticism because it seemed to the regime's critics that those settled in the urban core were more in need of recreational opportunities than those at the fringes of settlement. Initially, the why part of the scale question was answered by the entrepreneurial faction of the Corporate Regime who dominated the early years of park planning. Their park planning objective was to use the parks as naturalistic barriers to urban sprawl. But in the World War I decade, when sprawl leapfrogged the municipal park system, the Corporate Regime simply extended the naturalistic park idea to a regional scale. Professionals within and critics outside the regime wanted class-specific, managed recreational programs in the dual park systems.[19] Urban growth policy as land use controls was not at issue, but professionals differed from entrepreneurs in their belief that land use controls should serve a higher social purpose than nature preservation and managed growth.

These two elements of scale came together in the mid 1890s, just as the Corporate Regime assumed dominance in urban policy making and when guardianship of the Cleveland park system was assumed by the Board of Park Commissioners. The Board of Park Commissioners, acting on the advice of Commission staff member William A. Stinchcomb and his allies in the Chamber of Commerce, retained landscape architect E. W. Bowditch to craft a comprehensive design for the Cleveland park system. Bowditch came highly recommended because he was a member of Frederick Law Olmsted's design team for the Boston parks project.[20] The completed Bowditch design inspired John D. Rockefeller, the Shaker Realty Company, and Martha B. Ambler to make additional donations of land to the Board of Park Commissioners so that the design could be implemented, at least on the city's east side.[21] Late in the 1890s, the future of the park system seemed assured: it had a board of commissioners to give it structure, an ample amount of land at the city's periphery, an annual budget allocated by City Council, professional staff, the support of the Chamber of Commerce, and a comprehensive plan drawn by E. W. Bowditch in 1893.

Bowditch's design was influenced by the park planning philosophy of Bowditch's mentor, Frederick Law Olmsted. What Olmsted taught Bowditch was the importance of bringing nature to the city, and E. W. Bowditch's design for the Cleveland park system turned the city's topography toward naturalistic ends. The design imposed order and structure on the land already acquired by the Board of Park Commissioners and set a direction for further development and completion of the municipal parks system.[22]

E. W. Bowditch's design closely followed Olmsted's park plan for Boston. It proposed a circumferential chain of parks spanning the city's perimeter, linked to each other by a system of boulevards and to the city proper by radial connector streets.[23] (See figure 6.1.) The system began at Gordon Park on the city's east side and ended at Edgewater Park on the city's western perimeter. A boulevard connected each park site. East Boulevard was designed to connect Gordon, Wade, Shaker, and Garfield parks on the east side, and West Boulevard connected Brookside and Edgewater parks on the west side. Lay audiences, charmed by drawings of green spoked wheels, were easily persuaded to lend their support to the Bowditch rendering of a park system encircling the area of settlement.[24]

The language of the Board of Park Commissioners report explaining features of the Bowditch park plan was unrestrained: "The dream of a continuous bower of verdant foliage stretching from the lake on the east to the lake on the west; and encircling the city in a wide and graceful sweep far to the south; with a smoothly graded parkway to carry softly gliding wheels

Chapter 6: Urban Growth Policy I 109

FIGURE 6.1 Cleveland Park System and Cleveland Metropolitan Park System, 1930 (Courtesy of The Western Reserve Historical Society, Cleveland, Ohio)

over the score or more of miles intervening between the termini of the system; with a vast domain where all our people, without distinction of class or station, among flowers and trees, pleasant lakes, grassy lawns, rippling streams, purling brooks, and the songs of birds, may hold sway in pleasure and enjoyment of Nature's greatest bounties...."[25] Social bounties would also accrue because the park system would instill a "love of nature, of birds, of flowers, of noble trees, of green verdure and beautiful landscape, which lying dormant in some hearts—especially in those persons where sordid aims or surroundings have always been paramount...."[26]

But these social uplift goals of the plan were disingenuous. If by sordid persons the Corporate Regime park planners meant the city's inner-ring working class, the urban perimeter scale of intervention precluded them as beneficiaries. Working class families were not the owners of horses or carriages with "softly gliding wheels," and the trolley car system was just then extended to the site of the Wade donation. Even so, at a cost of seven cents a ride, a day in the park for the working class family was reserved for Easter Sunday or the Fourth of July, holidays when Bowditch and Stinchcomb must have taken the surveys which asserted that the parks were extensively used by the working class. Still, when the holiday day-trippers stepped off the trolley, picnic baskets in hand and rowdy gamins in tow, they were

110   Part Three: The Corporate Regime, 1895–1919

greeted by fences and "keep off the grass" signs.[27]

The sordid aims at issue were those of the real estate industry. Wade and Gordon, both members of the Board of Park Commissioners, were repelled by the design of real estate developments at the fringe of settlement, and both men as private citizens battled the vernacular in site design and residential architecture with their private parks and real estate development projects. When these individualist campaigns for land use control failed, the two opted for a collectivist resolution to the problem and pushed for the intervention of Corporate Regime governmental and civic institutions.

But the nature of the Corporate Regime's park planning policy and urban periphery scale of intervention sparked criticism because the twin park systems so plainly failed to serve the recreational needs of city residents. Under this arrangement, the cost of park building, site acquisition, and upkeep became the third largest line item in the municipal budget, taxpayer dollars spent liberally on parks for the benefit of a select few.[28]

Nevertheless, intervention at the urban periphery prevailed through the course of the Corporate Regime, and the twin park systems continued to function as interruptions in the city's sprawl. Compromises with critics, however, meant that the parks became multi-purpose recreational venues serving all classes of Clevelanders, a collectivity benefiting a collectivity.[29]

Function: Who Benefits

Tom L. Johnson's first directive as Mayor of Cleveland was for removal of the "keep off the grass" signs in the city's parks, a widely applauded symbolic act that spoke volumes about the beneficiaries of the municipal park system. Mayors Johnson (1901–1909) and Newton D. Baker (1912–1916) preferred a park system that would serve the recreational needs of the greatest number of Clevelanders. Johnson worked to bring the park system under the mayor's control and liberate it from the land use control policies of the Board of Park Commissioners and the chamber's Parks Committee, both of which were wed to naturalism and the socially exclusive intervention on the urban periphery. Newton D. Baker's interest in parks ran in the same direction, but, as a staunch ally of the professionals, Baker also sought to bureaucratize recreation.[30]

All Cleveland mayors, including Johnson and Baker, were under pressure from church and professional groups to root out gambling and vice and regulate the sale and consumption of alcohol and to find a moral alternative to such pastimes. While Mayor Johnson was inclined to wink at such activities, Newton D. Baker, serving as Johnson's city solicitor, was convinced that a park system undergirded by a comprehensive recreational plan could serve as an alternative to the gambling den, brothel, and saloon. During the Johnson administration, Solicitor Baker proposed bath houses at Gordon and Edgewater parks, playing fields accessible to working class neighborhoods, and supervised recreational programs at all parks in the system. To fill evening hour recreational needs, Baker proposed alcohol-free dance pavilions staffed by chaperons. Many of these ideas eventually materialized during Baker's mayoral administration. Mayor Baker unabashedly claimed credit for empty saloons and clientless gambling dens and brothels on summer evenings.[31]

In Johnson's administration, City Engineer and Parks Supervisor William A. Stinchcomb was assigned the thankless task of selling the idea of managed recreation to the chamber's committees on Parks and Municipal Art and Architecture. The two committees refused to respond to the idea of a comprehensive recreational plan. Indeed, many chamber members supported a lawsuit that reestablished the independent board of park commissioners. And even after Mayor Johnson at last regained control of the park system, Johnson, Baker, and Stinchcomb were forced to implement their recreational plans in piecemeal fashion. The Municipal Art and Architecture Committee foot-dragged Stinchcomb's plans for bathhouses at Edgewater and Gordon parks, repeatedly sending the hapless engineer back to the drawing board with orders to surround bathhouses with camouflage fencing and prim walkways and to festoon the serviceable buildings with costly architectural filigree.[32]

Frustration over park battles within the Corporate Regime finally led both parties in the conflict in 1911 to agree to endorse the recommendations of a chamber-sponsored survey of the city's recreational needs. The source of the tug-of-war was a rift within the Corporate Regime between entrepreneurs and professionals, which, in turn, was set against the more obstinate opposition of a vocal populist minority in city council. "The Cleveland Recreation Survey" effected an understanding between entrepreneurs and professionals and became the basis for consensus in park building and recreational planning.[33]

The Cleveland Recreation Survey (1911) proposed a class specific system of city parks undergirded by a recreational plan designed to serve the needs of all citizens. The recreational philosophy informing the survey was given a wide audience in George Burnap's book, *Parks: Their Design, Equipment, and Use* (1916).[34] The Cleveland Recreation Survey and Burnap's book emphasized the importance of employing recreation professionals within the municipal bureaucracy. This philosophy ratified the work of Tom L. Johnson, Newton D. Baker, William A. Stinchcomb, and their new-found ally, social worker George A. Bellamy, the director of Hiram House, Cleveland's first social settlement, and a strong advocate of organized recreation for inner city residents.[35]

The survey argued not only for a class-specific geography of parks but also a recreational strategy for each class. Working class parks should be built in working class neighborhoods and would offer municipally supervised baseball, football, and soccer teams in small neighborhood parks. The outer ring of parks was converted to middle class use, for Burnap contended that the middle class values of stability, order, and family should be promoted in parks devoted to their use. In the new century, with the growing accessibility of streetcars and the middle class moving out from the center of the city, the original peripheral parks in the Bowditch design were widely frequented by middle class families, while the working classes took over the vacated parks in-between.[36]

The municipal parks system, dismissed in the 1890s as a rich man's toy, no longer served the upper class by 1915; but the Cleveland Metropolitan Park District soon created an upper class recreational venue. When the special purpose parks district was created in 1917, the Metropolitan Park Board hired Frederick Law Olmsted, Jr. to create a design for a regional parks system. The Cleveland Metropolitan Park District fused many of the elements of Corporate Regime park planning philosophy. Structurally, the system was a special purpose district, financially and managerially independent of partisan politics and conventional units of government. The design retained the urban periphery scale of intervention and the goal of halting the spread of the vernacular in site design and architecture.[37] It was an article of faith that large-scale parks drove up the price of adjacent land, which also would serve as a damper on vernacular architecture.

The Olmsted design defined urban space in upper class terms as a nature preserve. The Corporate Regime, seemingly, was haunted by industrial era violence done to natural landscapes. Coal mining operations in southern Ohio and West Virginia and iron mining and timber cutting in the Upper Great Lakes irreparably transformed these landscapes, once mountainous and forested, into ersatz hills of oily black mine tailings and a horizonless plain of tree stump cemeteries. Cleveland's smoke belching factories and towering office buildings shrouded the city center in cloud and shadow. And the real estate industry, over which the Corporate Regime steadily lost influence, was doing damage to suburban naturalism, the locale where aging members of the Corporate Regime were seeking residential sanctuary as if in response to this environmental carnage. The Cleveland Metropolitan Park District arrived to preserve nature in the suburbs and furnish a setting for upper class recreation; the regional parks system became an allegorical mea culpa for past transgressions against nature.

The proposed regional park site, Cuyahoga and the adjacent counties, was a landscape portrait with Lake Erie as its vanishing point. The surface of the landscape is defined by the foothills of the Allegheny chain, imposing a rugged composition of hills and valleys in the eastern half of the topographical setting. These subside into gentler lakes plains in the west, trowelled at regular intervals by glacial outcroppings rising as terraces from the lakeshore. The Cuyahoga River, meandering north to the lake, flows through a dominating central valley separating eastern hills from western plain. Secondary defining breaks in the composition are rendered by Euclid Creek and the Chagrin River in the east, Tinkers and Chippewa creeks in the south, and the Rocky River in the west. Together, these secondary waterways form an enveloping ring around the urban region. This topographical sketch, highlighted by slashes of blue water, nature paints in with subtle shadings of forest green in the summer months, a riotous panoply of color in the fall, and stark counterpoints of black and white during the region's interminable winters, which yield only grudgingly to the pale greens and yellows of spring.[38]

Frederick Law Olmsted, Jr. and William A. Stinchcomb, who now worked for the Metro Parks, emphasized the secondary waterways as the key to the site. Olmsted, in particular, had a finely honed instinct for the relationship between topography and park planning. The restrictive topographical features of the site lent themselves to permissive park planning. No Clevelander, related Olmsted, "who has not tramped through the less accessible portion of those valleys and wound his way out to the brink of the enclosing plateau at the wider and more commanding spots can have any idea of the sylvan beauty of these valleys or of the sense of utter remoteness from the city which they make on the beholder."[39] Olmsted and Stinchcomb designed the park system around nine nature reservations, emeralds in the chain of secondary waterways—two parks anchoring the Chagrin River Valley and connected to the easterly flowing Euclid Creek, followed by Bedford, Brecksville, and Hinkley reservations surrounding the southerly Tinkers and Chippewa creek flowages, and ending in the west with Huntington Park and Rocky River Reservation, the largest of the nine. An internal system of boulevards built in harmony with site topography connected all the reservations and parks, while the entire emerald necklace was moored to the city proper through a series of existing radial streets and highways.[40]

The metropolitan park system was built on eight thousand acres of land.[41] Anticipating opposition from realtors, Olmsted warned his Corporate Regime clients that the land was currently inexpensive, but it should be purchased before real estate developers realized its potential. Stinchcomb, wise in the ways of local politics and more aware than Olmsted that the pendulum in policy making was swinging toward a regime dominated by realty interests, downplayed the potential value of the land. The park land was, he claimed, marginal for residential development, and housing built on land with such lackluster potential would fast deteriorate into slums, "a prospective burden upon the community, and a canker in the midst of the normal development around it."[42]

On the strength of these arguments the Board of Metropolitan Park Commissioners moved quickly to acquire land. Tax levies approved in 1917, 1918, 1920, and 1924 generated annual revenues of $830,000, and by 1929, the board had purchased the 8,426 acres necessary to build the system of reservations, parks, and boulevards.[43]

William A. Stinchcomb's premonition of a change in regimes and a shift in urban growth policy from one of land use controls to laissez faire in land development was no idle fantasy. Realty interests joined by disgruntled property owners brought four lawsuits against the Board of Metropolitan Park Commissioners between 1922 and 1932. Opting for a balkanized regional polity to sustain a divide-and-rule political strategy, the rising Realty Regime challenged the constitutionality of the special purpose regional park district, targeting within the more general indictment the district's powers of taxation and right of eminent domain. The real estate company suits flailed board members with charges of dereliction of duty and use of board positions for private gain.[44]

But the board carried the day, and the decision in the 1922 case set the legal standard for the other three cases. In *State, ex. rel. Stanton v. Cleveland Metropolitan Park District Board of Commissioners,* Ohio Supreme Court Justice R. M. Wannamaker ruled that the special purpose park district was created by the state legislature within the boundaries of the Ohio state constitution. Accordingly, the park district's powers of taxation and eminent domain were legitimate powers exercised by all governmental bodies.[45] The one case the Corporate Regime lost was to the Pontiac Improvement Company over an interpretation of eminent domain. The Board of Park Commissioners attempted to use its powers of eminent domain to buy a small section of a larger parcel of land owned by the company. The court ruled that the Park District was obligated to buy the entire parcel owned by the company.[46] Although the Stanton case gave the Board the powers it needed to build a park system, the Pontiac case demonstrated the growing willingness of the emergent realty interests to challenge the policy making authority of the Corporate Regime.

The Olmsted-Stinchcomb park design was created primarily to preserve nature, but the regional park system also served as a recreational venue for the local upper class. Hiking trails and bridle paths were added to the reservations, South Chagrin reservation hosted a polo field, and the Chagrin River Valley Hunt Club was granted access when it built its clubhouse and stables near a park entrance. By the 1920s, the two park systems served all classes of Clevelanders.

The Cleveland Park System and the Cleveland Metropolitan Park District were the two most visible examples of Corporate Regime urban growth policy. The parks were intended as land use controls, as bulwarks against urban sprawl, bad design in building architecture, and as visible examples of how urban space should be used. The two park systems failed as land use controls, failing to halt urban sprawl and bad design. At best, the two park systems temporarily interrupted urban sprawl, and, as a class-specific recreational plan was implemented, they moved farther from the entrepreneurs' original intent of preserving nature. The entrepreneurs originally believed that by acting as individuals they could create something in urban space that would benefit others as individuals, a philanthropic goal. They soon learned that a collectivity, an administrative structure, would be required as a vehicle to realize their goals of benefiting other individuals. The class-specific recreational plan supported by the professionals meant that the beneficiaries of the park system would not be individuals but rather collectivities, classes of people each with its own collectively defined recreational needs and wants. The park system came closest to matching the ideal of the middle class professionals who wanted a park system insulated from partisan politics, financially independent, and administered by professionals. Even if the two park systems did not quite square with the entrepreneurs' original intent, the region would be a far worse place to live without its two-strand emerald necklace.

# 7

URBAN GROWTH POLICY II
Land Use Controls at the Center

THE DUAL HUB APPROACH

*P*arks formed an important part of the Corporate Regime's urban growth policy, but other aspects stemmed from two influential early-twentieth-century city planning movements: the City Beautiful and the City Efficient.[1] The Corporate Regime embraced both, and the two models represent the divergent paths that land use control followed. Entrepreneurial land use controls—the central business district civic center (the Group Plan) and the University Circle satellite city, which together formed the Dual Hub—were bold but ad hoc schemes and illustrate the strengths and weaknesses of City Beautiful planning.

The chamber's professionals, for their part, pursued more measured, comprehensive land use controls in the form of building codes, sanitation codes, zoning, and city master planning, which, taken together, comprised the local expression of the City Efficient movement. The City Efficient would in addition impose institutional order; in Cleveland this was accomplished when, in the twilight of the regime, the beautification projects and the regulatory codes came together under an organizational umbrella beneath which urban growth policy was initiated by the Cleveland Chamber of Commerce, designed by the city planning commission, and implemented by the relevant departments of the municipality.

As allies in the same policy making regime, entrepreneurs and professionals united on the broad objective of controlled land use, but divided over means. Entrepreneurs would join land use controls with highly individualistic, short-term civic beautification projects, the model pioneered in the Cleveland Park System. Wary of partisan politics, entrepreneurs preferred project implementation in civic sector institutions free from the

Chapter 7: Urban Growth Policy II				117

influence of elected officials. They chose special purpose districts and private foundations to build the downtown Group Plan and the University Circle satellite city. Realizing late in the regime's tenure that entrepreneurial land use controls regulated too little of the city's land and at too high a price, professionals sought government implementation of comprehensive regulatory land use controls, which brought them into a protracted conflict with the emerging Realty Regime.

Entrepreneurs and professionals alike supposed that the two park systems, city and regional, would be forceful physical interventions to effect land use controls at the urban periphery, but land use control in the central business district was a more complicated matter. The central business district was an evolving geography tracking in apparently unpredictable directions. The geographical mutations of the central business district were a perplexing reflection of the deeper currents of local economic change.

The Historical Geography of the Central Business District

Cleveland's historic business center was the Flats, the place where commercial and early industrial era water and rail long-distance transportation networks fused; however, late-nineteenth-century changes in commuter transportation technology and in the industrial business organization transformed the city's historic business geography. Electric trolley lines built in the 1890s deposited their passengers at Public Square rather than in the congested Flats, where land was at a premium. This resulted in very high rush-hour pedestrian traffic densities at Public Square, prompting a reappraisal of the commercial and retail potential of the site.

Simultaneously, manufacturing concerns separated—both organizationally and physically—blue collar production from white collar office functions. Blue collar factory jobs remained in the Flats, but white collar management and clerical functions moved to the new multi-story office buildings lining Superior Avenue. Retailing and wholesaling, historically joined, now separated, with wholesalers moving from the Flats to more spacious loft-type buildings constructed on cheaper land between Superior and St. Clair overlooking the river, an area neatly cordoned by West 9th and West 3rd. Carriage-trade stores were in the vanguard of the revolution in retailing, and they, early in the 1890s, leapfrogged Public Square to form a line eastward on Superior in pursuit of guests lodging at the city's new hotels. Other retailers, lured by the vogue in department store groupings, clamored for Public Square frontage, the gateway to the traffic generated by the electric streetcar system. Unwilling to engage in a bidding war for the

118 Part Three: The Corporate Regime, 1895–1919

FIGURE 7.1 Cleveland central business district, 1900 (Courtesy of The Western Reserve Historical Society, Cleveland, Ohio)

high-cost land at the two Superior locations and Public Square, the financial community began erecting Greco-Roman style financial temples on cheaper land along East 6th and East 9th streets between Superior and Euclid avenues.[2] (See figure 7.1.)

At the new Public Square focal point, Cleveland's past and present were catalogued in warring land uses, pitting New England village, commercial hub, and modern industrial technology against each other. The northwest side of Public Square housed Old Stone Church, now a charming relic of the city's New England heritage, while on the northeast corner the new Italian Renaissance Cleveland Chamber of Commerce building was under construction. The east side of the square housed the decrepit commercial-era city hall building. The south and west sides of the Public Square were zones in transition, the objects of emerging retail and commercial claimants. The center, a pasture within memory of living Clevelanders and now a park, was giving way to the new vogue in garden formalism heralded by the recent completion of Soldiers and Sailors Monument (1893). The entire evolving business district, north and south, was surrounded by working class housing and the city's worst slums and basest examples of retail enterprise.[3]

A new spatial economic order grounded in land use specialization and competitive ability to pay rent was slowly evolving, but the logic of the new land use order was impossible to fathom because of the density and diversity of transportation routes and technologies at the site. Pedestrians mixed with horses, carriages, wagons, trolley cars, and even the occasional automobile in a hopeless tangle of conveyance.

To bring order to this chaos, land use controls had to be more visionary and more exacting in the central business district than at the urban periphery. In the city's center, entrepreneurs and professionals joined to create a new urban landscape in the form of a monumental civic center.

Simultaneously, entrepreneurial landscape revisionism erupted at the eastern periphery of settlement. E. W. Bowditch's design for the municipal park system was based on naturalistic premises and a naturalistic design. But even before the full realization of Bowditch's park design, entrepreneurs cast naturalism aside in favor of the idea of bringing educational and cultural institutions to a park-like setting at the eastern end of the Euclid Avenue trolley line. Together, the civic center and the cultural satellite city would form a dual hub. Both projects deepen our understanding of the values and divisions within the Corporate Regime.

The Downtown Civic Center

The idea for the downtown civic center was conceived in 1895 at the Beer and Skittles Club, a young professionals' drinking society which met in the convivial atmosphere of Frau Wohl's Hungarian Restaurant. Among the club members were Frederic C. Howe and Morris Black, two bachelors who founded the Municipal Association that same year. Howe and Black saw in the land use disorder of Cleveland's central business district a metaphor for the political chaos of the McKisson administration.

Howe, Black, and other members of the Beer and Skittles Club had heard rumors of several civic building projects that potentially might be joined to form a civic center.[4] The local rumor mill churned with the news that Congress would soon allocate money to build a federal court and customs house in Cleveland; meanwhile, municipal politicians launched trial balloons for a new city hall to replace the decrepit Victorian mansard roof monster at Public Square; a wish list authored by county officials included new facilities for court rooms, offices, and a jail; and the Cleveland Public Library Board sought a new building worthy of its growing collections. Several members of the Beer and Skittles Club were architects who saw in the rumored building projects an opportunity to build a unified civic center in Cleveland. To publicize the scheme, the Beer and Skittles Club sponsored a civic center design competition that drew numerous submissions from local architects, unexpected public enthusiasm, and the welcome editorial support of Liberty E. Holden, who not only published the Cleveland *Plain Dealer* but also ranked as an active and influential member of the Cleveland Chamber of Commerce.[5]

The chamber readily endorsed the civic center concept and took the next step of naming an ad hoc Committee on Grouped Public Buildings. Entrepreneur William Gwinn Mather was appointed chairman of the committee, and other entrepreneurs, architects, and an art history professor filled the other seats. The committee spent months laying the political groundwork for the project by seeking endorsements from prominent citizens and Corporate Regime civic organizations. Meanwhile, local architects hired by the committee drew preliminary designs, prepared cost estimates, assessed the impact of the civic center project on central business district development, and composed some preliminary designs which grouped the public buildings around an 11-acre mall stretching from Superior Avenue to Lake Erie.

The most important issue deliberated by the Committee on Grouped Public Buildings was organizational. The buildings were the projects of three separate units of government—federal, county, municipal—and the Cleveland Public Library, a special purpose district. Each institution was accustomed to acting independently, but the Committee concluded that an umbrella organization would be needed to make uniform building plans and locate the buildings in a site designed for the whole.[6] The Committee on Grouped Public Buildings recommended the creation of a quasi-public Group Plan Commission, similar to the parks commission, as the collectivity to oversee the implementation of the plan. The proposed Group Plan Commission would be supported by an appointed Board of Supervision responsible for the finished design.[7]

The response of the chamber membership and the public in attendance was enthusiastic. But swimming against the rhetorical currents in praise of the city, the design, and the vision of the chamber was former Mayor Myron T. Herrick, who offered a sober assessment of the land use control scheme. In Herrick's view, the site, stretching from Superior Avenue to the Lake, was too far removed from the emerging Public Square business district to have a positive impact on its development. The land at the northern end of the 10.8 acre site, Herrick warned, might belong to the railroads, in which case a protracted court battle would have to be fought with them testing the legality of the railroads' riparian rights. (In fact, it was.) Lastly, and perhaps most ominously in the short term, former Mayor Herrick did not think the quasi-public commission was constitutional. A similar body created for the municipal park system was at that moment in legal limbo as court cases challenging the legality of the park district dragged on. Failure to heed Herrick's warnings delayed the project by three years.[8]

In 1902, even as the last legal obstacles to a quasi-public commission were cleared away (though not the railroads' claims), the Group Plan project nearly collapsed when Congress unilaterally awarded the architectural commission for the federal court and customs house to Arnold W. Brunner of New York. An endorsement of the Group Plan Commission and Board of Supervision by Mayor Tom L. Johnson brought Brunner's project into the fold, and, following his instruction, the mayor's political ally, Councilman Frederic C. Howe, introduced the enabling legislation for the Group Plan, which was quickly passed by the Cleveland City Council. Simultaneously, the Cuyahoga County delegation to the state legislature won the approval of that body for the Group Plan on May 6, 1902, when it passed as Senate Bill No. 188. Governor George K. Nash appointed Daniel H. Burnham, John M. Carrere, and Arnold W. Brunner to the Board of Supervision. Each appointee had been actively involved with the City Beautiful Movement in other cities, and, of course, the appointment of architect Brunner incorporated the federal building into the group plan.[9]

On August 1, 1903, the Board of Supervision completed its work and presented the finished report and drawings to Mayor Johnson, followed a few days later by a public presentation at the Cleveland Chamber of Commerce Building. The by now less than novel idea was to group the public buildings along a central mall. The Group Plan drawn by Burnham, Carrere, and Brunner fixed the southern boundary of the site on Superior Avenue between Bond and East 3rd streets. It would extend north to Summit Street at the Lakefront. Four monumental buildings anchored the corners of the mall. The buildings on the Superior corners of the site were the federal building, already in the blueprint stages, and the Cleveland Public Library. The county courthouse and city hall were proposed for the northern corners of the site. Slightly north of these buildings, at the northern axis of the mall, the Board of Supervision envisioned a monumental railroad passenger terminal, a new element the architects identified as the keystone of the entire plan. The architectural commission had been awarded to Daniel Burnham. The east and west sides of the rectangular site were to be lined with other public buildings, including a civic auditorium, a board of education administration building, and others as yet undetermined. A uniform Roman Revival design was proposed for the buildings, with conforming cornice heights and construction materials. The open interior of the mall was an exercise in Baroque geometry incorporating walkways with fountains, monuments, and tree plantings, emulating Paris and the more recently redesigned Mall in Washington, D.C.[10]

The text of the Group Plan explained how the architects went about solving the design problem, the problem of "composition" as Burnham, Carrere, and Brunner called it. Cleveland impressed Brunner as ". . . a cubist—or post impressionist—or super impressionist picture, an extra set of arms and legs but no recognizable head. So we find miles and miles of streets extending in all directions but with no distinctive features or evidence of individuality. The Civic Center is where the city speaks to us, where it asserts itself. Here the streets meet and agree to submit to regulation. They resolve themselves into some regular form, the buildings stop swearing at each other, competition is forgotten; individuals are no longer rivals—they are all citizens."[11]

The orderly grouping of classical revival style buildings along the axes of a mall would achieve Brunner's goal of land use control. The aesthetic inspiration for the Group Plan, and the mall in particular, he said, "will recall in part many of the fine avenues we point to with pleasure, such as the Champs Elysées in Paris, or the Esplane in Nancy." But the Group Plan was not only a thing of beauty, he added, for it would stand "as an example of order, system and reserve, such as is possible here, [and] will be for Cleveland what the [Chicago Columbian Exposition] Court of Honor of '93 was for the entire country. . . ."[12]

The focal point of the Group Plan was the Mall. (See figure 7.2.) The north-south axis gave the composition of grouped buildings its harmony and balance. The Mall was to be lined with two rows of tall clipped trees to create the illusion of length, heighten the appearance of formality, and offer a visual contrast with the surrounding granite buildings. At the north and south axes of the Mall, the Group Plan architects recommended courts of honor. The north axis would have a quadrangle at its center and within the quadrangle were geometric paths circling formal gardens surrounding a monumental fountain. The extreme north end of the Mall would be dissected by an esplanade which formed a miniature east-west axis on the north side of the city hall and county buildings. The south axis of the Mall would form a nave in which an imposing example of civic statuary would be erected. The Mall was designed to be a visual experience in its own right,

Chapter 7: Urban Growth Policy II   123

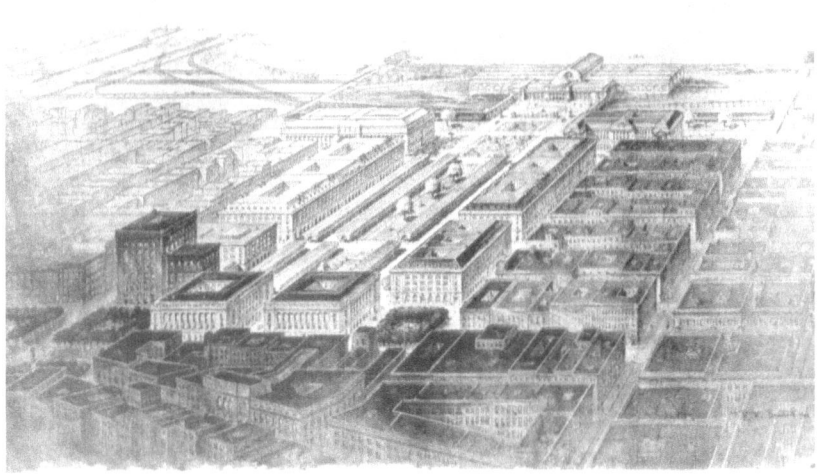

FIGURE 7.2 Group Plan of public buildings (downtown civic center), 1903 (Courtesy of The Western Reserve Historical Society, Cleveland, Ohio)

but more importantly, it brought the grouped buildings in orderly touch with one another and emphasized the lakefront horizon as the "composition's" vanishing point.[13]

Implementation of the Group Plan dragged on for nearly thirty years. The buildings anchoring the corners of the Mall went up relatively quickly. The county government, although committed to additional buildings on the west side of the Mall, could not pass levies to build them. Particularly noxious to the voting public was the plan to construct a county jailhouse on the west side of the Mall. A civic auditorium and a public school administration building eventually were built on the east side of the Mall. The crowning failure, however, was the Board of Supervision's (later the City Planning Commission's) failure to win an agreement from the railroad companies to surrender the land to build a rail terminal at the north end of the site, a legal obstacle former mayor Herrick foresaw in 1900. In 1918, an agreement was finally reached, but the terminal was built at Public Square (a defining regime succession conflict to be investigated in chapter 11). Delays extended the life span of the project beyond the longevity of the Corporate Regime. By the time the battle over the location of the rail terminal was fought, the Corporate Regime was in eclipse and public and institutional memories of why the project once seemed important had faded. By the 1920s the Group Plan was seen by the reigning Realty Regime as a sterile monument to a bygone era.[14]

University Circle

In the 1890s, as the entrepreneurs warmed to the idea of a central business district civic center, they simultaneously set in motion the plans for an educational and cultural satellite city on Cleveland's eastern border. The park-like setting of University Circle during the next twenty-five years became the home of more than a dozen of the city's leading cultural and educational institutions.[15]

E. W. Bowditch's 1893 plan for a naturalistic municipal park at University Circle had an unexpectedly short life. Though the original link in the municipal park system was provided by telegraph entrepreneur Jeptha H. Wade's donation of east side land bordering Doan Brook, a little noted caveat in the donation precipitated the sequence of entrepreneurial landscape revisionism. Wade donated the land to the city, to be sure, but he held in abeyance one parcel of the donation, the odd acreage surrounding a pond near Euclid Avenue, designated by Wade for an art gallery and grounds. Wade owned significantly more land east of the park site along Euclid Avenue, as well as land north of the site. His grandson and heir, Jeptha H. Wade II (1857–1926), formed Wade Realty to develop the land around the University Circle site as a residential enclave and through Wade Realty made other parcels available to institutions as they made their decisions to locate at University Circle. Jeptha H. Wade I (1811–1890), by virtue of his business, civic, church, charity, and other affiliations, cast a wide net in the fraternity of Cleveland entrepreneurs, and together they built University Circle.[16]

The key to the University Circle development was the commitment by Western Reserve College and the Case Institute of Technology to build new campuses at the circle. The schools were the magnets that attracted the other educational and cultural institutions.

Western Reserve College, originally located in Hudson, Ohio, was a Presbyterian college foundering under the weight of enrollment competition from other Ohio sectarian colleges. Jeptha H. Wade's pastor at Old Stone Church (First Presbyterian) in Cleveland was Hiram Haydn, who, like Wade, was a member of Western Reserve College's Board of Trustees. Haydn proposed moving the struggling college from Hudson to Cleveland. Haydn persuaded another one of his parishioners, entrepreneur Amasa Stone, to underwrite the relocation of Western Reserve College to University Circle (1882–1883). Later, as president of Western Reserve College, Haydn (1887–1890) and his successor, Charles Thwing (1890–1921), transformed the college into a university.[17]

The Case Institute was founded by philanthropist Leonard Case on land

Chapter 7: Urban Growth Policy II 125

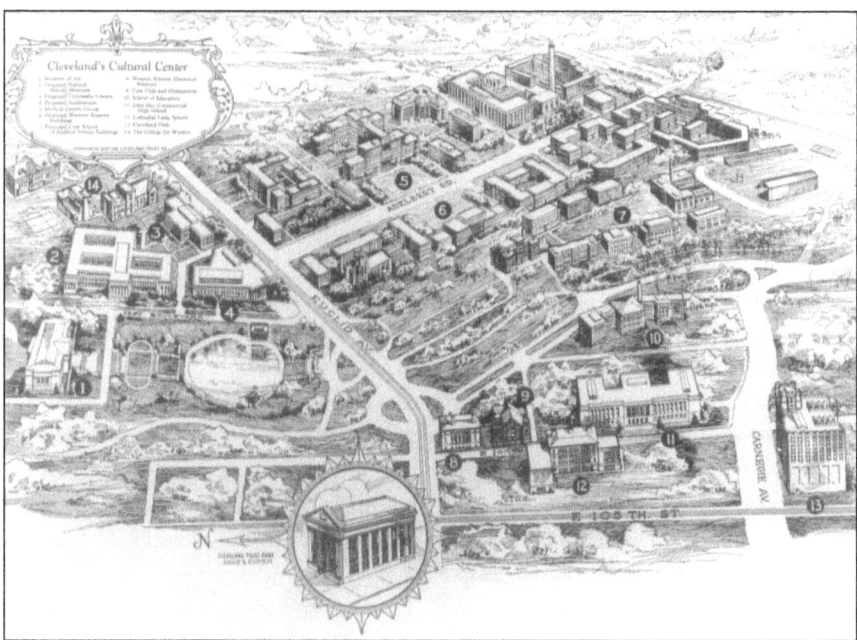

FIGURE 7.3 Artist's rendering of University Circle, ca. 1930—Cleveland Trust Bank advertising (Courtesy of The Western Reserve Historical Society, Cleveland, Ohio)

owned by Case on Superior Avenue near the future site of the Group Plan. When Case died in 1880, his land in the central business district was willed to the school, and it became the institute's endowment. Sale of this land, coupled with the fund-raising efforts of the Case Institute Board of Trustees, allowed the school to purchase the family farm of Liberty E. Holden, which bordered on the Wade allotment. The Case Institute moved to University Circle in 1885 when the construction of Case Main, the school's first classroom building, was completed.[18]

Entrepreneurs and their wives served on the boards of and were the major financial contributors to the Western Reserve Historical Society, the Cleveland Institute of Art, the Cleveland Museum of Art, the Garden Society, and the Musical Arts Society. When these institutions constructed their new buildings, they built them at University Circle. (See figure 7.3.) Hospitals, churches, public schools, and lesser ranking institutions of higher learning, themselves the beneficiaries of entrepreneurial philanthropy, followed in their wake.[19] Led by Jeptha H. Wade II, Wade Realty built grand apartment buildings and made lots available for the new University Circle mansions of the entrepreneurial class. A graceful new upper class district emerged in a park-like setting.[20]

By the late 1910s, however, University Circle looked like an urban land use ad hocracy. Entrepreneurial individualism was in danger of running riot. In 1917, the Cleveland Chamber of Commerce took notice and warned that a University Circle "plan of development" was in order. President Thwing of Western Reserve University, initially impatient with the idea of the chamber meddling in University Circle, acquiesced when two of the university's trustees, Samuel and William G. Mather, seconded the chamber's concerns. William G. Mather was chairman of the chamber's City Planning Committee, and he appointed a University Circle subcommittee chaired by architect Benjamin S. Hubbell.[21] Hubbell's firm had already been awarded commissions for the Cleveland Public Library in the Group Plan and several of the University Circle buildings, the most important of which was the Cleveland Museum of Art.[22] He brought to the enterprise the professional's ability to see the land use issue whole. Hubbell's goal as chairman of the University Circle subcommittee was ambitious; he would redesign University Circle as an educational and cultural City Beautiful twin to the downtown Group Plan.[23]

Hubbell's subcommittee created the University Improvement Company in 1919. The University Improvement Company was a privately held collectivity, an organizational entity which satisfied the entrepreneurs because of its independence from government and politics. The University Improvement Company brought an end to the warring land uses and imposed architect Hubbell's orderly professional design on the site. The University Improvement Company was a not-for-profit land bank serving University Circle institutions, and it served a valuable purpose in disciplining entrepreneurial individualism at University Circle.[24]

The entrepreneurial emphasis at University Circle was aesthetic and institutional and was realized piecemeal with the help of the University Improvement Company. The professionals hired to administer the nineteen University Circle institutions, however, had a larger and more comprehensive organizational vision; they saw in the autonomous University Circle institutions an opportunity to achieve the managerial goal of organizational synergy. President Thwing of Western Reserve University led the way. He formed male and female undergraduate colleges and founded a graduate school. Paralleling the wave of acquisitions, mergers, and horizontal integration in the world of business, Thwing and his successor Dr. Robert E. Vinson added schools of education, architecture, social work, law, and medicine.[25] These acquisitions created an opportunity for synergistic vertical relationships with other University Circle institutions in art, music, health care, social services, and secondary education. To cement these vertical organizational relationships and plan for a programmatic future, the professional administrators who headed University Circle institutions in 1925 formed the Cleveland Conference for Educational Cooperation, chaired by Newton D. Baker, the lawyer and former mayor. The institutions not already located at University Circle were lured there by Wade Realty, the University Improvement Company, and the opportunity to achieve organizational synergy afforded by the Cleveland Conference for Educational Cooperation.[26]

THE GROUP PLAN AND UNIVERSITY CIRCLE ASSESSED

The Corporate Regime, more than the regimes preceding it and those to follow, was the governing elite most concerned with the symbols of power and the regime most able and willing to erect them, symbols which today survive as an artifactual legacy of the era when they made urban policy.[27] The Group Plan and University Circle were symbolic representations of Corporate Regime governance, but more interestingly, the twin land use projects were emblems of the regime's intent to write an agenda for the future greatness of the city. Corporate Regimers were convinced that Cleveland could become a center of civic virtue, culture, and learning. Cleveland was conspicuously not a center of any of these things when the Corporate Regime came to power in 1895. Although the predecessor Populist Regime made many positive contributions to urban governance and advanced the art of urban policy making, the Corporate Regime dismissed populist political culture as grubby and wholly lacking in civic virtue. As a sprawling industrial boomtown with a large and disparate working class population, Cleveland struck Corporate Regimers as a seat of neither learning nor culture.[28]

The Group Plan and University Circle symbolized the aspirations of the regime rather than the reality of the city as they found it. The two developments became the charismatic twin loci of the Corporate Regime.[29] In the buildings that formed the civic center (including the Chamber of Commerce building) and University Circle, the leading men, the leading ideas, and the leading institutions came together to create an arena, a charismatic core, in which the plans that most vitally effected Clevelanders' present and future took place. One of the underlying principles of the regime was its desire to create social order. The geography of social order is patterned activity. The Group Plan and University Circle and the later developments in zoning and master planning were patterned activities and were emblematic of the social order the Corporate Regime was trying to create in Cleveland. To be sure, social order, defined by the regime as civic virtue, learning, and culture, was more a goal than a reality.[30]

Historians are inclined to exaggerate the impact of city planning generally and the City Beautiful Movement in particular. The historical literature suggests that in large measure the history of cities is the history of city planning. No untainted observer could possibly believe that city planning made a major contribution to the look of American cities. The City Beautiful Movement was not city planning. The Group Plan and the University Circle developments were projects rather than plans. They were, however, important mileposts on the road that led to city planning. The critique of contemporary professionals, perhaps, puts the City Beautiful Movement in a more balanced perspective. The monumental buildings, the gardens, the statuary, and formal malls brought land use controls to too little of the city's land, triggering the push from professionals for comprehensive zoning and city master planning, land use control efforts that were comprehensive yet flawed in their own way because they regulated the present rather than planned for the future.[31]

Central to the City Beautiful Movement was the physicalist fallacy that good design will have a spillover osmotic effect on neighboring land uses. Rarely was the osmotic effect realized. In a city sprawling over thousands of acres, the Group Plan and University Circle brought land use controls to no more than a few hundred acres of the city's land. The rest developed haphazardly, the result of marketplace decision making. Many of these decisions were made by the real estate industry, which scorned city planning generally and the City Beautiful movement particularly because the projects removed valuable commercial land from free market exchange and because the finished works seldom afforded opportunities for retail enterprise.[32]

Still, the City Beautiful Movement, and the downtown Group Plan in particular, meant something. In the Group Plan, the entrepreneurs attempted to redefine urban space and create a new urban landscape. Space, including built landscapes, operates in a dual manner. First comes the belief that space affects behavior; second comes its corollary, that man-made space can be made to affect behavior in deliberate ways.[33] This observation should not be overstated, especially keeping in mind the criticism of the physicalist fallacy leveled above, but the turn of the century educated classes did give varying degrees of credence to environmental determinism.[34]

Group Plan architect Arnold W. Brunner forthrightly stated what impact he thought the Group Plan would have on behavior. Brunner defined American democracy as inclusive rather than exclusive, but inclusion, he cautioned, would not be gained by downward leveling. To be included in the democratic experiment, the masses must be elevated. A civic center was a positive symbolic step toward elevating the masses. Brunner saw in the stateliness of the buildings and the order, harmony, and balance of the Group Plan design the elimination of conflict, rivalry, and competition. The patriotic legends emblazoned in granite on the buildings and statues of the nation's founding fathers adorning the Mall and the entrances to the buildings were meant to convey a shared historical experience. The Group Plan was the invention of an urban tradition where none had previously existed.[35] The design conferred upon the beholder a single title and a shared status: that of "citizen." Brunner's clients, the Corporate Regime, flattered themselves as being a broadly based, indeed representative, policy making group that carried the custodial obligation of elevating the masses until such time as the masses were able to assume their own responsibilities as citizens. Custodialism more than noblesse oblige motivated Corporate Regime entrepreneurs and middle class professionals. The alternative was class conflict, and the labor relations experience of the entrepreneurs taught that class conflict inevitably leveled rather than elevated. Custodialism was a talisman for all Corporate Regime policy making. The civic center was an upward step.

The Group Plan not only reveals the aspirations the Corporate Regime had for its fellow citizens but also reveals something about the regime itself. A frequently made observation about the City Beautiful Movement is that it was a reflection of its backers' "search for order," a characterization that is broadly true, but one that masks other shadings of meaning. City Beautiful designs emphasized centrality, horizontal rather than vertical monumentality, and physical separation of function. Centrality was an entrepreneurial objective, but it took architect Benjamin S. Hubbell to fully articulate it. Hubbell, coming to the projects with fresh insights some fifteen years after their inception, decoded the downtown civic center and University Circle as twin group plans. The two group plans were centralities linked by Euclid and Carnegie avenues, the two axial corridors that joined the two focal points of the design. The design not only satisfied the Corporate Regime's quest for order, but it symbolically called to the beholder's attention the central values of the entrepreneurs: civic virtue, learning, and culture. These were the values of the newly invented tradition that architectural symbolism would communicate to all citizens.[36]

Horizontal monumentality and separation of function are linked symbols. City Beautiful site design was formal yet expansive, and the buildings, while conveying mass, were low-rise, visual elements at odds with a city driven to vertical growth by high land costs. Expansive formalism in site planning and horizontal monumentality in building design visibly separated the City Beautiful projects from the rest of the congested, haphazardly constructed, vertically rising city. Horizontal monumentality was an attention gathering contrivance, a way of highlighting the values of the creators—civic virtue, culture, and learning. Because City Beautiful buildings were exclusively devoted to civics, culture, and education, these functions were spotlighted and cordoned off from the rest of the city's land-consuming activities—housing, industry, and commerce.[37] Some observers have found it odd that businessmen would sequester their City Beautiful projects, in both design and function, from the buildings in which their wealth was created. But this was merely a symbolic representation of the themes current in their business lives. The entrepreneurs were no longer active capital participants in the businesses they had created. Their indifference to economic development policy was a reflection of this new reality. The entrepreneurs flatly rejected Chamber of Commerce appeals to make capital available to new enterprisers, but they gladly channeled millions of their own dollars into the capital circuit which built the cultural and educational institutions at University Circle.

University Circle began not as a City Beautiful project but as a park. The late-nineteenth-century park planning movement brought nature to the city; parks were designed to be a relief from the remorseless advance of urban settlement. That appears to have been the intent of William Gordon, Jeptha H. Wade, John D. Rockefeller, and other entrepreneurs when they donated land for the Cleveland Park System, and it certainly was the intent of park designer E. W. Bowditch. Wade himself opened the door to landscape revisionism when he reserved a parcel of his donation for an art gallery. In the 1890s, even before the completion of Bowditch's design, the purpose of the park district was in the process of revision. Middle class professionals, as we have seen, wanted a functional park system, while entrepreneurs in the University Circle area embraced the revisionist idea of cultural and educational institutions in a park-like setting.[38]

Removing culture and education from congested urban centers to the urban periphery was an increasingly fashionable trend, a partiality which materialized earlier in such diverse places as Paris, New York, Chicago, and San Francisco. In Paris, the Opera House was built on a tightly bound site in deliberate contradistinction to the city around it. Similar design schemes in America were more expansive. In New York, culture and education, the Metropolitan Museum of Art and Columbia University, moved uptown to park-like settings. In Chicago, the Field Museum, the Museum of Science and Industry, and the University of Chicago (funded by former Clevelander John D. Rockefeller) moved south of the Loop to the park-like setting which had recently housed the World's Columbian Exposition. In the San Francisco Bay area, Stanford University and the University of California at Berkeley were built in park-like settings.[39] After more than two decades of transporting culture and education to parks, corresponding to the time when architect Benjamin S. Hubbell became chairman of the chamber's University Circle subcommittee, the park-like character of the University Circle development was nearly obliterated in a maze of construction. The city had come to the park. Hubbell and the entrepreneurs, using Wade Realty and the University Improvement Company, then attempted to bring their version of City Beautiful urban order to the design of University Circle.

University Circle eclipsed the original intent of the park design. University Circle was a satellite city devoted to culture and learning and with the addition of upper class domiciles became an extension of the city rather than a form of naturalistic relief from it. But it was to be a different kind of city, a deliberate break with the past and a harbinger of Cleveland's destiny. To entrepreneurs, University Circle symbolized Cleveland's future as a center of culture and learning. For the middle class professionals who administered the educational and cultural institutions, University Circle symbolized institutional synergy, a major breakthrough in organizational integration and cooperation that itself would be a break from the contentiousness of the recent past. These were far more important attainments than an open-space barrier to urban sprawl.

CONCLUSION: TOWARD THE CITY EFFICIENT

Mainstream Corporate Regime professionals, unlike architect Hubbell, reluctantly acknowledged that the grand development projects were diversions from the larger goal of land use control and the City Efficient. Outside the boundaries of the projects, land use development continued haphazardly and chaotically as always. Comprehensive land use control measures were needed, but progress toward this end was slowed because middle class professionals arrived at an understanding of comprehensive land use controls slowly and incrementally. A comprehensive, effective urban growth policy would be achieved only by means of public land use regulation. Government, shunned by entrepreneurs, was the only viable institutional vehicle available to achieve land use controls. Public land use controls were highly inflammatory politically, igniting conflict with small, vote-wielding property owners and a steadily widening community of real estate interests which in time would coalesce as the Realty Regime. Nevertheless, it was obligatory to work within the formal political system to achieve public regulation of land use. This is why, on so many issues, the middle class professionals were willing to make political accommodations with professional politicians, public servants, and populist elements.

Progress toward the City Efficient was slow because the techniques of land use control were new and untested. Public land use controls were initiated in the early years of the twentieth century and continued in fits, false starts, and conflict for nearly three decades, indeed, to the fag end of the Corporate Regime. The price paid for controlled land use was high, for a comprehensive policy of urban growth brought with it the ruin of the Corporate Regime.

The paternity of land use controls can be traced to the public health movement. The public health movement marched in twin columns: germ-theory-based epidemiology and the creation of healthful physical environments. The physical environment included both the workplace and residential quarters. In the early years of the century, state and federal governments responded to workplace public health issues, while the Chamber of Commerce professionals followed a course of investigation that tracked disease to slum ridden neighborhoods. What all such neighborhoods had in common was the dilapidated, overcrowded housing branded by public health crusaders as the incubator of communicable disease. Chamber committees and subcommittees worked on tenement housing codes, which led incrementally to citywide building codes and, finally, when the link was made between disease control and land use control, to citywide zoning. Zoning, in turn, seemed ineffectual and lacking in theme without a comprehensive city master plan. By the time institutionalized city master planning was accepted, urban problems were regional in scope, leading in turn to the regional planning movement of the 1920s. Political battles were fought at each stage in the evolution of land use controls. Tenement and building codes were grudgingly enacted in the first decade of the century, and a city planning commission was established during Mayor Baker's administration in 1915. Delaying tactics by small property owners and the real estate industry postponed zoning and city master planning legislation until the 1920s. In that decade, with the Realty Regime ascendant in urban policy making, the regional planning movement was crushed and the City Efficient with its core elements of zoning and city master planning was redefined in terms satisfactory to the Realty Regime.

8

THE PROFESSIONAL IDEAL TRIUMPHANT

The symbolic values represented in the design of the Group Plan and University Circle—civic virtue, culture, and learning—were put on trial in Corporate Regime service distribution and wealth redistribution policy. If democracy indeed leveled upward, then the masses must be educated and the very poorest must be given a leg up on the social ladder. True to its beliefs, the Corporate Regime reformed the Cleveland Public School System and built an entirely new charity edifice.

That the Corporate Regime was not omnipotent, even in its heyday, can be seen in its limited ability to make the delivery of urban services more efficient. Although the regime clearly dominated urban policy making, it did not have a comparable ability to dominate policy implementation and the bureaucratic operations of the municipality. The city government remained a constant irritant to the Corporate Regime, even though service delivery improved considerably during the years of the regime's policy making primacy. The source of irritation was that the municipal government remained to a significant degree captive of populist political culture and highly independent mayors. Repeated attempts at municipal charter reform misfired, and populists retained their influence as elected officials and as public servants within the bureaucracy.

The regime was also split between entrepreneurial and professional approaches to the delivery of services. In electoral politics as well as within the service delivery departments of the municipal bureaucracy, Corporate Regime professionals made accommodations to populist political culture in the interest of consensus building around broad urban policy goals, especially those related to urban growth policy. For more than half the quarter century that the Corporate Regime made policy, the mayor's office was occupied by Tom L. Johnson (1901–1909) and

Newton D. Baker (1912–1916). Often at loggerheads with the Chamber of Commerce, both men nonetheless made cabinet appointments of exceptional quality, expanded civil service, and implemented business management techniques and modern accounting systems. While the entrepreneurs shunned Johnson, professionals made accommodations with both administrations. This was in the main a successful political strategy but one that frustrated the impatient entrepreneurs who eventually lost interest in the municipality and concentrated instead on policy areas—the land use development projects, the public school system, and wealth redistribution in the charity system—where they could more reliably affect outcomes. Although professionals practiced a strategy of accommodation in electoral politics and within the municipal bureaucracy, the triumph of middle class professionalism was nearly total in the delivery of public educational services.[1]

THE PUBLIC SCHOOL SYSTEM

Gains won by the middle class professional schoolmen did not materialize quickly or in a conflict-free environment. Yet control of the school system was essential if the Corporate Regime was to modernize the organization and reconcile a welter of public demands for educational services and fulfill its custodial destiny of elevating the masses. Three layers of Corporate Regime control eventually materialized: (1) structural control over the system of governance, (2) consensus on the school system's educational mission, and (3) the introduction of modern management techniques. The campaign for structural control was won during the municipal charter reforms of the 1891–1905 period. Programmatic control was secured between 1891 and 1915 when the Corporate Regime reconciled public demands for a more broadly based institutional mission with actual programs. Following the recommendations of the Cleveland Foundation Survey of 1915, management controls were established by means of pedagogical reform and regulation of budgets and costs.[2]

Structural Reform

Three episodes of municipal charter reform gave the Corporate Regime structural dominance over the public school system. The 1891 Federal Plan reduced the number of school board members from forty-two elected by ward to seven members elected at large, a structural reform which purged

Chapter 8: The Professional Ideal Triumphant   135

the school board of populist and sectarian influences. A temporary setback occurred in 1901 when Tom L. Johnson's political coattails proved long enough to elect a suspect slate of school board candidates in an at-large election. With a political base built on the support of middle class professionals and the populist-leaning lower middle class, the Johnson school board included two reform minded lawyers, a minister, a librarian, and a college student. The new board members were broadly representative of the city's new social geography. A new anti-Johnson municipal charter enacted in 1905 mandated the familiar seven-member board, but the new charter skirted the controversial at-large representation issue by requiring at-large election of five of the board members, while throwing a bone to the populist idea of geographical representation by having one member each chosen from the city's east and west sides. During the balance of the Corporate Regime, the demographic composition of the school board came more and more to resemble the demographic composition of the Corporate Regime itself. The several elected boards were composed primarily of male corporate managers and lawyers and women active in Corporate Regime cultural and charity organizations. Except for the lone west side representative, all lived within a one-mile radius of University Circle.[3]

The Evolving Institutional Mission, 1891–1915

Structural reforms purged the school board of populist membership, but they did not expunge populist influence from the school system. The importance of the populist era in the history of Cleveland public education was that it prompted a wide-ranging community debate over alternative educational agendas. These agendas were given shape, focus, and advocacy by the professional schoolmen hired to administer the Cleveland Public School System. The community-wide debate survived the departure of populist school board members and culminated in an entirely new educational mission for the Cleveland Public Schools.[4]

From the onset of the Populist Regime in 1878 to the Cleveland Foundation Survey of 1915, several alternative programs and services came under review, discussion, debate, and, finally, implementation. The first matter was agreement on the constituencies to be served by the public school system. This issue in turn provoked debates over which programs would best serve which groups of students. Corporate Regime traditionalists, unwilling to commit dollars to nontraditional students and programs, held that all constituencies would be best served by an unadorned school system which simply taught the three R's. But the educational expectations of public school constituencies and the expertise of the professional schoolmen had grown too sophisticated during the course of the unfolding industrial era to be placated by threadbare pedagogical homilies. Immigrant leaders, for example, demanded English-language instruction for children and adults alike, while labor spokesmen pursued evening and weekend classes for adults and children obliged to participate in the work force. With compulsory school attendance laws in effect, special provision would have to be made for the instruction of incorrigibles who might otherwise be ignored or expelled by the system. In an industrializing city, manual training became a highly important educational issue for both labor and management. A handmaiden of corporate managerialism and the emergence of retailing and services was a growing demand for a cadre of white collar workers with "commercial competencies" which could be learned in the public school system before entering the white collar labor force. Employers, clamoring for a trained work force, broadly supported the educational demands of immigrant and labor groups. Turn of the century public health crusaders and charity agency workers targeted the neighborhood elementary school as the organizational base from which to deliver the message of preventive health care and the delivery of basic family social services.[5]

The Merchant Regime had defined the mission of the public school system as education in the service of good citizenship. The new demands in the Populist and Corporate regimes meant that the mission of the public school system must be redefined and more broadly configured to include training for children and adults from all social classes for diverse roles in the industrial workplace and society. School superintendents Andrew Draper and Lewis H. Jones (1891–1902) thoroughly overhauled the educational delivery system, efforts calculated to offer something to all public school constituencies. Thereafter, until the Cleveland Foundation Survey of 1914, their successors, public school superintendents William H. Elson and James Frederick, made the commitment of bricks, mortar, and dollars to the broad based educational programs designed by Draper and Jones.[6]

When Superintendent Jones pledged to rid the public schools of the "uneducated and unthinking classes," he was issuing a politically expedient rejection of the departing populist school board and not a blanket rejection of the public's increasingly divergent expectations for the public school system. The actions of the schoolmen spoke more loudly than their words. Draper and Jones implemented the populist educational agenda. Manual training classes were offered. "Steamer Classes" in English-language instruction combined with an evening program for immigrant students harked back to the days of the old populist school board. Special

Chapter 8: The Professional Ideal Triumphant   137

programs designed to lure dropouts back to the school system also materialized. The middle class social service constituency was served when classes for the disabled were offered and, by allying with the Visiting Nurses Association, health education programs and physical education programming were implemented. In response to new child learning theories developed in universities, the kindergarten idea was incorporated into the curriculum. To house the new programs, superintendents William H. Elson (1906–1911) and James Frederick (1911–1914) built manual training and commercial high schools and six new kindergartens.[7]

Large-scale programmatic and physical expansion of the Cleveland Public School System addressed the demands of the various constituencies for broad based educational services, but it helped that this local educational agenda was also the agenda of an emerging national public education establishment. Symptomatic of the growing professionalization of education, the aim of the national public education establishment was to standardize the delivery of educational services across the nation. The education establishment emerged from the cooperative relationship between education programs in universities, foundations devoted to the study of educational issues, and administrators in public school systems. Schoolmen moved freely between the institutions and exchanged experiences and ideas which in time evolved into a national education agenda. The fully realized national public education agenda included scientific management, vocational education, vocational guidance, intelligence testing, standardized examinations, educational tracking, and standardized educational materials.[8]

Superintendent Andrew Draper was one of the new schoolmen. His career straddled public school administration, the university, the private foundation, and legislative lobbying for improved educational standards and programs. In 1894, in a career change not uncommon among schoolmen, Andrew Draper left the Cleveland Public School System to become President of the University of Illinois. Other local schoolmen followed similar career paths. Superintendent Jones left Cleveland in 1902 to head the Michigan State University Normal School and Frank Spaulding (1916–1920) left the Cleveland superintendency to accept a faculty appointment at Yale.[9]

If the institutional mission of the Cleveland Public School System between 1891 and 1915 broadened in response to public demand and the new educational standards formulated by the national education establishment, criticism of the local public school system continued almost unabated. Even though the schoolmen responded affirmatively to the concerns on the local public education agenda with new programs and physical facilities, annual enrollment surges amounting to nearly ten thousand students a year placed growth pressures on the system that led inevitably to mishaps in service delivery, inefficiencies that provoked renewed criticism of the public schools. Critics pointed to the system's high dropout rate and low participation rate (students enrolled relative to the number of children in the school age population cohort).[10] The Orth Commission, appointed in 1905 by lawyer and school board president Samuel P. Orth, was created to respond to just this sort of criticism. The Orth Commission's report reaffirmed the school board's commitment to a broad based educational agenda but promised greater efficiencies in service delivery.[11] The enrollment increases and attendant service delivery inefficiencies, however, continued to rack the system until 1915, when the Cleveland Foundation intervened unilaterally with a comprehensive survey of public education in Cleveland.[12]

Management Controls, 1915–1920

The Cleveland Foundation was established in 1914 by Frederick Goff, banker to the entrepreneurs, and it became the social policy research arm of the Corporate Regime. One of the first tasks the new foundation took on was the comprehensive survey of the Cleveland Public Schools. The commission for the survey was awarded to Leonard Ayres of the Russell Sage Foundation, a key institutional link in the national education policy network. Ayres, in turn, dispatched a team of expert schoolmen to Cleveland to study the city's public schools, and between 1915 and 1916, the Russell Sage Foundation consultants wrote a series of reports which set the course for a managerial revolution in the Cleveland Public School System. The school board, initially stung by the reports, intemperately accused the Cleveland Foundation of meddling, but yielding to irresistible pressure from the Corporate Regime, the school board sheepishly hired Frank Spaulding as the superintendent to implement the management recommendations of the Cleveland Foundation Survey.[13]

Schoolman Spaulding was an efficiency expert enamored of Frederick Winslow Taylor's new science of management. He labored under the illusion that a soulless management system designed by Taylor for business organizations could be transported wholesale to the public school system. Schoolmen like Spaulding and the staff and professional consultants employed by the Russell Sage Foundation were oblivious to the fact that a management system appropriate for an organization engaged in the manufacture of nuts and bolts was inappropriate for an organization that educated children. Yet Taylor's management system was uncritically appropriated by educational organizations.[14] Taylor's system of management armed complex business organizations engaged in manufacturing with tall, top-down command and control line hierarchies supported by heavily layered staff bureaucracies.[15] This bureaucratic, impersonal system of organizational management was imposed on the Cleveland Public Schools by Superintendent Spaulding, who, as the man atop the command and control hierarchy, held the reins of organizational control firmly in his grasp. The unaddressed issue was that the industrial management model unnecessarily distanced the recipient of the service from those responsible for providing it, transforming what was once a personal relationship between teacher and student into an impersonal relationship between students and teachers on the one hand and layers of faceless schoolman-bureaucrats on the other.[16]

Taylorism empowered the superintendent by disempowering school boards, principals, teachers, students, and parents. By explicitly separating policy setting from daily management functions, Spaulding became nearly independent of the school board. Under the pre-Spaulding administrative system, the school district was organized by geographical district with a relatively autonomous district superintendent in charge of the locality, administrators whose offices were in the neighborhoods and who were recognizable and accessible to students and parents. Teachers in this decentralized system were acknowledged as professionals with responsibility for setting classroom standards and for evaluating student progress. Spaulding replaced this structure with a top-down command and control administrative hierarchy purloined from corporate organization charts, a model in which the company president at the top of the chart placed vice-presidents in charge of the chief functional operations of the business, and so on down through lesser ranking functionaries on the organizational ladder until the widget at last rolled off the assembly line.

In the Cleveland Public School system, Spaulding replaced district superintendents with assistant superintendents for budgets, curriculum, instruction, and buildings.[17] Assistant superintendents reported directly to the superintendent, and their offices were placed near Spaulding's in the newly constructed school administration headquarters building on the Mall downtown. From these offices, assistant superintendents for curriculum and instruction reduced school principals to middle management overseers and teachers to white collar labor. The assistant superintendents for curriculum and instruction created the matrix of educational programs that would become the "one best system."[18] District-wide intelligence testing, standardized examinations, educational tracking, and standardized instructional materials installed a standard curriculum and a Taylorized instructional process which degraded the teacher's role in evaluating student performance and progress and designated students as mere products of an educational assembly line. Apprehensive students and parents were now routinely referred "downtown" with concerns or complaints. The added costs of the new centralized management operation were charged against the budgets of the individual schools.[19]

Frank Spaulding's downtown budget office gave the superintendent control over the school system's finances, and budgets came more and more to drive all operations of the school system. The corporate organizational model and the Cleveland Foundation surveys emphasized the importance of rigorous business-like fiscal controls and strict accountability for monies spent. The tax avoidance strategies and tax burden shifting tactics of the Corporate Regime put the public school system on a tight fiscal leash.

The schoolmen countered with suspect productivity measures and evasive accounting practices in their attempts to squeeze more money from taxpayers. Productivity measurements were one of the hallmarks of Taylorism, and Tayloristic schoolmen developed their own productivity measurements. The annual reports of the superintendent fairly bristled with these statistics. Annual reports ran to hundreds of pages of tables accounting for nearly every conceivable activity of the school system, tables introduced by lengthy, densely written obfuscations rendered in a pseudo-scientific managerial jargon that only accidentally resembled the English taught in public school classrooms.[20]

Enrollments were counted and categorized and cross-tabulated in a variety of imaginative ways but rarely the same way two years running. The budget was sensibly split into capital and operating accounts and in the operating accounts enrollments were joined to dollars to fashion productivity measurements. Per capita spending per student was touted as the most important productivity measurement because it could be used to track the overall spending of the school system. In reality, the most important productivity measurement was the student-to-teacher ratio, for it drove the operating budget and had far-ranging consequences for the capital budget. Extreme fluctuations could take place in the student–teacher ratio and yet not be discernible in per capita spending tabulations. The superintendent was under constant pressure to keep the budget under control, and per capita spending was a way to evaluate the superintendent as watchdog of the public purse. The schoolmen, fatefully, suffered from edifice complexes, and the showiest educational edifice of the era was the high school. In order to build high schools and professional reputations and still keep per capita spending and high school student-to-teacher ratios impressively low, student-to-teacher ratios were driven skyward in elementary schools. By manipulating this student–teacher productivity measure, per capita spending increases were held to politically acceptable levels, and superintendents won rave reviews for their prudent fiscal management from school boards, the public, and potential employers.

Not everyone in the public was so persuaded. The statistics and productivity ratios derived from them formed a double-edged sword upon which the schoolmen eventually impaled themselves. The productivity ratios exposed the hollowness of Frank Spaulding's claim that a "one best system" could be all things to all people. Private and suburban schools spent far more per capita than the Cleveland Public School System, and these schools had far lower student–teacher ratios than did the Cleveland system, most conspicuously at the elementary school level. Because the private and suburban schools were not required to spend on manual training and commercial programs, evening classes, classes for immigrants and incorrigibles, and social service functions, they got far more per dollar spent. Middle class parents who made the connection between the quantitative claims of the schoolmen and qualitative results observable in their children moved expeditiously to the suburbs. At the close of the Corporate Regime, Cleveland public elementary schools were experiencing their first losses in enrollment.[21]

However much the public school system became a captive of the professional ideal of the schoolmen, the goals of the entrepreneurs nonetheless were realized in the system. The entrepreneurs wanted a public school system that was accessible to the masses and that delivered a quality education, was well managed, and fiscally responsible. The entrepreneurs saw in the public school system the institutional means for elevating the masses. With a public school education and hard work the humblest of toilers could himself become an entrepreneur and a contributor to the betterment of society, a captain of industry and employer of labor who had earned a position inside the policy making boardrooms of the buildings lining the Mall and gracing the park land at University Circle.

WEALTH REDISTRIBUTION
The Scientific Management of Charity

Scientifically managed wealth redistribution was the final policy achievement of the Corporate Regime. During its years of policy making ascendance, the Corporate Regime rationalized a charity system composed of a welter of warring public and private, often sectarian, organizational elements, a network further splintered by debates over the philosophy of charity. The notion of wealth redistribution itself was at the core of the philosophical and institutional discord.

Wealth redistribution is an economic act directed toward a social beneficiary. Plainly put, haves give to have-nots. This, in the language of economics, is a one-way transfer of wealth. Unlike other economic relationships, there is no mutuality of exchange between giver and receiver. In all other areas of urban policy—economic development, urban growth, and distributive services—there is exchange value for a dollar spent. Dollars spent on economic development return profits to owners and jobs to workers. Urban growth policy plots out rational and pleasing uses of urban space with results both tangible and intangible that are cast to a widening circle of beneficiaries who see in the spatial benefaction a utilitarian exchange value for money spent. Distributive services are measured in the public mind with mathematical precision: services improve in accordance with the amount of money spent and just as predictably worsen during moods of fiscal retrenchment. Wealth redistribution offers no such exchange value. The individual beneficiaries do not reciprocate; nor, in the short term, do the monies spent appear to improve the human or social condition.[22] Frustration inheres in wealth redistributive policy.

Wealth Redistribution Policy Reprised

Frustration with wealth redistribution policy was common to all policy making regimes, and it led mostly to angry finger pointing and convulsive debates over blame. Americans believe that for every condition there is a cause and for every cause a cure. But wealth redistribution policy is thwarted by the lack of consensus over cause and cure. The core purpose of wealth redistribution policy is to alleviate poverty, a goal which raises a twofold debate. First is the matter of poverty itself. Why are some people poor? Once widows, orphans, the chronically infirm, and the handicapped are dispensed with, the debate turns to the matter of why there are such unexplainable numbers of able-bodied poor people. Two contradictory and mutually exclusive answers to this question shaped an important part of the debate over wealth redistribution policy. The poor are poor either because of (1) personal failure or (2) failure of the economic system. The policy maker's causal preference is important because it guides the choice of remedial vehicles and institutional agendas. Until the Corporate Regime, Cleveland's wealth redistribution policy floundered on these contradictory claims of cause and cure. The ideals which motivated policy making in each of the regimes differed on the causes of poverty and therefore on remedial policies.

The Corporate Regime in the matter of wealth redistribution policy was philosophically at odds as between entrepreneurs and professionals over the causes of poverty, though far less so on the mechanics of fund-raising, the organization of institutional delivery systems, and the direction of wealth redistribution policy.

Cleveland entrepreneurs readily agreed with the sentiments of Reverend Thomas Robert Malthus, who declared in 1798 that "Dependent poverty ought to be held disgraceful."[23] Wealth was a reward for personal achievement and poverty a punishment for personal failure. Early in their involvement with the local charity movement, Cleveland entrepreneurs parroted the sentiments of English liberals, from Malthus to Chamberlain.[24] When turn of the century English liberalism became tainted by the socialist attempt to lay the blame for poverty on industrial society and by its advocacy of state collectivist remedies, Chamber of Commerce entrepreneurs probed modern psychology for answers. Modern psychology was seductive because it scientifically set normative standards for individual and family behavior and judged as abnormal and deviant those who failed to conform to such norms. Social psychology put a modern face on the causal relationship between personal failure and poverty.[25]

Entrepreneurs, however, also believed in the old fashioned virtues of reciprocity, their own as well as that of dependent groups. Entrepreneurial reciprocity required service to society, and an element of that service was the amelioration of poverty. Judgments about the origins of poverty, moral or scientific, did not absolve the entrepreneurs of their obligation. Entrepreneurs were at heart optimists who wanted to believe that poverty was only a temporary condition. The poor were lacking only in opportunity. Hard work and education would manufacture the opportunities needed to lead the dependent classes out of poverty. The public school system was the long-term remedy for poverty, but short-term relief fell to the network of private charitable agencies. Entrepreneurs thought that this heretofore directionless network must be taken in hand and directed toward getting the dependent claimants back on their feet.[26]

The professionals were far less sanguine about the origins of poverty. It was not a simple matter of either/or. Moral frailty, social deviance, and the industrial system were all valid explanations of poverty. Unlike their entrepreneurial colleagues, many professionals had first-hand experience working with the poor. When lawyer Frederic C. Howe arrived in Cleveland, he took up residence at Hiram House in the decaying Central neighborhood and volunteered his evenings and weekends working with the social settlement's clients. There he began to appreciate the fact that many of the impoverished clients of the settlement house were neither depraved nor deviant. Still, he agreed to serve on the board of the Charity Organization Society (COS), a board composed chiefly of entrepreneurs.[27] One fund-raising letter sent out by the COS was returned to Howe with a stern rebuke, written by Dr. Louis B. Tuckerman. A physician, religious leader, and reformer active in the public health movement, among other, more radical causes, the doctor's letter to Howe laid the blame for poverty squarely on the steel and coal magnates who served on the COS board. The COS, Dr. Tuckerman charged, was merely an ill-disguised attempt to sweep the human refuse of industrial society off the street and hide it in charitable agencies, an effort now capped by the appalling insult of petitioning middle income people to pay for the sins of the plutocracy. Howe was chastened, and he joined other professionals in laying the blame on industrial society, though not directly on the individual entrepreneurs who served on the board of the charity organization society.[28]

Realists among the professional classes appreciated the fact that the inequities of industrial society were not going to be remedied at the local level. Many professionals were too beholden to entrepreneurs to too loudly lay blame, while some, such as Starr Cadwallader, the director of Goodrich Social Settlement House, George Bellamy of Hiram House, and James Jackson of Associated Charities, feared government participation in wealth redistribution policy as much as they feared poverty itself. What professionals discovered is that they could either fight entrepreneurs in a winless battle over blame or join them on the common ground of organizational process. Aid to the impoverished if not the cure for poverty could be improved through effective fund-raising and efficient redistributive agencies. It would mean, however, that wealth redistribution policy would attack symptoms rather than causes.[29]

The Cleveland Chamber of Commerce confronted the wealth redistribution problem in its Committee on Benevolent Associations, established in 1899. Composed of entrepreneurs and professionals, the Committee on Benevolent Associations for a period of twenty years worked toward solutions to the problems that had frustrated wealth redistribution policy in each regime: management, fund-raising, service delivery, and policy research, problems exacerbated by the proliferation of social service agencies as the city's population grew in size and diversity. The major religious denominations had charitable arms; immigrant groups created benevolent associations; labor groups had affiliated welfare agencies; professional organizations aided their pet populations; and businessmen's service clubs performed their acts of charity and benevolence. Some of these agencies were highly exclusionary, while the clientele of others overlapped. Some were highly efficient as service providers, while others were sloppy, inefficient, and soft-hearted. Entrepreneurs were drawn into redistributive policy because they were the most visible beneficiaries of the new industrial order, and they quickly became the beleaguered targets of the fund-raising campaigns of every charitable organization. Professionals were more troubled by the sheer proliferation of organizations, the wasteful duplication of effort, the competitive bickering among the agencies, the amateurishness of the service delivery staff, and the lack of a coherent policy direction. Entrepreneurs and professionals alike suspected that clients exploited these weaknesses to their own advantage, which, of course, they did.[30]

After years of drift in a sea of trial and error, the Chamber of Commerce's Committee on Benevolent Associations at last took heed of the lessons learned from failed past attempts to centralize wealth redistribution policy. In a series of bold strokes between 1913 and 1917, the committee at last resolved the issues of management, fund-raising, service delivery, and policy research. It did so by helping to organize the Welfare Federation, the Community Chest, the School of Applied Social Sciences, and the Cleveland Foundation.[31]

The Welfare Federation (initially, the Federation for Charity and Philanthropy and today the Federation for Community Planning) was the umbrella organization that coordinated charitable fund-raising, accredited agencies, set operational standards, and distributed money to agencies meeting its standards. The importance of the Welfare Federation was that it adapted the corporate planning model to wealth redistribution policy. One of the responsibilities of the Welfare Federation was to approve all agencies seeking funds. A Welfare Federation seal of approval meant that the agency had submitted a plan stating its goals and objectives supported by a budget detailing its capital and operational needs. A parallel to the managerial revolution occurring in the public school system, the charity agency budget became the means for achieving organizational accountability. From the myriad agency plans, the Welfare Federation staff prepared a single, comprehensive wealth redistribution policy budget and proceeded to raise the money to fund it.[32]

Fund-raising campaigns led by the Committee on Benevolent Associations and later the Welfare Federation made impressive gains over the ad hoc and inefficient nineteenth century methods of charitable money grubbing, but in 1919, when the Committee reassigned fund-raising to the newly created Community Chest, charitable solicitation reached a new and far more sophisticated level.[33]

Community Chest fund-raising directed a new stream of money into philanthropic agencies, money that augmented the public tax dollars flowing into public education and public charities and eased the fiscal burden on the entrepreneurs who were channeling their philanthropic capital into University Circle. The Community Chest employed professional fund-raisers who brought modern marketing techniques to the task of charitable fund-raising and, most significantly, spread the cost burden of wealth redistribution well beyond the entrepreneurial class. The professional fund-raisers targeted entirely new categories of contributors and tailored marketing strategies to reach each segment of the solicitation market.

Entrepreneurs remained an important segment in the fund-raising campaign, but the marketing strategies of the professional fund-raisers shifted the cost burden of wealth redistribution to new categories of contributor. Middle income households were identified as a significant but largely untapped segment and fund-raising campaign strategy dictated a door-to-door campaign carried out by an army of neighborhood volunteers. The most significant marketing breakthrough, however, came with the campaign to raise funds from the employees of major businesses. White collar employees of corporate and professional organizations were required by management to pledge a percentage of their annual salaries. The last year of Welfare Federation fund-raising yielded $250,000, a sum far exceeding that of any previous campaign. But the Community Chest in its first year alone raised $4 million to fund wealth redistribution policy, and the amount soared every year thereafter.[34]

The staffing of wealth redistribution agencies remained a problem until the founding of the School of Applied Social Sciences (SASS) in 1913. A college within Western Reserve University, SASS trained professional social workers to staff welfare agencies. Prior to 1913, agency staffs were likely to be composed of volunteers, such as Frederic C. Howe at Hiram House, clergymen, well-intended amateurs, and salaried but untrained social workers. But social work was evolving into a profession at the turn of the century. Late in the old century, charity organization societies conducted in-house training programs for their workers, the approach taken by James Jackson of Associated Charities in Cleveland before he came up with the idea of establishing the School of Applied Social Sciences as a two-year graduate program to train professionals in social work, public service, and public health care.[35] Within five years, two of SASS's three divisions, the programs in Municipal Administration and Public Service and the Course for Public Health Nurses, were dropped for lack of enrollment, but the Family Welfare and Social Service Division for the training of social workers went forward with considerable success.

In the early years of SASS, social work education sought to blend the practical with the academic. Its twenty-seven faculty members were drawn from traditional academic disciplines in the university and in part from practitioners in Corporate Regime businesses and civic sector organizations. Political scientist Raymond Moley, economist Charles C. Arbuthnot, and sociologist James Elbert Cutler (who was also the school's first dean) allied with Samuel Scovil of Cleveland Electric Illuminating Company, investment banker Warren S. Hayden, Mayo Fesler of the Civic League, Munson Havens of the Cleveland Chamber of Commerce, and City Engineer William A. Stinchcomb to train social work students in the broadest possible application of their discipline.[36]

The SASS curriculum was grounded in the new institutionalism gaining currency in universities. Core courses in government, municipal government, sociology, social institutions, and the child and the community were paired with social issues such as labor, socialism, and the factory system, and to these the curriculum linked such courses as municipal administration, the administration of social legislation, household administration, playground management, charity organization administration, and case work with families so as to maximize the program's key concern—organizational management.

Institutionalists skated on thin ice. Their approach implied that social ills could be remedied by social institutions, but institutionalism also strongly suggested that poverty and other social maladies were rooted in society and its institutions rather than in individual behavior. Early master's degree students under the direction of Professor Mildred Chadsey studied neighborhood life and workplace environments and made the connection between society and the individual. By 1920, the first forty SASS graduates were so trained.[37]

In the 1920s, however, the emphasis in SASS shifted from institutionalism to case management and social psychology.[38] Agency management remained an integral part of the curriculum but courses in psychology, case studies, interviewing techniques, counseling, and case management steadily replaced the study of institutions and institutional behavior. Masters essays, now case studies of dysfunctional families and individuals, reflected the trend. The new approach was geared toward setting standards of normative behavior for families and individuals. The social ills that had earlier been blamed on industrial society could now be ascribed to the deviant behavior of individuals or groups of individuals. Modern psychology offered the hope that these deviancies could be treated and corrected by the new generation of social worker–counselors. Ironically, Corporate Regime wealth redistribution policy began by holding society accountable and ended by laying the blame on individuals.[39]

148 Part Three: The Corporate Regime, 1895–1919

The work of Corporate Regime wealth redistribution policy was at last completed in the 1920s, just as the regime was slipping from power. Wealth redistribution policy rested in the hands of the private sector, which satisfied the entrepreneurs in the regime. At the same time, its managerial efficiency and operation as one collectivity (the system) serving another collectivity (classes of clients) satisfied the bureaucratic impulses of regime professionals. It was a remarkable edifice. The Community Chest Fund raised funds; the Welfare Federation provided planning, budget making, and operational oversight; SASS trained professional staff; and the Cleveland Foundation conducted policy research with surveys of the public schools and criminal justice system. This policy edifice, despite the commanding federal role in wealth redistribution policy since the 1930s, survives to this day.

CONCLUSION: THE ACHIEVEMENTS OF THE CORPORATE REGIME

The Corporate Regime was the most dynamic and effective of Cleveland's policy making regimes and the regime whose policies had the most far-reaching impact. The economic development, urban growth, service distribution, and wealth redistribution policies, for good or ill, cast a long shadow over Cleveland a century after their inception.

Yet it was a regime that accomplished much despite internal divisions and debate. The entrepreneurial element within the regime argued that, to the extent practicable, policy making should be an individual enterprise contributing to the well-being of individuals. As organization builders themselves, entrepreneurs appreciated the importance of individuals acting together in an organizational conduit to achieve important goals from which individuals would benefit.

But the entrepreneurs divided over the proper organizational conduit. The faction represented by Tom L. Johnson relied heavily on the state to achieve individualist goals. This was anathema to the faction headed by Cleveland Chamber of Commerce entrepreneurs. For them the organizational conduit must be removed from the perils presented by public institutions and elected officials. The proper conduit was the voluntary civic organization, the nonsectarian organization, the special purpose district, or the private foundation. Only in these organizations could self-interest be put aside and could civic virtue flower.

Critics, of course, might claim that these organizations were too narrowly representative of a single class and its values. But professionals, whose numbers were most dominant late in the Corporate Regime, did not rise in opposition to the values or the conduits chosen by the entrepreneurs. For the professionals, organizations were both ends and means: one collectivity benefiting another collectivity. The goal of the professionals was to improve organizational efficiency and spread the benefits of regime policy making as broadly as possible to as many groups as possible.

Corporate Regime economic development policy did not engage the attention of professionals; instead, they deferred to the superior business wisdom of the entrepreneurs. Corporate Regime economic development policy, in truth, died of individualism. The telling moment came when the entrepreneurs refused to make venture capital available to the Cleveland Chamber of Commerce to attract new enterprises. From then on, Cleveland's ability to attract new businesses was left to chance, and the fate of the largest local employers was in the hands of multilocational corporations.

Professionals played a much more important role in urban growth policy. Both parties to the regime agreed that land use controls were the essence of growth policy. The entrepreneurs wanted to bring order and civic virtue to the city by way of example, as demonstrated particularly in the parks systems and the twin group plans; their commitment was measured by their lavish redirection of capital from business investments to philanthropy represented in University Circle. Assigning both order and virtue to institutions, the professionals sought to achieve land use order through comprehensive building regulation, zoning, and city planning; they sought to promote civic virtue by means of establishing cooperative relationships between more conventional institutions, such as the municipality, the public school system, higher education, and cultural institutions. In this manner, urban growth policy was eventually co-opted by the professionals and the professional ideal.

Entrepreneurs shied away from service distribution policy except to lend support to political structural reform measures intended to disempower populists. Tom L. Johnson was the lone exception. As mayor, Johnson appointed qualified professionals to head executive departments and attempted to spread the professional ideal of order and efficiency throughout the municipal bureaucracy. He paved the way for Newton D. Baker and the Chamber of Commerce professionals to establish productive working relationships with civil servants within the municipal bureaucracy, the result being improved efficiency in the delivery of services but not the wholesale purging of populist influences. Of all municipal institutions, the public school system most notably became the instrument of the professional ideal, the universalism of which provoked a crisis of expectations in the public school system by regime's end.

Wealth redistribution policy was the most unqualified success of the Corporate Regime. It was a unique blend of entrepreneurial vision and professional managerialism. The fund raising edifice was a triumph of burden shifting from the rich to the middle class, the Welfare Federation a victory for order and organizational efficiency, the Cleveland Foundation a unique attempt at policy research, and SASS a model of what could be achieved through institutional cooperation. The entire wealth redistribution edifice was a triumph over both sectarian charity and philanthropy and government interventionism.

But the Corporate Regime did not survive its successes, and, as it turned out, it ended more with a whimper rather than a bang. The founders of the regime got old, retired to the suburbs, or simply moved on to other venues. There was a sense also that the job was finished. Economic development policy would go on as before. The public land use controls were in place or soon would be. The new city manager system in government would be a trusted vehicle to implement land use controls and deliver services efficiently. And the new wealth redistribution system was working beyond anyone's best expectations.

Part Four
The Realty Regime, 1919–1929

9

ORIGINS OF THE REALTY REGIME

In the 1920s a new and more sophisticated real estate industry exploited Cleveland's new urban geography and promoted the making of policy on a regional scale. The real estate industry, moreover, spawned a new generation of prominent businessmen, the founding fathers of the Realty Regime which dominated urban policy making from 1919 to 1929. The regime owed its origins to the early-twentieth-century transformation of real estate business practice.

THE EMERGENCE OF THE REAL ESTATE INDUSTRY

The real estate industry escaped from its late nineteenth century status as a small-scale, highly competitive industry subdividing land in the unbuilt outer city to become a much-larger-scale, operationally integrated, twentieth century business, an industry skilled in exploiting commercial opportunities in the central business district and suburban residential real estate. The real estate industry, in contrast to the industries sustaining the Corporate Regime, was a local-sector industry.

Ownership in the real estate industry was more representative of the city's population than any other business, explaining why realtors understood the city and its decision-making process so well.[1] Real estate industry entrance requirements were minimal. Almost anyone could enter the business and many did. Hard work, diligence, and imagination were rewarded. First and second generation immigrants were attracted and found themselves on an equal business footing with native born Anglo-Saxon competitors. Immigrant surnames were far more common in real estate than in export sector industries.

The real estate industry was the core around which the Realty Regime formed. The industry consisted of a growing cast of players, including, roughly in order of appearance, those who bought and sold land and buildings, the building industry, street railway operators, retailers, law firms seeking to replace departing corporate clients with developers, banks as the circuits of capital shifted from primary to secondary, the media for the advertising dollars the realty coalition generated, and increasingly in the 1920s, public officials, most notably those serving the suburbs.[2]

All held in common the small business philosophy of the real estate operator. Even though the scale of development projects and capital requirements greatly increased in the twentieth century, the size of the firm remained relatively small, in contrast to the bureaucratic magnitude of the multilocational export-sector manufacturing corporation. Small local-sector businessmen and export-sector big businessmen did not operate in the same ways. Local-sector small businesses were far more oriented toward short-term goals. Real estate development projects had a comparatively short life span and were completed in discernible phases. Beyond the principals, accountants and salespeople were the only full-time employees, and salespeople were usually paid commissions rather than salaries. Professionals such as lawyers, engineers, and architects were hired as independent contractors for the duration of their phase of the project only. General contractors were hired for the building phase, and subcontracting was their responsibility. Capital requirements were met sequentially by banks and other financial institutions and were likewise short term in duration. The sales component of the development returned the project to the parent firm. Payrolls for the real state operator were small, and accounting was relatively simple. No elaborate line and staff management organization existed, and the business operations did not operate according to a fixed long-term plan.[3]

If there was little organizational difference between nineteenth and twentieth century real estate businesses, it was because the early industrial era realty firm was hindered by lack of capital, knowledge of the economics of the business, and a guiding set of business practices. The nineteenth century real estate operator was a subdivider who dealt in raw land, relying on guesswork and ethical corner cutting to make his way. The residue of mistakes, unfulfilled hopes, and broken promises left turn of the century realtors with unsavory reputations. Twentieth century real estate firms overcame these burdens by learning the economics of the business and by professionalizing their operations. These lessons reaffirmed that businesses could remain organizationally lean even as the scale of operations increased many times over.[4]

The credit for this impressive transition must go to national and local real estate professional organizations. These organizations schooled realtors in the economics of the business and supplied them with a much needed code of ethical standards (1913). Local real estate boards proliferated in cities and towns across the county, culminating in the founding of the National Real Estate Board (1908). The mission of the national organization was both informational and educational. The National Real Estate Board promoted urban land economics as a formal academic discipline with abstract theories crucial to daily practice in the real estate industry.

For these services, the National Real Estate Board relied heavily on Richard T. Ely, the University of Wisconsin economist who pioneered the study of urban land economics. Ely was the principal in a private consulting firm, the Institute for Research in Land Economics and Public Utilities, which served as a consultant to the National Real Estate Board for monographs on urban land economics, real estate taxation, and zoning. Ely was also the designer of the real estate courses taught by the National Real Estate Board. John R. Commons, Ely's University of Wisconsin colleague in economics, shared his knowledge of real estate taxation and public utility valuations expertise with the National Real Estate Board. Both economists were Johns Hopkins University Ph.D.'s, graduate professors, and founders of the American Economics Society. They trained the first generation of land economists and used their professional network to lobby for university and business college courses and programs in urban land economics and real estate business practices. The National Real Estate Board networked with collateral organizations, including the National Municipal League, the National Conference on City Planning, the American Institute of Architects, and others to broaden the knowledge base of the industry and to promote its goals. Ely and Commons were frequent visitors to Cleveland, and one of their protégés, Edward W. Bemis, was the city's water commissioner.[5]

The Cleveland Real Estate Board

The most important local professional organization was the Cleveland Real Estate Board, which originated as an offshoot of the Building Trades Association. By the 1910s the Cleveland Real Estate Board (CREB) was an independent association with its own meeting rooms, dining facilities, officers, and committee structure. In the 1920s, CREB took positions on public issues, but from its inception, the main work of CREB was the professionalization of the real estate industry.[6]

CREB membership included realtors, lawyers, bankers, builders, architects and engineers, retail businessmen, and public officials. Organizationally,

CREB, like the Chamber of Commerce, was a federation of divisions representing the major market segments of the industry, including subdividers, suburban real estate development and sales, commercial properties, and industrial real estate. In the 1920s CREB formed committees to study public issues such as zoning, taxation, city planning, legislation, highways, and a changing kaleidoscope of ad hoc issues. The work of the committees provided the basis for the positions the organization took on public issues.[7]

In its drive to professionalize the real estate industry, CREB gathered and compiled a trove of literature on urban land economics and wrote standards of ethical practice for the industry. As a field of academic inquiry, urban land economics came into its own during the 1920s. CREB disseminated this knowledge by scheduling leading scholars and practitioners as speakers at well-publicized and well-attended lunches (many of these speeches were printed verbatim in *The Cleveland Realtor*, the house newsletter of CREB). Richard T. Ely, the University of Wisconsin land economist, and J. P. Goode, a University of Chicago geographer, headed the list of distinguished academic speakers, but the roll also included such local experts in urban land economics as realtor Stanley L. McMichael and lawyer Robert Bingham. Curiously, speakers from the Ohio Grange, a farmers' organization, often addressed CREB. The Granger orators, who had probably been denounced by the fathers of those sitting in the CREB dining room as hayseed radicals, had three interests in common with the realtors: an appreciation of the value of land, a strong aversion to real estate taxes, and a passion to shift the tax burden to other forms of wealth.[8]

Dissemination of information was a major goal of the CREB. *The Cleveland Realtor* was the single most important source of information, but local newspapers also assisted. Stanley L. McMichael was assigned to the real estate beat by *The Plain Dealer* in 1907. By World War I, each of the city's newspapers featured real estate reporters and published Sunday real estate supplements. Not uncommonly, newspaper articles explained complex issues of land economics theory. In the 1920s, McMichael, now a realtor himself, and lawyer Robert Bingham formed a publishing company to print articles, pamphlets, and books on land economics and real estate written by the pair. CREB was a major market outlet for their works.[9] It was also an outlet for the ideas of John A. Zangerle, the Cuyahoga County auditor and sometimes the nemesis of the real estate industry, who was a respected land economist and a feared land valuation expert. Zangerle frequently addressed CREB meetings, and his speeches and journal articles appeared in *The Cleveland Realtor*.[10]

The most pressing practical need facing the realtors was a scientific, reliable method of fixing and forecasting land value. Early in the 1920s,

CREB formed a valuation committee and encouraged all members to submit their real estate transactions to study and evaluation by the committee. The committee used these transactions to experiment with techniques of scientific real estate appraisal. By the mid 1920s, the committee had enough confidence in its appraisal methodology to challenge valuations and appraisals made by the county auditor.

Tax relief was only one goal of this process. Appraisal techniques were used to set land valuations, the very heart of the real estate business. Land valuations could be aggregated and charted over time to monitor the trajectory of the real estate business cycle. Land valuations, moreover, were crucial for fixing the ratio of site value to improvement value. Thus the realtors could resolve the dilemma of land use potential in the "margins of transference," those places in a city where land appears to be in transition from an older to a newer use. The trick was figuring out which type of land use, older or newer, would prevail in the margin of transference. Formulating and testing such hypotheses in land economics was probably the most important work performed by CREB.[11]

Professionalization also meant setting ethical business practices. The unsavory reputation of real estate salespeople was the industry's weakest link. Shady sales practices were often the result of ignorance of the product combined with market and credit pressures; however, the minimal entrance requirements of the industry also attracted the unethical. CREB promoted licensure of real estate agents, and a CREB committee created to study the problem found that real estate salespeople lacked an understanding of the product they sold and had no standardized procedure for selling properties. CREB offered seminars for salespeople in which they would be instructed in the elements of land economics. CREB wrote standardized sales contracts to guide a sales transaction through its several stages, affording legal protection for seller and buyer. CREB recommended that candidates for licensure enroll in CREB land economics seminars and submit to tutoring by legal consultants in the art of drafting contracts. CREB encouraged all member real estate firms to send their sales personnel to it for training. Despite some initial opposition, these procedures won the day, and the real estate industry steadily became more professionalized and respected.[12]

The Real Estate Lawyer

The legal profession played a crucial role in the emergence of the real estate industry. CREB welcomed attorneys as members and retained the

Thompson, Hine, and Flory law firm as legal counsel. Lawyers were important for standardizing sales procedures and cleaning up the image of realtors, but they had other more far-reaching contributions to make. During the 1910s and after, lawyers became indispensable to the real estate industry. Although real estate developers played the entrepreneurial role in bringing large-scale real estate developments to fruition, lawyers served as vital middlemen in the process, working out the details with all parties to the transaction. Lawyers devised new methods of finance, land assembly techniques, and tax relief schemes. They were the first to see that finance, land assembly, and taxation were interrelated parts of a whole.

Several local law firms and lawyers specialized in real estate law. The two most prominent law firms were Thompson, Hine, and Flory and Baker Hostettler. The founder of the Thompson firm, Amos Burt Thompson, was a specialist in land valuation, taxation, and the ninety-nine-year leasehold. Robert Bingham, whose interests included land economics and land parcel assembly, was an associate in Thompson's law firm.[13] Newton D. Baker, the protégé of Tom L. Johnson and former Cleveland mayor, returned to his law practice at Baker Hostettler after service as Woodrow Wilson's secretary of war and found his corporate and labor client list dwindling, a repercussion of the devolving export sector of the local economy. He soon replaced departed corporate clients with real estate clients. Baker represented the Ambler Realty Company in its landmark suit against the suburban village of Euclid's zoning law and throughout the 1920s represented the vast Cleveland real estate development interests of the Van Sweringen brothers.[14]

Amos Burt Thompson's contributions to the real estate industry grew out of his attempts to assemble Euclid Avenue land parcels for real estate developers. Thompson and his clients envisioned a retail and commercial corridor that would extend from Euclid Avenue at Playhouse Square (E. 18th Street) to Euclid Avenue and East 105th Street, including the westerly portions of Chester and Prospect running parallel to Euclid. The land between Playhouse Square and East 105th Street was given over to high-grade residential and apartment land uses, the western end of which included the Euclid Avenue "Millionaires Row." Thompson saw the corridor as the city's most important area of land use change. By the early 1920s, Playhouse Square and East 105th already were retail, commercial, and entertainment districts. Thompson sought to connect the two centers with a continuous corridor of retail and commercial land uses. (See figure 9.1.) His real estate clients were people who could make this development a reality.[15]

Serious obstacles stood in Thompson's way. One worry was the gravitational pull of the Van Sweringen Terminal Group project at Public Square,

Chapter 9: Origins of the Realty Regime   159

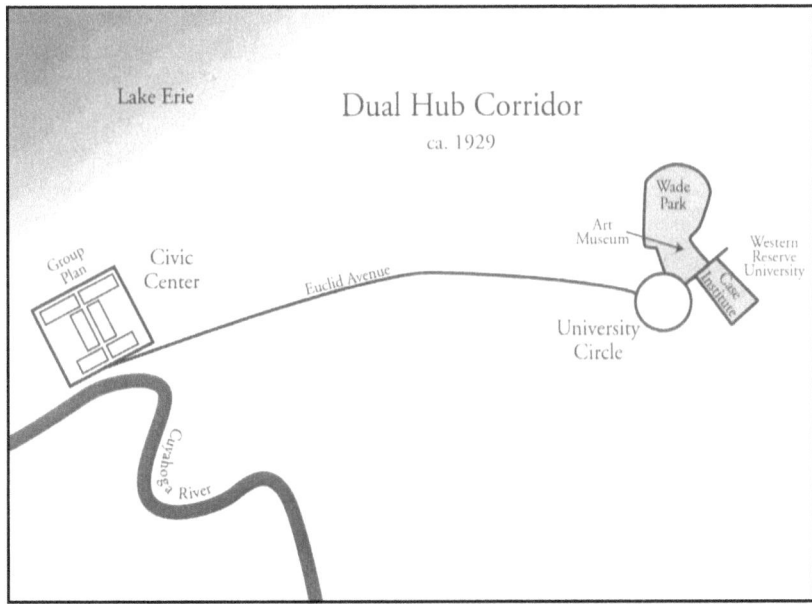

FIGURE 9.1 Map of Euclid Corridor, E. 18th to E. 105th (ca. 1929)

a development that included not only a rail terminal but also office buildings, a hotel, and a department store. Thompson dispatched this worry with a new research tool, vehicular and pedestrian traffic counts on Euclid Avenue throughout the 1920s. Gathered at quarterly intervals through the year and at various hours of the business day, these traffic data convinced Thompson that Euclid Avenue could sustain eastward commercial and retail development even in the face of the gravitational pull of the Van Sweringen project.[16]

A second obstacle was posed by the site-to-improvement ratio, that is, the value of the land relative to the value of the structure built upon it. Thompson energetically assembled valuation data on every Euclid Avenue lot from Playhouse Square to East 105th. Chester and Prospect avenues were also included. He compared three sets of valuation data: his own, those of CREB, and those of the county auditor. These data convinced him that the value of the improvement (the existing residence) was declining in relationship to the increasing value of the site (the lots). A clear message was received: it was time to change the nature of the improvement.[17]

This created a third obstacle: how to wrest the residential land at issue from its present owners. Here Thompson teamed with Frederick H. Goff, a lawyer and president of Cleveland Trust bank. After the passage of the federal income tax law in 1913 and the progressive wartime amendments to the legislation, lawyers scrambled to find ways to protect wealthy clients from the "confiscatory" impact of federal income and inheritance taxes. One legal device employed was the living trust, pioneered by Goff in Cleveland. The living trust was designed to retain the pecuniary rewards gained from accumulated assets. Wealthy Cleveland Trust customers were encouraged to place their assets, real and portable, in trust accounts with the bank, naming the bank as trustee. The bank provided daily management of these trust accounts. The living trust device reduced federal tax liabilities solely to income earned by the trust, and taxes on the principal were avoided. The trust was also perpetual, and when such customers died their heirs continued to collect the income from the trust and—a matter of no small consequence—paid no inheritance taxes on the assets in the trust. By the 1920s, many of the Euclid Avenue residential properties were in trust accounts managed by Goff's bank.[18]

This was when Thompson, inspired by favorable site-to-improvement ratios, sought to acquire Euclid Avenue properties on behalf of his clients in the real estate development business. The site acquisition process was now simplified because he did not have to negotiate with scores of owners; he had only to deal with Goff and a handful of bankers like him. Thompson soon discovered that trust managers and individual owners were also aware of the improving site-to-improvement ratios, but they were unwilling to sell the land. Hurdling this obstacle was Amos Burt Thompson's finest hour as a lawyer. Thompson's solution was the ninety-nine-year leasehold, a sublimely simple solution that allowed all parties to have their cake and eat it too. In a ninety-nine-year leasehold arrangement, the owner of the property leased the land to a developer for a period of ninety-nine years in exchange for an agreed-upon annual ground rent. The developer-lessee, under the terms of the contract, was then free to make any improvement on the land he desired. The developer-lessee also benefited by being freed of the burden of raising capital to buy the initial land. The ninety-nine-year lease allowed Thompson and Goff to make prime Euclid Avenue land available for retail and commercial development.[19] If the ninety-nine-year leasehold doomed the showcase mansions on the Euclid Avenue Millionaires Row, seldom did the owners raise their voices in protest. Instead, they cheerfully took up residence in new mansions at University Circle.

Amos Burt Thompson promoted the full range of tax advantages to be gained from the ninety-nine-year leasehold. Local real estate taxes could be avoided by the lessor by passing the obligation along to the lessee. Real estate tax liabilities were sometimes negotiated with the parties in which they agreed to split the obligation, with the lessor paying the land portion of the tax and the lessee paying taxes on the improvement. The federal tax

Chapter 9: Origins of the Realty Regime   161

burden could also be eased. Because no property actually changed hands in the leasehold arrangement, the owner did not have to pay federal capital gains taxes. Owners were liable for federal taxes on the rental income only. The lessee, on the other hand, was able to use the rental paid as a deduction on his federal income taxes. For the lessee, there were also rental costs which could be deducted from the federal tax obligation. Most leasehold contracts contained clauses allowing the lessee to sell his lease to another purchaser. This was frequently done, and there were tax advantages in doing so. Regardless of the tax bracket of the seller, the tax on the sale of the lease was capped at a rate of 12 percent. For wealthy individuals, this sort of transaction made a great deal of sense. Robert Bingham reported that many leaseholds were arranged for that sole purpose.[20]

Robert Bingham was Amos Burt Thompson's law associate and a perceptive student of real estate values. If Thompson's approach to values was grounded in the minutia of statistics and the fine print of the tax code, Bingham's evolved from a macro level appreciation of urban growth patterns. Bingham's books, articles, CREB speeches, and office memoranda reveal that he was a keen student of urban structure. He took notice of the corollary relationship between changes in city structure and improvements in land values. Bingham and his publishing partner Stanley L. McMichael observed that in the commercial era the nation's cities were walking cities dependent on long-distance transportation connections. The land where these routes fused was the highest valued in the city. But the industrial city was dominated by large export-sector businesses and the technology of electricity, which allowed for both horizontal and vertical real estate development. Central business district land values were the chief beneficiary. Bingham saw the city of the 1920s increasingly as the creature of the automobile, resulting in a more sprawling city than the hub and spoke configuration of the streetcar era, and making attractive real estate transactions at the unregulated edges of settlement. Urban expansion, structural change, and increases in land values were related, but these elements were a volatile mix, a mix, however, that Bingham believed could be stabilized by using the regulatory powers of government. Bingham was one of the first people in the real estate industry to see the compatibility between public land use controls and profit.[21]

Bingham's initial appreciation of the role that government might play in urban growth was financial. Bingham was an advocate of public spending on infrastructure to artificially stimulate urban growth and consequently increase land values. He was almost indiscriminate in his enthusiasm. He endorsed bridges linking east and west sides, streetcar and interurban links to the suburbs, suburban street and highway linkages, and expansion of utilities. Bingham championed a network of commuter transportation linkages regional in scope. All of these strategies would lead to more land sales and higher land values.[22]

Bingham's notions were not unflawed. Improved infrastructure tempted the real estate industry to bring land into production too soon, accounting for the boom and bust cycles in the real estate market. Bingham's support of both rail and highway transportation was also blemished because the market could not sustain both. As more and more highways were constructed and streets were paved to accommodate the automobile, streetcar ridership precipitously declined, culminating in the last illness of the privately owned transit companies. Municipal ownership followed in the 1940s.

In any case, Bingham's strategies became policy in the 1920s, and in the short term, thanks to growth, increased allocation of land, and soaring land values, Cleveland took on the appearance of a boomtown, paradoxically one with a stagnant export sector. In Bingham's analytical framework, local government should be the ally of the real estate industry. Only government could regulate land use and raise the large sums of money necessary for infrastructure improvements and subsidized rail rapid transit.[23]

Real Estate Finance

Lawyer Robert Bingham thought on a grand scale and so in his way did lawyer turned banker Frederick H. Goff. In 1908 Goff left the private practice of corporate law, in which he was a specialist in mergers and financial reorganizations, to become president of Cleveland Trust Bank. It was a good fit because Cleveland Trust had historically supplied capital for corporate expansion, mergers, and reorganizations. Within a decade of Goff's arrival, however, the corporate banking business eroded, and Goff scrambled to find new business for the bank. Goff led an aggressive campaign to expand the bank's branch operations and increase the number of individual accounts. In the early 1920s branch banks mushroomed from fifteen to fifty-two and individual depositors from 70,000 to 397,000. These marketing changes, however, did not by themselves compensate for the loss of corporate loan customers; but the expanding branch operations of the bank taught Goff some lessons about the market implications of Cleveland's changing geography. Cleveland was now an urbanized region and real estate was the wave of the future, and Goff had capital for real estate investments in the living trust accounts managed by the bank.[24]

Chapter 9: Origins of the Realty Regime   163

Yet there were constraints on Cleveland Trust's entry into this market. Federal legislation prohibited national banks from making loans on real estate, restrictions which were not lifted until 1928.[25] Goff circumvented this legislation by acquiring non-national banks, Lake Shore Banking and Trust Company and Garfield Savings and Trust, institutions that could make real estate loans. Other Cleveland national banks followed suit, acquiring through merger or acquisition small building and loan companies, savings and loan companies, and citizens' savings banks. Goff and other local bankers then redefined the taxonomy of loans to include site acquisition loans, construction loans, bridge loans, corporate restructuring loans, and home mortgage loans, among others.[26] In the newly restructured banking industry, subsidiary savings and loans could make loans the parent national bank could not make.[27] Making use of these loan options, a group of investors represented by Amos Burt Thompson bought the $4.5 million Discount Bank Building at Superior and East Ninth with an out-of-pocket cash investment of $100,000.[28] The heavily mortgaged Van Sweringen empire was the most extreme local example of creative loan making by a labyrinthine corporate pyramid of holding companies.[29] These creative credit arrangements allowed the real estate industry to remain organizationally small even as they increased their operational scale.

The local real estate capital market reached completion when local banks and law firms entered the municipal bond market. The Realty Regime's aggressive regional urban growth policies, particularly infrastructure spending, were dauntingly expensive. To keep tax rates low and actual costs camouflaged, the Realty Regime favored heavy borrowing rather than taxing for capital improvements. The City of Cleveland carried a sizable amount of bonded debt, most of which had been acquired to fund the projects of the Corporate Regime, so the Realty Regime shifted the debt burden to the county and suburban municipalities, creating a rich market in suburban municipal bonds. Federal tax law made municipal bonds tax exempt, which created a boon for trust account managers in the 1920s.[30] For banks generally, the municipal bond not only carried federal tax advantages, but was computed in the bank's accounts as an asset against which additional loans could be made. Banks were not only purchasers of municipal bonds, some could also serve as underwriters. To avoid the bond default fiascos of the mid-nineteenth century, federal and state law required the hiring of independent bond counsel to review each issue of municipal bonds. Local law firms specialized as bond counsel. The municipal bond market financed massive infrastructure investment throughout the 1920s and created a wealth of business opportunities for banks, trust account managers, and law firms.[31] Frederick H. Goff was the financial genius behind the complex transition Cleveland's banking industry made from corporate to real estate investments. His innovations made financing large-scale real estate developments feasible and the rise of the Realty Regime inevitable. Goff's career in law and banking illustrates the transition in policy making dominance from the Corporate Regime to the Realty Regime. The fact was that power was shifting in the Cleveland community, and Frederick H. Goff did much to make this transition a reality. Lawyers Frederick H. Goff, Amos Burt Thompson, and Robert Bingham made very tangible contributions to the growth of the real estate industry and the rise of the Realty Regime.

Boosterism and advertising were less tangible elements of the real estate business in the 1920s. CREB developed a flair for both, each of which masqueraded as economic development policy. In 1926, the *Cleveland Realtor* noted in the city a flagging civic spirit and a pervasive sense of pessimism about the future. In response, CREB raised $75,000 in contributions and hired an advertising agency to sell Cleveland to Clevelanders. These ads trumpeted the city as the new Athens and as a vessel of civic progress. The good feelings generated by the advertising helped sell real estate, even though the market for industrial real estate did not improve and neither did the manufacturing sector.[32]

Stagnation in the export sector of Cleveland's economy facilitated the rise of the Realty Regime. Policy making dominance and policy priorities could not be established, however, until the real estate industry learned its own business. In the first two decades of the twentieth century, the industry learned the interdependent relationship between city structure, commuter transportation, land values, and the highest and best use of land. This knowledge taught that there were two places where profits were most reliably made: the central business district and the unsettled fringes of urban land. Packaging land and financing real estate deals through infrastructure building and creative loan making were learned in the 1920s. In that decade, because of increased automobile usage, urban settlement became regional, and the policy making regime that came with it operated also on a regional scale, though not in the way regional reformers had anticipated.

During the 1920s, real estate men became the most visible and prominent businessmen in Cleveland. The Van Sweringens, Cragins, Amblers, Halles, and Laronges became the successors of the Rockefellers, Chisholms, Mathers, Severances, and Hannas. Their visibility and apparent wealth made them business leaders and policy makers. The organizations the realty men founded became the institutional base of the Realty Regime.

THE RISE OF THE REALTY REGIME

"Real Estate men are the city builders of modern times," Stanley L. McMichael and Robert F. Bingham proclaimed in their book, *City Growth and Values*. "Assuming the places of kings and emperors, who fostered and promoted growth of ancient times, the real estate subdivider and the business district operator now sway and direct the future of towns and cities in the making."[33] More than just drumming the booster's hollow washtub, the two realtors were sounding the arrival of a new generation of urban policy makers.

In the 1920s the Realty Regime took the policy setting reins in hand and proved the incantations of McMichael and Bingham nearly right. Although the Realty Regime was a polyglot group composed of realtors, builders, bankers, lawyers, retailers, and the newspapers, the dominant element was the real estate developers, the "subdividers" and central "business district operators" celebrated by McMichael and Bingham. The Realty Regime came to power when the Corporate Regime abdicated its leadership position in policy making. Throughout the 1920s the Realty Regime governed key policy setting institutions, and from these positions new economic and social policies followed. The new policies emphasized low real estate taxes, urban growth over economic development, and a social program of fiscal parsimony and self-interest.

The Guard Changes

The most visible members of the Realty Regime were the large-scale developers such as the Van Sweringens and men bearing the names of downtown stores. Familiar names of bankers and lawyers also appeared on committee rosters and special purpose district boards, suggesting continuity between old and new regimes; but the nature of the legal profession and the banking business had now switched from a reliance on export-sector clients to a dependence on local-sector clients. The new guard emasculated the Cleveland Chamber of Commerce and transferred policy making power to the Cleveland Real Estate Board. Real estate men captured the Chamber's Committee on City Plan, the City Planning Commission, the board of the Metropolitan Park District, Cleveland's city manager system, and mayoralties and city council posts in the suburbs. From these policy-setting perches a new urban policy emerged. Implementation followed a familiar course: commanding influence in the political decision-making process followed by wholesale changes in urban

166   *Part Four: The Realty Regime, 1919–1929*

growth policy and unheralded yet far-reaching changes in service distribution and wealth redistribution policies.[34]

Transition in the Voluntary Civic Sector

In the corporate era, the Cleveland Chamber of Commerce had been the cornerstone of urban policy making. Two parallel trends at work in the 1920s explain the decline of the chamber: first, the executive board and the committees of the chamber were gradually taken over by the real estate men; second, and paradoxically, was that the chamber became far less influential in policy making, giving way to upstart civic organizations dominated by the real estate industry.

Beginning in the late teens and through the 1920s, the power of the Corporate Regime was diluted by the growing presence of the real estate men on the executive board and key committees of the Cleveland Chamber of Commerce. Real estate developers, department store owners, newspaper publishers, and lawyers and bankers with ties to the real estate industry gradually replaced Corporate Regime members. The Chamber's City Planning Committee by 1918 was chaired by real estate developer O. P. Van Sweringen, and soon his business ally William Van Aken was added to the roster. In 1926, both Van Sweringen brothers, Oris Paxon and Mantis James, were awarded the Chamber's Cleveland Medal for Public Service. The citation proclaimed that the brothers Van Sweringen were "masters of business, builders of great enterprises, eager participants in every movement for a better Cleveland,"[35] a citation reflecting both the changing leadership and a disturbing inability to distinguish between deeds which fostered urban growth and those which nurtured economic development.

Other than laud real estate operators, the chamber found itself with less to do. Policy was in the main set. Corporate era reforms were institutionalized, and the policy setting apparatus gave the appearance of being "a machine that would go of itself."[36] The most conspicuous example of the chamber's declining influence was its inability to pass the zoning ordinance which it wrote and for which it lobbied. The Chamber's Committee on City Plan had advocated a zoning ordinance since 1922; despite the advocacy of the organization, no zoning ordinance passed until 1928. On this issue, the chamber was a house subtly divided against itself. The Realty Regime members of the chamber quietly but firmly opposed zoning within the chamber but campaigned loudly outside the organization with the public, politicians, and municipal bureaucrats to block its passage. Real estate men altered the chamber's city planning philosophy during the Realty Regime.

Simultaneously, the chamber's policy setting influence weakened. Its role changed from a proactive organization to a reactive organization, a reflection of the organization's growing loss of leadership, power, and influence. As the decade of the 1920s progressed, the chamber lost its institutional memory, unable to recall what issues it had supported or why, despite the bountiful documentary evidence kept on file in its Public Square headquarters. The chamber's shortcomings came to public attention, however, when *Finance and Industry*, a publication of the Federal Reserve District, openly criticized the chamber for failing in the 1920s to assume a leadership role in civic affairs. The newsletter charged that the chamber could no longer bring together other civic organizations and leaders to set policy.[37]

Stanley L. McMichael noted this too, and wrote a brief admonition that serves as a barometric measure of the decline of the Corporate Regime and the rise of the Realty Regime (and its self-serving guiding philosophy). McMichael observed that "The hustle and bustle of a decade of engagement in a business and real estate boom and the partial recovery therefrom has definitely dimmed the splendid civic spirit for which Cleveland was formerly noted. We still have the high grade public spirited men and women we have always had," McMichael explained, "but their energies have in part been deflected away from civic progress toward more selfish channels."[38] Seldom at a loss for a remedy, McMichael noted in 1929 that "With executive talents, secretarial staffs, and adequate personnel in the way of committees, an organization can adopt a plan, develop and embellish it, and turn it over in a finished state to the legislative and executive bodies of a city government to put into effect."[39] "A sharp reawakening of civic mindedness is needed in Cleveland," he added. McMichael then told his listeners that "the movement might just as well emanate from the Cleveland Real Estate Board as elsewhere."[40] This was the ultimate humiliation for the chamber and recognition that institutional policy leadership had long since passed to CREB and the Realty Regime.

The Corporate Regime gave birth to modern city planning: policies and plans that originated in the parks and city plan committees of the Chamber were institutionalized in the City of Cleveland Public Park System, the Cleveland Metropolitan Park System, and the City Planning Commission. In the 1920s, the Corporate Regime lost its dominance in all three. The Cleveland Parks System became the ward of the municipal bureaucracy. Control of the board of the Metropolitan Park District was divided between a professional civil servant (Stinchcomb), a corporate lawyer (Andrew Squire), and a realtor (Louis A. Moses).[41]

The City Planning Commission, created in 1915, was urged on the municipality by the Corporate Regime. The City Planning Commission was appointed by the mayor and was composed of six directors of city departments and five prominent citizens. Francis F. Prentiss, an industrialist, was the first chairman. The others included Morris A. Black, also an industrialist and an early supporter of the Group Plan and housing reform. H. M. Farnsworth, William G. Mather, industrialist and philanthropist, and O. P. Van Sweringen rounded out the group. With the exception of Van Sweringen, the citizen commissioners were all important members of the Corporate Regime. In 1919, Van Sweringen became chairman of the City Planning Commission. Thereafter, the composition of the commission changed and the number of commissioners increased. The expanded membership roster retained Black, Farnsworth, Prentiss, and Mather but also included a larger number of architects. Most significantly, however, realtors Joseph Laronge, Raymond T. Cragin, and real estate lawyer James Metzenbaum were added to the list of policy makers. In 1924, after the municipal charter reform campaign that gave Cleveland a city manager form of government, William R. Hopkins, a real estate operator, became city manager and permanent chairman of the City Planning Commission.[42]

Governmental Institutions

The city manager system (1924–1931) itself represents an important institutional change. The city manager system was the brainchild of the Cleveland Citizens League. An institutional creation of the Corporate Regime, the Citizens League (formerly, the Municipal Association) was designed to promote structural reforms aimed at purging local political institutions of populist influences. The Citizens League was less influential in the 1920s than it had been in the decade of its founding. Those manning the Citizen's League in the 1920s were younger, less influential lawyers and rising corporate branch plant managers. The Citizens League and prominent members of the Corporate Regime endorsed the city manager system. What attracted the Citizens League to the city manager system was its obvious organizational resemblance to the industrial corporation and the fact that the city manager was to be a nonpartisan professional, preferably an out-of-towner.[43]

Much of the enthusiasm for the city manager plan came from the Cleveland Real Estate Board, but its motives differed from those of the Citizens League and Corporate Regime leaders. These became apparent once the city manager charter was approved. The CREB threw its weight behind the appointment of William R. Hopkins as city manager. Hopkins was county chairman of the Republican Party and a member of city council. In private life, Hopkins was an energetic real estate developer and a member of the CREB (realtor and savings and loan operator Clayton C. Townes was chosen mayor under the city manager plan).

The hiring of Hopkins, of course, was a milestone in the establishment of a Realty Regime in Cleveland.[44] The selection of William R. Hopkins as city manager destroyed whatever hopes the remnants of the Corporate Regime had for the city manager system. As city manager, Hopkins was an enthusiastic supporter of land development schemes, including the construction of a lakefront stadium and the airport which bears his name. But Hopkins was not the impartial, professional executive the Citizens League had campaigned for. Hopkins was a real estate operator first and a professional politician second. Impartiality and professionalism barely registered with him.[45]

Other significant political institutions fell under the sway of the Realty Regime. Most suburban mayors and many suburban city councilmen were realtors. Edward A. Weigand, a large-scale suburban subdivider, was elected mayor in Lakewood. Realtor William J. Van Aken was elected mayor of Shaker Heights in 1923, and his business partners, Max Rudolph and Carl Palmer, were elected to the city council. The Shaker Heights mayor's office and even the first public school classrooms were housed in the Van Sweringen real estate company offices.[46]

Defanging the Cleveland Chamber of Commerce, appointments to key special purpose districts, dominance on the City Planning Commission, and control of political offices throughout the county announced the arrival of the Realty Regime. What more was needed was a central, guiding policy-making intelligence. This was provided by the Cleveland Real Estate Board.

The CREB was to the Realty Regime what the Cleveland Chamber of Commerce had been to the Corporate Regime. It played not only a key role in the professionalization of the real estate industry but also an equally important role in the policy setting of the Realty Regime. In the 1920s it operated in much the same way that the chamber had operated three decades earlier. CREB had a network of policy-specific committees which studied issues and made recommendations to the CREB board. The CREB board then took official positions on all public policy issues. From this series of position statements, spanning a period of fifteen years, the policies of the Realty Regime emerged.

Toward a New Policy Orientation

Led by CREB, the Realty Regime set goals and developed policies which it implemented throughout its institutional network. The 1920s have been dubbed the automobile age, and the Realty Regime saw policy making in regional, automobile-city terms. The automobile was the agent responsible for the dramatic change in city structure already visible when the Realty Regime came to power, and the Realty Regime tailored its policies to exploit the new structure. The region-wide institutional foundation of the Realty Regime gave it the appearance of fragmentation between city and suburban entities, but policy itself was internally consistent and regional in scope. The twin pillars upon which all Realty Regime policy rested were taxation and transportation. These two core policy issues reveal the Realty Regime's ambivalence toward government. The low realty tax philosophy of the Realty Regime was usually rationalized by anti-government laissez faire rhetoric. But the Realty Regime supported virtually all government spending for transportation improvements. By the time William R. Hopkins took office as city manager, the Realty Regime had concluded that local government was an important conduit to policy implementation.

10

GETTING DOWN TO BUSINESS
Economic Development and the Financing of Urban Growth Policy

This chapter brings together the Realty Regime's economic development policy and the initial stages of its expansive urban growth policy. Economic development policy was based on misreadings of such elements of economic development as transportation, economic trends, and the business organization. The regime failed to understand that a key element in Cleveland's economic development was its ability to adapt to changing transportation technologies. The regime also failed to perceive the changing themes of the post World War I economy and the new vertically integrated business organization. The most critical misreading came when the regime substituted urban growth policy for economic development policy, a mistake which obliged the regime to use tax reform and municipal budgets to raise the large sums necessary to finance its urban growth policy.

ECONOMIC DEVELOPMENT: THE LOST POLICY

Any economic activity that did not put money directly in the pockets of realtors failed to kindle the interest of the Realty Regime. Urban growth did generate pecuniary rewards, and the self-interested thinking of the Realty Regime deflected its attention from economic development policy to urban growth policy. But the shortsighted substitution of urban growth policy for economic development policy stemmed also from other factors.

Cleveland's economic development in the 1920s was shaped by three forces, one misunderstood by the regime and the other two not comprehended at all. First, the Realty Regime failed to understand that Cleveland's economic development was tied more to the city's ability to keep pace with technological innovations in long-distance transportation than to long-distance transportation per se. Second, Cleveland's economic development during the course of the Realty Regime was affected by the swings of long-wave cycles, national, perhaps international, economic phenomena not well understood by anyone. These undulations crested in 1920 and fell thereafter, with devastating results for Cleveland's economy. Third, the Realty Regime did not appreciate the consequences of the organizational and managerial changes taking place in multilocational businesses. These changes shifted economic development policy making from the Realty Regime to corporate managers who, like the realtors, were unaware that their decisions shaped Cleveland's economic future. The managers focused narrowly on the economic health of the companies and ignored the local impact of their business decisions.

Long-Distance Transportation: The Past as Present and Future

Cleveland's economic development paralleled advances in long-distance transportation technology, the surfaced road, the canal, and the railroad. By the 1920s the link between transportation and industry was a litany tirelessly repeated in noon hour oratory, Fourth of July celebrations, and election campaigns. The point obscured by the orators was that earlier economic development policy tied the city to *innovations* in long-distance transportation technology. The Realty Regime missed the point. They saw Cleveland's future economic development tethered to the older technology of water and rails. They were oblivious to the new technological innovations in long-distance transportation, the truck and the airplane. Not linking Cleveland to the new transportation technologies contributed to the listless pace of economic development.

The rail transportation element in the Realty Regime's economic development policy was set by the Van Sweringen brothers, Cleveland real estate operators but also the builders of a Cleveland-headquartered railroad empire. The Vans invested heavily in traditional modes of long-distance transportation, and after their purchase of the Nickel Plate Railroad in 1916, they devoted the next decade to consolidating their ownership of other railroads serving Cleveland. Ultimately, these acquisitions gave the brothers, who confided to a local reporter that their favorite authors were Rand and McNally, a near monopoly on rail transport throughout the northeastern quadrant of the country and a commanding presence in the Trans-Mississippi West. The Van Sweringen rail empire was financed through an elaborate pyramid of holding companies originating in Nickel Plate Securities, extending to the notorious Allegheny Corporation, and culminating in an apex formed by the Vaness and General Securities corporations.[1] Initially, the heavily mortgaged Van Sweringen railroads were profitable, transshipping thousands of tons of freight and depositing 2 million passengers annually in Cleveland.

With the city's long-distance transportation connections locally owned and headquartered, Realty Regime policy makers assumed that the economic development of the city was assured. But just as the Van Sweringens were assembling their debt-burdened railroad empire, the industry itself was proving overbuilt. Warning signs were ignored. As the use of trucks, cars, and planes increased, railroad traffic steeply declined in the late 1920s and profits with it.[2]

At the same time, Cleveland's tradition of relying heavily on water transportation continued. Because the Cuyahoga River was historically linked to the harbor complex, the Chamber of Commerce, as in the past, supported projects coupling river straightening and harbor improvements; but the Cleveland Real Estate Board only paid lip service to harbor improvements and adamantly refused to endorse tax increases and bond issues to straighten the river.[3]

The Realty Regime was not opposed to water transportation connections. Instead, CREB supported the grandiose St. Lawrence Waterway Project, which would be paid for by federal rather than local taxes. The Realty Regime felt that river and harbor infrastructure were already built and that rail infrastructure was safely contained in the Van Sweringen rail empire.[4] The St. Lawrence Waterway Project was Realty Regime economic development policy at its most visionary.

Closer to home, the Realty Regime shunned other new long-distance transportation technology—flight facilities. In 1926, the *Cleveland Realtor* reported that other cities had left Cleveland behind in the development of air transportation. Cleveland, the paper concluded, needed an airport.[5] The city lagged in the development of air service because the city's banks refused to loan money to finance the routes. When William B. Stout, a pioneer in the air passenger business and airplane manufacturing, came to Cleveland to raise money to finance his routes, he was turned down by Cleveland banks. Stout went next to Detroit, where he received the financial backing of Henry Ford, a man in the flight-related finished metals products industry, an entrepreneurial type in short supply in Cleveland.[6]

Cleveland banks no longer supplied investment capital to industry because their assets were committed to the Van Sweringens and other real estate developments. The pool of potential venture capital held by the

174   Part Four: The Realty Regime, 1919–1929

entrepreneurs was now invested either as passive capital or was channeled into the University Circle institutions.

Long-Wave Rhythms and Short-Term Cycles

Quite apart from Realty Regime reliance on railroads and water connections, Cleveland's economic development was adversely affected by long-wave up and down rhythms in the international economic system. A long-range up rhythm[7] of approximately fifty years ended abruptly in 1920. It was during this long-range rhythm that Cleveland experienced its industrial revolution. The economic factors that paced this long-wave rhythm—railroad construction, iron and coal extraction, and metals making—formed the core of Cleveland's economy. As the long-range rhythm ended, railroad construction, iron and coal extraction, and metals making entered a steep downward slide beginning in 1920, bottoming out in 1930. The effects of the long-range rhythm limited the city's economic development policy options throughout the decade.[8]

Simultaneously, a cyclical stagflation crisis hit the nation's economy in 1918–1919, bringing with it more immediate local repercussions. Policy makers could measure the stagflation crisis in the sharp increases in prices paid for goods and services, soaring municipal operating budgets, spiraling debt, higher interest rates, strident employee demands for increased wages, and a drop in housing starts. But Realty Regime growth policy led by infrastructure spending helped pull Cleveland out of the stagflation crisis. Bridge building, streetcar line extensions, street and highway construction, and utilities installations created the jobs and profits fueling what became a decade-long city building boom encouraged after 1921 when the Federal Reserve lowered interest rates. Throughout the decade, the long-range economic rhythm had a negative impact on the city's economic development, but the correction of the shorter term economic cycle created a building boom in Cleveland and a false sense of prosperity.[9]

The Impact of Vertical Integration

The Realty Regime could have improved the relative competitive position of Cleveland's export sector by heeding the new technologies in transportation (trucks and planes) which were responsible for the decline of the railroad industry. However, the fate of the export sector was also swayed by a newly evolving business organization, the institutional offspring of

America's second great corporate merger wave, surfacing shortly before World War I and cresting in the late 1920s.[10] Many of Cleveland's entrepreneurs, as noted earlier, sold off their businesses during the initial merger wave. The consolidation process in durable goods industries continued and was largely completed during the second merger wave in the 1920s, in which large companies integrated their operations from raw materials sourcing to finished products distribution. Independent Cleveland companies in minerals, shipping, metals making, and metals fabrication stood as signposts along the road toward vertical integration and were easily absorbed into giant vertically integrated combines.[11]

Vertically integrated corporations in steel, electricity, autos, and communications inaugurated a new phase of managerial capitalism. Operating decisions rested in the hands of salaried managers who were also the designers of these giant oligopolistic combines, enterprises which competed with one another for market share and profits by means of functional and strategic effectiveness. "Functional" competition meant improving the product, streamlining the processes of production, sophisticated marketing, timely and cost conscious purchasing, and stable labor relations. "Strategic" competition compelled professional managers to make quick decisions about when to enter and leave markets. Corporate functional and strategic decision making brought local geographical repercussions which, almost unnoticed, substituted for the economic development policy in most cities, including Cleveland.[12] Vertically integrated businesses hired many white collar managers and functionaries who more than offset the loss of blue collar jobs in the 1920s. The bountiful market in upper middle class suburban residential real estate that enriched Cleveland's real estate operators during the decade was the local effect of the organizational and managerial employment in export sector industries. The corporate managers residing in these suburban dwellings made economic development policy for urban America from their offices in the central business district.[13]

Functional strategic decision making in a vertically integrated organization became a key element in the urban economy. Corporate decisions about where to locate the production, distribution, back office, and headquarters functions of the modern industrial enterprise replaced local economic development policy. These decisions affected countless other decisions by managers in ancillary industries and services. For example, the decision by the Ford Motor Company (and later GM) to build an assembly plant in Cleveland influenced the locational decisions of parts makers and paint and tire manufacturers.[14]

In the 1920s Cleveland was the beneficiary of management decisions made in other cities. The cloud on the horizon was the sensitivity of managers to growing and declining markets. As long as Cleveland was perceived as a growing market and an advantageous point of distribution, it would benefit from managerial decision making. Even in the 1920s, however, production and distribution facility decisions were predicated on market size, availability of land for single-story production facilities, and integration into the emerging auto and air transportation network. Doubts had already been expressed about Cleveland because of the inability of the industrial real estate market to generate sites for single-story production facilities and the apparent local indifference to the new transportation technologies.[15]

Reliance on traditional forms of long-distance transportation to achieve development failed the Realty Regime and failed Cleveland. The realtors were working with an industrial era understanding of the metals making corporation that required rail and water transportation. Both of these the Realty Regime believed to be in good shape, a belief that jaundiced its view of air transport. The emergence of the modern vertically integrated industrial enterprise doomed local control over economic development policy. As a result of these factors, Realty Regime economic development policy came more and more to be linked to urban growth. Most of the issues the regime supported in the name of economic development were in fact infrastructure schemes designed to achieve urban growth.

FINANCING THE REALTY REGIME I: REVENUES

Analysis of the urban growth policy of the Realty Regime begins with a journey through the jungle of tax avoidance and tax burden shifting. Indeed, no policy-related issue claimed more of the Cleveland Real Estate Board's energy than taxation. Taxation had a dual importance: it was crucial to the real estate industry's matrix of profit and loss calculations, and it also was central to public policy making because taxation redistributes wealth from one group to another, determining, in effect, which groups will pay for the urban policy preferences of the regime in power.

It was an article of faith with Realty Regime members that the local tax structure inherited from the Corporate Regime redistributed wealth from themselves to wealthier individuals, multilocational corporations, utilities, and the service-consuming public more generally. The Realty Regime's attempts to shift the tax burden involved it in a hard fought tax reform war waged in four successive fronts: (1) a losing battle against wealthier individuals and corporations—the core of the Corporate Regime—to shift the burden of local taxation from real to personal property; (2) a fight to achieve an objective, scientific method of property tax valuations and from these valuations a determination of the taxable percentage of the market value; (3) the struggle to achieve a fair ratio between site and improvement taxes, and (4), during the darkest hour when the tax war seemed lost, a successful last ditch campaign to shift the burden of the real estate tax from large to small holders of realty.

Real vs. Personal Property

One of the unsung accomplishments of the Corporate Regime was its success in shifting the burden of local tax incidence (who pays) from themselves in the form of personal property to others in the form of real property.[16] The tax dollars that supported Corporate Regime public policies came mainly from the real estate tax, a classically suave example of the regime in power shifting the tax burden from themselves to those at the margins of power.

In the closing decades of the nineteenth century, the "property tax" was the largest single source of municipal revenues, amounting to some 60 percent in Cleveland and most other cities.[17] The term "property tax," however, is a misnomer because it embraces two antagonistic elements: real property and personal property. The real property tax was a measure of the tax burden of real estate holders, while personal property tax was a measure of the tax burden of individuals and corporations. Therefore, the assertion that the "property tax" contributed some 60 percent of all municipal revenues between 1870 and 1930 needs to be separated between shares paid by real estate taxes and those paid by personal property taxes.

The many varieties of personal property included individually owned household items, bank accounts, stocks, and bonds; in addition, such corporate holdings as machinery, inventories, bank accounts, stocks, and bonds were also classified as personal property. This was the wealth (earlier identified as active capital) which the Corporate Regime heralded as good capital and which as such should be shielded from the grasp of the local tax collector. The Corporate Regime regarded real property, in contrast, as passive (bad) capital which richly deserved the attention of local officials. Three classes of real property were taxed: income-producing property; property bought for resale; and owner-occupied residential property. In Cleveland, uniquely, the ninety-nine-year leasehold constituted a fourth form of taxable real estate.[18]

As early as 1895, at the very dawning of the Corporate Regime, the ratio within the property tax between real estate taxes and personal property taxes was shifting to the detriment of real property holders. During the decade of the 1890s alone, the share paid by personal property tax slumped to 39 percent of the whole. Two decades later, Amos Burt Thompson, in testimony before the state's Special Joint Committee on Taxation in 1917, charged that the value of personal property on the county tax duplicate was less than the deposits in Cleveland banks, the deposits themselves representing only a fraction of the total of personal property owned by Clevelanders. Thompson offered the joint committee data showing that county real estate tax now amounted to 75 percent of local taxes, while the portion paid by personalty had eroded to a negligible share.[19] The difference between Thompson's 75 percent figure and 100 percent was made up by various local user taxes.[20] These statistics testify to the ability of the Corporate Regime, during its heyday dating from 1895 to 1917, to shift tax incidence from themselves to the then less powerful holders of realty. Corporate interests justified this on the grounds that personal property was active capital and an asset to the export sector of the economy while real property was passive capital held in the main by greedy land speculators and franchise-holding monopolists who fittingly deserved punitive taxes.

This shift explains why Ohio Grange orators were popular speakers at Cleveland Real Estate Board (CREB) luncheons in the 1920s. Grangers and the farm interests they represented had more experience than any other political interest group in matters of land taxation. For half a century, Grangers opposed real property taxes because they made real property owners pay the cost of government services which benefited corporate interests more than farmers. Granger rhetoric argued for a "fairer" system of taxation in an attempt to shift the weight of tax incidence from land holders to individuals and corporations. This goal could be achieved in three ways: through a fairer, more scientific system of real estate appraisal; by collecting the widely evaded personal property tax; and by taxing other forms of wealth. Initially, at least, the second and third parts of the Granger testament had more appeal to the Cleveland Real Estate Board than the first.[21]

Fired by Granger rhetoric, CREB and its allies in the city attacked the tax evasion artifices of Cuyahoga County's wealthy individuals and corporations. In doing so, they locked horns with John A. Zangerle, the formidable Cuyahoga County auditor. Zangerle was a man of many talents, a local legend in the newly emerging field of real estate appraisal, a lawyer, a land economics expert, and, like his critics, a part-time real estate operator.[22] Zangerle was not out of sympathy with the claims of the realtors, but he was far more realistic about the possibilities of tax burden shifting than his critics in the real estate industry.

CREB repeatedly pushed for greater reliance on the personal property tax, a stratagem Zangerle scorned.[23] Zangerle's calculations showed that a rigorously enforced personal property tax would yield little more money than the tax was already generating. The personalty held by individuals was difficult to assess and was in any case too easily hidden from the tax collector. The truth was that individuals held only a small fraction of the total value of personalty, a portion estimated by Zangerle in 1924 to be only 11 percent.[24]

Corporate personalty was the key element in the personal property tax. The seven wealthiest individuals in Cleveland held personalty amounting to only $14.2 million; but the share value of the seven largest corporations headquartered in Cleveland totaled $71.7 million.[25] Even this latter figure was an underrepresentation. According to Zangerle, corporate personalty was assessed by a flawed formula. Corporations were assessed only in terms of their local plant, capital equipment, and inventories. These assets did not reflect the real worth of the company. In a speech before his critics at CREB, Zangerle explained that the true worth of the corporation was not the value of its personal property in Cleveland, or even its stock, but rather the value of its stock plus its debentures (bonded debt).[26] The personal property of the Standard Oil Company, to cite one of Zangerle's examples, was valued at $6.4 million, but the value of the company's shares was $19.25 million, meaning that in shares alone there was an untaxed "corporate excess" of $12.845 million.[27] Zangerle was also keenly aware of the local tax implications of the multilocational corporation. Those seven Cleveland companies cited above whose Ohio shares were worth $71.7 million had out-of-state operations totaling $60.9 million in share value. In 1919, even before the merger wave of the 1920s was felt, Ohio assets were just 54 percent of the corporate total. The problem was, Zangerle told his listeners, that existing state tax law was not in synch with the multilocational corporation.[28]

Zangerle proposed a comprehensive set of tax reforms, including graduated personal and corporate income taxes and taxes on inheritances and decedent estates. He advocated registration fees and property taxes on automobiles. Zangerle also saw that public utilities, franchises, building and loans, commercial banks, and corporations used sleight of hand accounting techniques to avoid paying their share of local taxes. To cut through the dubious accounting, Zangerle told the state legislature's Joint Tax Committee that these businesses should be assessed at their market value, that is, share plus debenture value. Corporate book value, another option presented to the legislators, Zangerle opposed because book value was based more on the sorcery of company accountants than on business reality.[29]

These reforms never materialized during the course of the Realty Regime. CREB and its Cleveland and Granger allies lobbied hard with the state legislature for passage of a tax reform package similar to that proposed by Zangerle, but it was blocked by corporate interests in every legislative session. With the battle to shift taxes from real property to personal property apparently lost, the Realty Regime turned to the first point in the Granger testament: fair, objective, and scientific real estate appraisal.

Appraisals

The real property tax was levied against four forms of real estate: (1) income-producing property; (2) property bought for resale, including vacant land; (3) residential property; and (4) the ninety-nine-year leasehold.[30]

John A. Zangerle had a simple, yet fair, solution to the problem of valuating all four forms of real property for tax purposes. Appraisals of value should be based on the most recent sale of the property.[31] That way the value of real estate was set by impartial market forces based on bargaining between buyer and seller that seemed fair and objective and could be used to set valuations for all four forms of real property.[32] The Realty Regime, unsympathetic to Zangerle's procedure, charged that the auditor's method was simplistic because it treated all four forms of real property as one when in fact they were significantly different. The real estate industry argued for a real estate tax appraisal system sophisticated enough to recognize the differences between the four forms of real property.[33]

INCOME-PRODUCING PROPERTY

In Cuyahoga County, income-producing property, like all other forms of real property, was taxed on total value of the property based on its most recent sale. The consequences of property re-evaluation after a sale were that businessmen either sustained lower after-tax profits or, more commonly, they retaliated by passing these costs on to consumers in the form of higher prices. The real problem, however, was that the real estate tax was calculated on the value of the entire asset, rather than the income generated by the real property asset.[34] The real estate industry claimed owners and consumers could both benefit if the American system of taxing income-producing properties followed the English example. In England, only the income derived from the property was taxed, not the total capital value of the property, the American practice.[35] CREB lobbied hard but in the end failed to change the tax laws on income-generating property.

UNIMPROVED PROPERTY

The taxation of unimproved land was an inflammatory issue in both corporate and realty eras. The great disparities of wealth characteristic of the industrial era were attributed by many reformers to the unearned increment in rents and land sales reaped by the holders of unimproved land. Reformers prescribed very high taxes on unearned increments, the proceeds from which would be used to solve social problems. Some of the more imaginative critics blamed profits in undeveloped land for suburbanization, and suburbanization in turn for the maladies visited upon inner cities.[36]

The Realty Regime saw things differently. Viewing these matters as both taxpayers and profit seekers, the Realty Regime claimed that real estate taxes on unimproved land were counterproductive. The real estate operator who bought unimproved land was celebrated by his fellows as a fearless, risk-taking entrepreneur, a long-odds gambler who put his capital on the line when he invested in unimproved real estate. Because unimproved land generates no income, the real estate tax is felt keenly. From an accounting standpoint, taxes are temporary losses and are added to the cost of the property. If, for example, the property taxes amount to 3 percent annually, nearly 17 percent would be added to the cost of the land over a period of fifteen years. Realtors therefore opposed paying taxes on non–income-generating land. Real estate taxes forced land into the market too soon and into expedient rather than higher and better uses as claimed by tax reformers. The Realty Regime argued for not taxing vacant land until the time of sale and then, at the time of sale, imposing a fair capital gains tax. Here again the Realty Regime failed. The public and the county auditor were too finely attuned to the twin evils of speculation and unearned increments to allow changes in the practice of taxing unimproved land.[37]

SITE VS. IMPROVEMENT TAXATION

The 1911 Tax Commission raised real estate taxes on sites and lowered them on improvements. This was a strategy calculated to reward improvements and punish speculators tempted to hold sites vacant or in low-order uses until market conditions ripened. CREB reacted to the punitive effects of site vs. improvement taxation, but it failed to devise a sound alternative solution to the problem. While the Realty Regime thought sites were too heavily taxed, the real estate industry was unwilling to shift the burden to improvements. High real estate taxes on sites impeded land parcel assembly, and high taxes on improvements worked against the principle of highest and best use. Because the Realty Regime lost the battle to shift the tax burden from all forms of real property to personal property, site vs. improvement taxation was a crucial issue, but it stymied CREB. The organization was unable to develop a position on the issue that would satisfy land owners and site developers. This dilemma caused the Realty Regime to fight for personal property tax reform long after it was obvious that the Regime would not be able to shift the burden of taxation to personal property.[38]

THE NINETY-NINE-YEAR LEASEHOLD

Appraisal techniques and site vs. improvement taxation loomed large in ninety-nine-year leaseholds. The first problem involved assessing the value of the site. Since no sale actually occurred, the actual market value of the land was murky. The county auditor's position was that the market value of the land was the same as the value of the lease. For example, under a standard ninety-nine-year lease, a $100,000 property would pay $777,000 in rents over the term of the lease. Accordingly, the property was assessed at $777,000. Lawyers Amos Burt Thompson and Robert Bingham complained bitterly that since in a fee simple sale the market value of the land would be $100,000, that sum should be the assessed value, not the $777,000 tabulated by the auditor.[39]

Lessees fought in vain for assessments calculated from current marketplace value. The ninety-nine-year leasehold, of course, was in some measure designed as a tax avoidance scheme: leaseholds commonly transferred the tax obligation from the owner of the site to the owner of the improvement because the owner of the improvement received better tax treatment than the owner of the land. Nonetheless, the lessees fought to reduce their tax obligations. Unable to sway the county auditor, Thompson and Bingham altered the standard leasehold contract so that the tax burden was shared, the lessor paying taxes on the site and the lessee paying on the improvement. This was not an ideal solution, but it allowed ninety-nine-year leasehold arrangements to continue. In the 1920s, however, federal tax advantages for both parties outweighed the local tax liabilities Thompson and Bingham fought against.[40]

Shifting the Tax Burden

Historians as well as contemporary observers have documented a shift in the burden of the real estate tax from large to small real property holders in the 1920s. The simplistic system of real property tax assessments that became the bane of the Realty Regime most significantly made no distinction between income-generating commercial property and non–income-generating residential property. All forms of real estate were taxed at the same flat rate. Factories worth in excess of $100,000 were taxed at the same $19.30 rate that owner-occupied houses valued at under $10,000 were charged. Throughout the 1920s, however, the Realty Regime was able to hold down increases in commercial property assessments by filing an avalanche of appeals and bargaining outcomes with civil servants in the auditor's office. The Cleveland Association of Building Owners and Managers (CABOM) also took aim at the evasive tax accounting techniques of the utilities companies, who dodged personal property taxes and paid little in real estate taxes. Obviously CABOM, as the representative of large realty holders, participated in shifting the burden of real estate taxation to smaller taxpayers and found scapegoats to blame for the result.[41] What could not be won from the holders of personal property was won from the small holders of real estate. This was a less than ideal solution to the problem of regressive local taxation, but it did succeed in easing the burden on large realty holders.[42]

THE CONSEQUENCES OF SHIFTING THE TAX BURDEN

A price was paid for the victory. Richard T. Ely, a University of Wisconsin economist, told a CREB lunch hour audience that the local low-income housing shortage was caused by inequitable real estate taxation. "Better housing," Ely said, "means reconstruction of taxation. Our American system of taxation nearly everywhere, and I think I may say, especially in Cleveland and Chicago, is antiquated, resulting in unjust distribution of the public burden."[43]

Ely calculated that the burden of real estate taxation had shifted to home owners in the course of the decade that the Realty Regime had been in power and calculated that Cleveland, like many other cities, was also undergoing a crisis in the supply of low-income housing. The real estate tax structure, he said, contributed to the low-income housing crisis. For low-income owners of low-income housing, the tax was an additional expense that could not easily be borne by financially strapped families. For those who invested in low-income rental properties, the tax cut into profits that were already razor thin and unattractive compared to alternative investments in middle-income rental housing. The real estate tax also contributed to the crisis in the construction of new low-income housing because the high cost of inner city land, inflationary construction costs, interest, and taxation narrowed profit margins to unappealing levels. There were far more profitable investments to be made in other forms of real estate where the tax burden could be more easily absorbed or passed on to more affluent buyers or tenants.[44]

The decade-long war to shift the tax burden from real property to others ended inconclusively. The campaign to tax personal property failed. So too did the battle to achieve more sophisticated formulas for property valuation, formulas which would make fine-grained distinctions between the four forms of real property. Because the Realty Regime's tax reform agenda was conflicted, the outcome of the struggle to achieve some form of parity between site and improvement taxation was muddled. In the end, the real estate tax burden was shifted to the owners of residential real estate, a hollow victory because home owners became highly sensitive to policies which would raise their property taxes. Because the Realty Regime advocated urban growth and service distribution policies that were highly dependent on infrastructure spending financed from the real estate tax, alternative means were sought to camouflage the cost of urban growth policy making.

FINANCING THE REALTY REGIME II: MUNICIPAL BUDGET EXPENDITURES

The narrow purpose of tax reform was to improve real estate industry profits, but the broader goal was to increase the flow of revenue needed to finance urban growth policy. The failure of tax reform led the Realty Regime to resort to schemes which would exploit fiscal opportunities on the expenditure rather than revenue side of urban finance. Rebuffed in its attempt to tax and spend to finance its policies, the Realty Regime, not unhappily, resorted to the practice of borrowing and spending, municipality by municipality.

Manipulating municipal expenditures was an easier task than changing tax laws, but legal obstacles nonetheless existed. These were state-mandated municipal expenditure limitations. Such expenditure limitations dated from the 1911 Smith Act, which limited local tax increases for operating budgets to one percent but allowed an additional one half of one percent for sinking fund charges and interest on debt.[45]

State-mandated municipal tax ceilings brought a renewed sensitivity to the distinctions between operating and capital budgets. Neighboring states learned early that tax limitation laws such as the Smith Act did not limit overall municipal spending. While the tax ceilings held operating budgets in check, municipalities resorted to various forms of capital budget borrowing to circumvent caps on operating budgets. "Public finance," a New York legislative committee found, "is made within budget but public overseers have adopted a more relaxed attitude toward capital budgets and municipal debt."[46]

Post–World War I inflation placed heavy upward pressure on municipal budgets. Relief came at last from the Gardner Act (1920), which released cities from tax ceilings on debt. In the aftermath, Cleveland's debt soared (although it was brought under control late in the decade). Operating budgets were subject to Smith Act ceilings, but the Gardner Act liberated capital budgets.[47] The Realty Regime became the vocal public champion of fiscal restraint in operating budgets, while with less ceremony it liberated capital budgets in municipalities everywhere in Cuyahoga County. At a time when Cleveland's bonded indebtedness rose to $137 per capita, suburbs such as East Cleveland reached $153, Lakewood, $175, West Park, $217, and Cleveland Heights a pace-setting $470.[48] Suburban capital debt was the handiwork of the Gardner Act, and the Realty Regime made fiscal policy regional in scope, for the Realty Regime viewed city and suburban budgets as a single fiscal pot. The Realty Regime postured as operating budget slashers in both Cleveland and the suburban municipalities because operating budget increases made an immediate, highly visible impact on vote-casting taxpayers, and were in truth restrained by the Smith Act. Capital budgets were another matter.[49]

Suburban capital budgets were the Realty Regime's piggy bank. Home rule municipal charters, the Gardner Act, and the tax-free municipal bond gave the Realty Regime virtually a free hand in developing the suburbs and in creating the balkanized urban regions we know today. Municipal charters opportunely separated municipalities from school districts, giving municipalities and school districts separate taxing authority. Although the Smith Act restrained municipal operating budgets, it did not affect school district operating budgets, which soared through the 1920s. The Gardner Act, however, was the key to municipal finance because it permitted almost unrestrained capital-expenditure borrowing for both municipalities and school districts. Suburban mayors, councilmen, and school boards were largely members of the Realty Regime, and they used suburban capital budgets and school operating and capital budgets to develop a place-specific regional urban policy.[50]

Because they were highly visible to the taxpayers, suburban municipalities had tight operating budgets, and most suburban municipal operating budgets were only a fraction of the school district's operating budget. Suburban municipal operating budgets were held up to Cleveland's political leadership as models of fiscal restraint. Capital budgets painted a far different picture. Suburban municipalities borrowed heavily for growth-related schemes designed to lure home buyers to the suburbs. Infrastructure spending for the delivery of services was also a major suburban expense, and it was purchased though the capital budget and financed with tax-free municipal bonds. School districts borrowed heavily for buildings and equipment. Municipal bonds, in addition to the appealing tax advantages, were sold as safe investments because of the affluence of the resident population and the community's potential for growth.[51]

Municipal bonds created a booming business for a local underwriting community composed of bankers, lawyers, and brokers.[52] The most attractive aspect of capital-budget bonded debt was that the real costs of government could be hidden from suburban taxpayers for decades, perhaps until another regime was on watch.

CONCLUSION

The Realty Regime's dubious economic development policy and an urban growth policy grounded in the maze of municipal finance had long-term effects on Cleveland, possibly even greater than the more conspicuous achievements of the Corporate Regime. Realty Regime economic development policy, perhaps, should not even by dignified by the word "policy" because the regime had so little understanding of what economic development was and the institutions responsible for shaping it. The realtors were, for the most part, small businessmen in the local rather than export side of the urban economy. They did not understand the great changes taking place in the modern business enterprise during the 1920s. Nothing about these giant combines resembled Realty Regime businesses. Most of all, the Realty Regime did not understand that corporate decisions about where to locate the parts of the business enterprise governed local economic development policy. Instead, the realtors focused on something they did understand, urban growth policy, which they substituted for economic development. Urban growth policy as city building did have good economic results, but the results came at a cost. This realization is what drove the Realty Regime's taxation and municipal finance campaigns. The regime's urban growth policy would be expensive (as well as profitable), and it schemed to pass the costs on to others, to the living in the form of tax burden shifting, and to taxpayers not yet born in the form of municipal bonds.

11

LAND USE CONTROLS IN AN ERA OF CHANGING CITY STRUCTURE

*T*he Realty Regime pursued what it regarded as a laissez faire urban growth policy that aimed to link more closely the suburbs and the central business district. This was accomplished by battering down existing planning and zoning land use controls and by staunchly advocating such infrastructure improvements as bridge building projects, utilities extensions, and commuter transportation schemes connecting suburbs to central business district. The policy making machinations of the Realty Regime helped suburbs and the central business district but ignored the city of Cleveland's residential neighborhoods.

THE CHANGING CITY STRUCTURE

Bridges and Utilities

In the industrial era, bridge construction and utilities installation were interwoven with economic development. During the Realty Regime, in contrast, these forms of infrastructure served urban growth policy. The Realty Regime rarely failed to endorse a bond issue for bridge building, although a bond issue to build a Lorain-Carnegie bridge spanning the Flats and connecting east and west sides was defeated in 1926 and again in 1928. Here the Realty Regime was divided against itself, between suburban subdividers and central business district boosters.

The Cleveland Association of Building Owners and Managers (CABOM) represented the owners of central business district real estate and strongly opposed the issue because the bridge would allow traffic to skirt the central business district. Subdividers and the Cleveland Real Estate Board (CREB) were strongly in favor of the Lorain-Carnegie bridge. The subdividers sought an uninterrupted flow of traffic to the land they would develop in the suburbs, east and west, a business objective the bridge would advance. CREB's campaign broadsides insisted that the bridge would trigger industrial development in the valley below, immediately south of the central business district.[1]

Utilities provided another form of linkage to the suburbs. In 1925, Cleveland was served by 281 miles of water pipe. In 1926, not a single foot of new pipe laid was in the city of Cleveland. All additional mileage was built in the suburbs. Gas, electric, and telephone lines followed. The Realty Regime read the annual reports of the utilities companies with glee, carefully noting miles, feet, and volume added to existing service lines. It was clear that while utilities might stimulate industrial development, the most important beneficiaries were residential suburbs.[2]

Streetcar Suburbs

As the first policy makers to view suburbanization as a positive force, the Realty Regime saw commuter transportation as the backbone of their urban growth policy. The Realty Regime came to power during a transitional era in commuter transportation technology. Cleveland was evolving from a city of electric streetcars to a city of automobiles, from moderately high density close-in living to lower density suburban living. The Realty Regime was uncertain which transportation technology best suited its growth policy goals. Which form of energy—coal and electricity or oil and gasoline—should drive the system of commuter transportation? Which form of commuter transportation—rail, buses, or autos—was deserving of the Realty Regime's support? Unable to forecast the future, the Realty Regime indiscriminately supported any and all forms of commuter transportation.

The much-envied Van Sweringens preferred streetcars. One of their suburban real estate developments, Shaker Heights, made money only after the Van Sweringens linked it to the central business district with separate-grade-level rapid transit service. Thereafter, suburban subdividers and central business district real estate operators endorsed rail linkages between suburban residential development and retail and commercial growth in the central business district. Realtors unable to finance their own separate-grade rapid transits pressured the streetcar companies to extend their lines to the suburbs.[3]

Chapter 11: Land Use Controls 189

The transportation advantages of streetcars were obvious, but no less important to the real estate industry was the positive impact that streetcars had on the value of land bordering the tracks. Automobiles and bus lines did not have a similar impact because their routes could be changed at whim. This was the core reason behind the Realty Regime's initial enthusiasm for streetcars. So lucrative was the market in adjacent real estate that in some cities street railway companies formed realty company subsidiaries to exploit the increases in land values. In Cleveland, however, capital-starved street railway companies were not involved in land development activities. In the 1920s most Cleveland street railway companies were coping with declining ridership, and without real estate development to fall back on, the financial future of the transit companies was clouded.[4]

The Realty Regime, despite the ample early warnings audible in the thunder of the gasoline engine, kept pressure on the street railway companies to expand their services into the suburbs. Realtors acknowledged that in general land values in most parts of the inner and outer city were lowered by the expansion of the transportation system into the suburbs. But this was offset by the rise in values of commercial property bordering the streetcar lines and suburban lots. The commercial and entertainment district forming at Euclid Avenue and East 105th Street was a prime example. A new transit line could increase the value of commercial property between 20 and 40 percent in as little as two years.[5] Suburban land connected to the city by streetcar lines positively boomed in value. A larger social benefit was also claimed. Transit allowed the population of the city to decentralize and achieve more uniform growth and lower density living.[6]

In the 1920s street railway companies remained under intense pressure to extend their lines to the suburbs, a task more difficult to achieve than was initially appreciated. Cleveland street railway companies were restricted by the capital requirements and monopolistic competition limitations imposed on them by the 1909 Tayler Grant.[7] The competitive limitations placed on the companies by federal judge Robert Walker Tayler were outmoded by the 1920s. Streetcar companies were too small in size and were limited by the Tayler Grant to paying 6 percent dividends, a rate unattractive to investors in the 1920s bull market. The challenge of raising capital limited the ambitions of the companies. To make matters more difficult, realtors insisted on low fares to the suburbs, while the owners preferred a zone plan of escalating fares.

Public ownership was an alternative. Made possible by state-enabling legislation in 1922, and advocated by such local reformers as Peter Witt, Tom L. Johnson's streetcar commissioner, the realtors pursued a policy counter to self-interest when they vehemently opposed public ownership on the grounds that acquisition would not only raise taxes but also that the system would fall prey to the incompetent administration of the municipality.[8]

A far more serious problem for the streetcar system was competition from the automobile and bus. By the mid 1920s there was one automobile for every eight persons in Cuyahoga County, and bus service was extensive and growing. These alternatives were also promoted by the Realty Regime. Streetcar companies suffering from limited capital and, facing the challenge of the automobile, saw their ridership steadily decline through the decade.

The Van Sweringens attempted a rescue of the street railway system in 1929 when they bought the Cleveland Electric Railway Company and merged it into their own system, giving them a virtual monopoly on streetcar service in Cleveland. But in 1930, just a year after the merger, the *Plain Dealer* reported that the Van Sweringen transit system was losing money.[9] Within the year, the entire Van Sweringen empire collapsed, leaving the fate of Cleveland's streetcar system hanging in the balance.

Rails and the Central Business District

Central business district real estate operators spent the decade trying to improve the transit system that served the downtown. The most enduring and least practical of these was the central business district subway scheme. The first subway franchise was granted in 1909. In 1916 voters approved a subway plan to connect Public Square with the Detroit-Superior Bridge, and city council approved final plans in 1917, but the project was shelved when America entered World War I. In 1919, immediately following the war, entrepreneur Charles A. Otis was appointed chairman of the Rapid Transit Commission, and it quickly acted to revive the downtown subway project. The fading Corporate Regime was divided on the commission's recommendation and consequently on support for the bond issue needed to fund the project.[10] The Chamber of Commerce endorsed the bond issue, but the Civic League, for so long a core organization in the Corporate Regime, broke ranks. It cited high interest rates, postwar shortages of labor and materials, and the free ride handed to the suburbs, which were not required to pay their fair share as reasons for its opposition, and the issue failed.[11]

The Otis Commission responded by allying itself with emerging realty interests to continue the fight. CREB, the Euclid Avenue Association, the Cleveland Association of Building Owners and Managers, and after 1926, City Manager William R. Hopkins all enlisted in the subway project campaign. Financing continued to be the sticking point. Early in the history of the project, realtors withheld support because the subway would be financed with public monies and because regime leaders were rightly skeptical about the retail traffic potential of the underground service.[12] City Manager Hopkins, seeking a middle ground compromise, proposed a public–private partnership in which the streetcar companies and the taxpayers would share the development costs. The Euclid Avenue Association, addressing the retail traffic concern, made support contingent on a Euclid Avenue subway line heavily dotted with stations. Reformers remained opposed. Peter Witt and other municipal socialists supported the subway project in principle but made their endorsement contingent on public ownership.[13]

The standoff was at last broken in 1928 when commercial realtor Raymond T. Cragin assumed the chairmanship of the subway commission. Cragin recast the subway proposal to make it more palatable to a broader coalition of groups. His idea was to build an underground skeleton linking downtown subways to the rapid transit system, with tunnels originating at Public Square to serve heavily trafficked stations at Union Terminal, Euclid and East 22nd Street, East 12th and Superior, Ontario-Central Market, and the Detroit-Superior High Level Bridge (now at last built). A failed bond levy in November of 1929 convinced Cragin that alternative sources of financing would have to be secured. To finance the scheme, a $30 million capital commitment from the Cleveland Railway Company was secured, the remainder to be raised from a one-cent surtax on fares. Real property owners applauded the proposal once they realized that the real estate tax would not contribute one cent of the cost. To temper the doubts of the municipal socialists, Cragin's proposal would award ownership and operations to the Cleveland Railway Company for thirty-five years, after which the municipality would assume ownership and operational control. The Cleveland Real Estate Board and the Cleveland Builders Exchange endorsed the Cragin proposal straightaway. The fate of the subway project, however, was tied to the business fortunes of the Cleveland Railway Company, and when the Van Sweringens bought the company in 1929, the prospects for the downtown subway appeared bright. Just months later, though, the Van Sweringen empire crashed and with it the Cleveland Railway Company and the dream of a subway in downtown Cleveland.[14]

Automobile Cleveland

The Great Crash of 1929 and the automobile spared Cleveland an investment of untold millions in an ill-conceived transit scheme for a central business district that would soon enough forfeit many of its charms to suburban rivals. The automobile was the prime culprit in the decline of the central business district, and the Realty Regime was its principal advocate. Throughout the 1920s scores of levies for street construction, paving, and street widening appeared on city, suburban, and county ballots. The Realty Regime endorsed each and every one. Seldom did levies fail.[15] Automobile registrations explained why. In the five-year interval between 1921 and 1926, automobile registrations increased from 91,000 to 210,000, an increment of 24,000 cars a year.[16] "Then came the auto," Stanley L. McMichael observed in 1928, "an element which in the past 10 years has done more to upset, disrupt and change customs, habits and real estate promotional work than any other single thing ... in the history of cities."[17]

The Realty Regime anticipated the impending auto-induced revolution in city structure. Physically, no sector of the city went untouched. And none more so than the central business district. The central business district, already a mess, was snarled by competing modes of transportation. The tangle of trolleys, cars, buses, and even horses led McMichael to conclude in 1923 that "the solution will be found only in broader decentralization when downtown sections will be made up largely of banks, office buildings, hotels, restaurants, and a few small shops." The "largest retail enterprises, such as department stores, specialty shops, etc., will move to the outlying business districts."[18] In McMichael's crystal ball was the multinucleated urban region.[19] The benefits, however, were unevenly distributed because Realty Regime transportation policy was indiscriminate. As noted above, the Realty Regime loved autos and supported all levies and bond issues for street and highway building. They also enthusiastically endorsed bus lines, street railways, rapid transits, subways, and interurbans. This eclectic transportation policy had the desired short-term effect of decentralizing the population and increasing suburban land values. From a peak in 1910, population densities in Cleveland steadily declined from 38 people per acre to a 1930 average of 18 people per acre as land values at the periphery of settlement rapidly rose.

If an unsystematic commuter transportation policy achieved urban decentralization, it had unwelcome consequences for the transportation industry. Even a population increase of 150,000 between 1920 and 1930 provided an insufficient base of ridership to support all modes of commuter transportation. In this market environment, if one form of commuter transportation succeeded, another must fail. As streets were paved and highways built, auto registrations and bus ridership increased while ridership on streetcars and the interurban fell precipitously. Streetcar and interurban companies edged toward insolvency.[20]

Late in the decade, the Realty Regime realized that its transportation policy was out of control. The more judicious members of the regime called repeatedly for county, regional, state, or even federal highway planning commissions. These appeared too late to remedy the situation. Too engrossed in tabulating profits from suburban real estate deals, most realtors ignored the impending crisis in transportation. Commuter transportation was at a crossroads. Short-term preferences prevailed.

THE BATTLE AGAINST LAND USE CONTROLS

Corporate Regime urban growth policy was regulatory, grounded in a comprehensive set of land use controls, including real estate taxation, city planning, and zoning. The urban growth policy of the Realty Regime, by contrast, began as a laissez faire rebellion against land use controls but ended with acceptance of noncomprehensive, place-specific land use control mechanisms. The Realty Regime aimed to emasculate all forms of public and quasi-public land use control. When the tax reform battle was lost, the anti–land use control campaign was directed against the master planning, zoning, and regional planning policies of the deteriorating Corporate Regime. Planning and zoning threatened laissez faire urban growth,, and regional planning threatened place-specific urban policy.

City Planning

When the real estate industry first seriously confronted the issue of land use controls (1910s), it came out in opposition because controls transformed a dynamic market in land into a static market. The short history of the real estate industry taught that profits were found in the dynamics of a changing urban structure. Land use controls froze the existing structure. The free play of the market in land created a natural, organic city plan with free-form zones of land use. But the boom and bust of real estate business cycles from 1917 through the 1920s also taught a contrasting lesson—that market behavior is not perfect. By the middle years of the decade, the more astute realtors took a new position on land use controls: A static market was desirable in the suburbs, and master planning and zoning offered protection against downside risks inherent in the business cycle and other forms of market irrationality; in the city core, where a dynamic market was still preferred, planning and zoning remained taboo.[21]

Cleveland's park planning and City Beautiful Movements were the initial steps toward comprehensive land use controls. Municipal park planning in the 1890s and regional park planning in the World War I decade roused the opposition of suburban subdividers. In the 1890s the real estate industry was too embryonic to challenge the land use control peril posed by the municipal system of parks. But the 1917 plan for the Cleveland Metropolitan Park System, created by design consultant Frederick Law Olmsted, Jr. and civil servant William L. Stinchcomb, anticipated the opposition of a more highly organized real estate industry. In defense of the regional park scheme, the planners said that the park system would be constructed on land marginal to any purpose other than parks. They drew the potential critics' attention to the positive business advantages of a park system.[22] The residential value of land bordering the park system, Olmsted and Stinchcomb predicted, would sharply increase, claims seconded by three important real estate industry opinion makers: Stanley L. McMichael, Robert Bingham, and Amos Burt Thompson.[23] When Louis A. Moses, a suburban subdivider, was appointed to the three-person regional park board, opposition was expected to evaporate.

The real estate industry rank and file were unimpressed with the promises of the planners, the assurances of industry spokesmen, and even with representation on the park board. The Board of Park Commissioners was sued repeatedly by real estate interests, and between 1922 and 1932 no less than four of these lawsuits reached the Ohio Supreme Court. These lawsuits challenged the land use control authority of the special purpose park district. The case which proved to be the landmark was *State, ex. rel. Stanton v. Cleveland Metropolitan Park District Board of Commissioners*. The plaintiffs argued in this and subsequent cases that the Cuyahoga County Commissioners violated the state constitution by turning over state powers to an appointed board of park commissioners. The decision dealt the anti–land use control forces a solid defeat by upholding the constitutionality of the state enabling legislation that had created the park board.[24]

The Realty Regime came away from this defeat sure in the knowledge that the court system would not be an ally in the battle against land use controls. Fifth column bureaucratic infighting and full scale legislative battles would prove more successful. The war of attrition against city planning and zoning was won on these fronts.

Challenging the City Beautiful

The 1903 Group Plan was the next step after the failed battles of the nineties toward city planning and a broader agenda of land use controls.

The Group Plan met with very little opposition. Conceived by the Chamber of Commerce during the heyday of the Corporate Regime and with carefully orchestrated public support, the classical design of the civic center conjured up appealing public images of ancient Athens and Rome, the Columbian Exposition, and the unfolding revival of Washington, D.C. The Achilles' heel of neoclassical design was that it symbolically scorned business. Neoclassical design celebrated order, balance, and harmony in civic buildings, theaters, arenas, and stadia, but shunned the grubby reality of trade.[25]

In 1903 it made little difference that architect Daniel Burnham's classical civic center design ignored trade because, in an era of evolving city structure, no one knew where the central business district might settle or what functions it might or might not have. By 1917, when it was time to site the union terminal, these questions were answered. Cleveland's circulation system now began and ended at Public Square, not the isolated lake end of the Mall where Burnham's plan would locate the terminal. Modern retailing in the form of department stores and specialty shops, the seed of the circulation system, blossomed in the Public Square–Euclid corridor and fed on the pedestrian traffic alighting there. The marketing needs of the retail and real estate industries mandated a Public Square location for the union terminal and its two million annual passengers, precisely where the Van Sweringen brothers proposed to build their office building, hotel, and department store complex.[26]

Cleveland City Council, after six weeks of debate between pro–lakefront and pro–Public Square forces, passed an ordinance on October 23, 1918 changing the site to Public Square, but the ordinance, in response to the public controversy generated by the issue, also set a referendum election for January 6, 1919, a contest won handily by the pro–Public Square forces (a two-thirds margin).[27] But the proposal also required the approval of the Interstate Commerce Commission, which held two hearings on the matter in 1921. At the first, Corporate Regime opponents of the Public Square site prevailed. But at a second hearing before the entire commission, the Realty Regime, champions of the Public Square site, won the day.[28]

Defining the City Efficient

The organizational ethos of the Corporate Regime ushered in a fight over another stage in city planning, the City Efficient's ideal of comprehensive land use controls on a regional scale. Progress toward the realization of the City Efficient's regional philosophy was a tortured process that reveals the conflict between corporate and realty urban growth policy. Public officials in the 1910s found themselves caught in the middle of the policy conflict between a declining Corporate Regime and the emergent Realty Regime.

The debate over the limits of the City Efficient began in 1910 with a letter from State Representative Frederic C. Howe, intended to update the chamber's Committee on Municipal Art and Architecture on House Bill #147, which granted cities the power to plat undeveloped land as many as three miles from the city limits. Howe believed that rational urban development on the European model could be achieved through the controlled use of land. He saw in the legislation an opportunity for Cleveland to lay plans for the suburban development of the forested heights area overlooking the city proper. Howe envisioned the county commissioners, township and village trustees, and Cleveland's Board of Supervision uniting to draw an ambitious comprehensive regional plan.[29] This legislation was followed in 1912 with new home rule charter reforms allowing municipalities to create city planning commissions.[30]

The two legislative enactments, bolstered locally by the lofty planning ambitions of Howe and the Municipal Art and Architecture Committee of the Cleveland Chamber of Commerce, served mostly to muddy the waters of comprehensive city planning. The 1910 legislation implied that cities could plan for development outside their boundaries, while the 1912 legislation allowed for the creation of municipal planning commissions, bodies with jurisdiction limited to the municipality's political boundaries. Moreover, the charge given to the planning commission was vaguely defined. Was the planning commission to operate in the City Beautiful tradition of aesthetics or was it to be a comprehensive planning body?

Throughout 1913 and 1914 the Municipal Art and Architecture Committee, supported by the local chapter of the American Institute of Architects, pressured Mayor Newton D. Baker to endorse a municipal ordinance creating a city planning commission, where, presumably, these conceptual imbalances could be righted.[31] The Municipal Art and Architecture Committee badgered the mayor by insisting that the planning commissioners should be "men of the highest standing," readily identifying them as Samuel L. Mather, Jeptha Wade, F. H. Goff, Z. Z. Norton, and Ambrose Swasey, members all of the Corporate Regime. Men of this quality could surely sort out exactly what a planning commission was.[32]

In May of 1914 the city council passed an ordinance creating a city planning commission without defining what kind of planning it should undertake, but it was Mayor Baker, as it turned out, who defined the role of the City Planning Commission. In a testy appearance before the Municipal Art and Architecture Committee on August 5, 1914, and in an accompanying memorandum, Mayor Baker spelled out his approach to city planning and made clear that he would not appoint a City Planning Commission until his definition of city planning was accepted. His appearance accomplished three things: (1) it marked the transition from City Beautiful to City Efficient planning; (2) it defined the geographical scope of city planning; (3) it forced the Corporate Regime to recognize the policy making legitimacy of the municipal bureaucracy and emergent realty interests.[33] The mayor criticized City Beautiful planning because it was impractical, expensive, and elitist. City Efficient planning, by contrast, addressed the city as a functional core of land uses knit together by a circulation system. But Baker rejected City Efficient planning *on a regional scale* for political reasons. The citizens of Cleveland, he argued, deserved to have their interests represented on a City Planning Commission, not diluted either in membership or mission by suburban interests. Baker would limit city planning geographically to the city of Cleveland and not the County of Cuyahoga or the more expansive region within the boundaries of the metropolitan park district, jurisdictions advocated by the chamber and *The Plain Dealer.*

Baker also argued that City Planning Commission membership should not be narrowly limited to the Corporate Regime activists recommended by the Chamber of Commerce, but should be broadened to include real estate interests and key civil servants whose departments represented the public interest and who eventually would be responsible for implementing a city plan. When the Municipal Art and Architecture Committee reluctantly agreed to the mayor's preconditions, Baker at last appointed four of the men originally recommended by the Chamber, six City of Cleveland department heads, and real estate developer Oris Paxon Van Sweringen.[34]

Shortly after Mayor Baker appointed the planning commission members, the chamber changed the name of its Municipal Art and Architecture Committee to the Committee on City Plan. The work of the Committee on City Plan and the City Planning Commission briefly ran parallel. Both approached City Efficient planning from the same textbook perspective which assumed that city planning originated in a vision of an evolving circulation system and concluded with a formal taxonomy of land uses and regulations. But the chamber's Committee on City Plan soon divided over its mission. Some members of the committee became lost in a sea of aesthetic minutiae which diverted it from its primary task of master planning. The remainder were soon captive of a new fad in land use regulation, zoning.[35]

Zoning

New York City passed the nation's first citywide zoning ordinance in 1916 to control the spread of nuisance land uses, namely, the spread of Chinese laundries into high-grade retail districts. But in the process New York's city fathers discovered that a comprehensive zone plan categorized existing land uses into a serviceable taxonomy of land use controls. It is not an exaggeration to say that the zoned land use concept swept the country like wildfire. Scores of cities between 1916 and 1920 enacted zoning ordinances.[36] So too did several Cleveland suburbs, but not the city itself. Zoning in Cleveland fell hostage to both a conceptual misunderstanding and to a power struggle between the decaying Corporate Regime and the emerging Realty Regime. Corporate Regime members of the chamber's City Plan Committee confused zoning with city planning.[37] The Realty Regime itself temporarily divided between one faction opposed to all forms of land use control and another favoring planning and zoning in this order of precedence. Both factions agreed on the tactical wisdom of stalling zoning in Cleveland.[38]

The Realty Regime, gaining ascendancy in policy making, held off zoning in Cleveland from 1919, when the state legislature first considered zoning enabling legislation, until 1929, when the Cleveland City Council at last enacted a zoning ordinance. By this time fourteen of Cleveland's suburbs had enacted zoning ordinances, and the balkanized institutional base for place-specific urban growth was in place. A place-specific urban growth policy was made possible by the Ambler court decision in 1926.[39]

Village of Euclid vs. Ambler Realty

In 1923 the Ambler Realty Company brought suit against a zoning ordinance enacted by the Village of Euclid. The Village of Euclid, a largely undeveloped suburb, bordered Cleveland's east shoreline industrial corridor. The question was posed: Would Euclid develop industrially like the neighboring district of Cleveland or would it follow the pattern of existing suburbs and develop as a residential area? Rather than wait for a free market decision, the Village of Euclid in 1922 chose to legislate an orderly spatial outcome.[40] The zoning ordinance adopted by the Village of Euclid recognized six categories of land use: (U-1) single family residential, (U-2) two family residential, (U-3) multiple family residential, (U-4) commercial and retail, (U-5) warehouses and light manufacturing, and (U-6) heavy manufacturing and penal institutions. The zoning ordinance was cumulative. Uses permitted in U-1, for example, were allowed in any of the other zones. Conversely, a use permitted in U-4—an office building in this instance—would not be permitted in U-3, U-2, or U-1.[41]

The Ambler Realty Company owned sixty-eight vacant acres in the Village of Euclid zoned under the new ordinance as U-2, U-3, and U-6. The bulk of the tract was zoned U-2 and U-3 and therefore could not be developed for industrial purposes. Because the acreage owned by the company was in the path of the industrial corridor, Ambler wagered that this vacant land would develop industrially. Gross revenue considerations fanned the desire. The market value of industrial land (U-6) was $10,000 an acre, in contrast to residential land (U-1, U-2, U-3) which was valued at $2,500 an acre. Ambler's tract had a potential residential value of $170,000, in contrast to a projected industrial value of $680,000. The Ambler Realty Company, driven by these "bird in the bush" computations, complained to the village government that the zoning ordinance not only crippled the company with a loss of $510,000 in potential gross revenues but also deprived the company of the right to use its property as it saw fit, an elemental American liberty protected by the Fourteenth Amendment.[42]

The Village of Euclid reminded Ambler that the Fourteenth Amendment contained a "due process" clause that reined in absolute claims to property rights. The zoning ordinance created a zoning appeals board, which the Village contended was the due process mechanism. Thus thwarted, the Ambler Realty Company brought suit against the Village of Euclid.[43]

Village of Euclid v. Ambler Realty Company had a tortured legal history. Although the U.S. Supreme Court ultimately handed down a landmark ruling on behalf of the Village, both the Ohio Supreme Court and the Cleveland Federal District Court earlier decided in favor of Ambler.[44] In both of these courts, the Village's case rested on a narrow definition of property and a broad definition of the police powers of government.[45] The Village claimed that zoning protected the public welfare, in this specific instance from nuisance land uses. Property, however, was narrowly defined. The Village contended that so long as Ambler retained the title to its property and had not been physically deprived of it, no invasion of property rights had taken place.

The Ohio court replied in a decision laced with savory ironies. The state court observed that the Village's case rested "on a mistaken view of what is property and of what is police power. There can be no conception of property aside from its control and use, and upon its use depends its value," the court said.[46] Euclidean zoning deprived property owners of control, use, and value.

This was certainly the kind of broad definition of property that hardliners in the Realty Regime were seeking. Although served up in a surly manner, there were also morsels for the moderate gatekeeping faction of the Realty Regime to savor. "In the last analysis," the court complained, "the result to be accomplished [by zoning] is to classify the population and segregate them according to their income and status in life."[47]

The United States Supreme Court reversed the earlier decisions. Written by Mr. Justice Sutherland, the majority opinion emphasized that the police power of government was a beneficial force. The zoning ordinance was seen by the court as an attempt to use police powers to regulate nuisance land uses in the general interest of the public. This regulation was, in the court's view, within the boundaries of the government's police powers, "a valid exercise of authority," concluded Justice Southerland. In reaching this conclusion, the Justice observed that since Ambler had not sold any land in the sixty-eight-acre tract for any purpose, the company had not made a case for loss of property. Significantly, the use of planning and zoning as land use controls and tools of social management was ignored by the court. So too was the relationship between planning and zoning. *Village of Euclid v. Ambler Realty* sanctioned zoning as a police power of government but would leave "other provisions to be dealt with as cases arise directly involving them."[48] The Ambler decision gave a free hand to suburban gatekeepers who wanted to legislate economic and social outcomes in urban space. The Ambler decision provided an institutional basis for the place-specific urban growth policy of the Realty Regime.

A price was paid by city planning advocates on both realty and corporate sides of the zoning issue. After Ambler, city planning would be confused with zoning to the detriment of the former. Virtually all municipalities in Cuyahoga County would enact zoning ordinances long before city plans were drawn.[49] The Ambler decision trumped the regional planning and regional land use controls of the Corporate Regime. Regional planning and zoning were now impossible.

CONCLUSION

The urban growth policy of the Realty Regime greatly altered the regional geography. Railways, interurbans, streetcars, rapid transits, street and utility extensions, highways, and bridges paved the way for the exodus of population from Cleveland to suburban Cuyahoga County. This massive public investment in infrastructure improvements led Cleveland out of the stagflation crisis of 1917–1919 and into the building boom–led economic upturn of the 1920s. Infrastructure investment was only the threshold of Realty Regime urban growth policy. Transportation linkages would create the dynamic market in central business district and suburban real estate that the regime sought. The land use controls of the old regime—city planning and zoning—threatened a potentially dynamic market in land with stasis. The fight against land use controls propelled disparate real estate interests into a powerful policy making regime. The anti–land use crusade, however, had an unintended outcome. The crusaders themselves converted to the religion of the infidels. Beginning tentatively in the suburbs and reaching a crescendo after the 1926 Ambler decision, the Realty Regime embraced city planning and zoning—zoning more zealously than planning—because liberally defined nuisance factors were more critical to business success than free market dynamism in urban land. As Realty Regime members became suburban mayors, city councilmen, and school board members, it also became apparent that it was from these home ruled independent villages and municipalities that place-specific distributive and redistributive policies could be set.

12

THE BALKANIZED METROPOLIS
The Realty Regime Victorious

The Realty Regime in the 1920s gave the appearance of being anti-institutional. Appearances, however, were deceiving: the anti-institutionalism of the Realty Regime was only directed toward regional policy making institutions. The regime substituted suburban village and municipal policy making institutions for more threatening regional policy making institutions. Realty Regime policy making originated in balkanized suburbs, and the benefits of growth policy and service distribution and wealth redistribution outcomes were directed toward middle and upper class suburban constituencies.

THE REVOLT AGAINST CORPORATE REGIME POLICY MAKING INSTITUTIONS

Corporate Regime urban policy making was dependent on institutional means of implementation. If the regime meant to extend policy making to the metropolitan region, then regional institutions were imperative. This was the purpose of the annexation, regional planning, and metro government movements. Annexation, the most uncomplicated of the three, simply extended existing institutions to the suburbs. Regional planning and metro government, on the other hand, required an entirely new institutional order.

The Failure of the Annexation Movement

Annexation was the first expression of Corporate Regime regionalism.

Requiring little reflection and no tactical changes, annexations were appealing because they simply extended the policy status quo into the suburbs. Annexation assumed a heightened importance in the 1910s when, for the first time, suburban population growth rates surpassed those of the city. Post World War I era Cleveland was the sum of no less than thirty-seven annexations, propelling the city from an area of less than one square mile in 1814 to an urban surface of nearly 72 square miles in 1915. Even though Cleveland made an additional thirteen annexations between 1916 and 1931, adding another 21 square miles of land and 218,000 souls, the Chamber of Commerce at the end of World War I rightly sensed that the annexation movement had run its course.[1]

Four postwar trends doomed the annexation movement: (1) an intensification of racial, ethnic, and class antagonisms; (2) new laws that facilitated incorporation and made annexation unworkable; (3) improved suburban services,[2] and (4) the struggle for control of the urban policy setting apparatus pitting the declining Corporate Regime against the emergent Realty Regime. The former favored annexations and the latter opposed them.[3]

Ethnic, class, and racial antagonisms intensified in Cleveland after World War I. The decade and a half before the war witnessed the greatest influx of foreign immigrants in Cleveland's history, and the war decade itself saw a dramatic increase in the city's black population, the result of local industries recruiting badly needed war industry workers from the rural south. The years immediately following the war were marked by labor unrest and political radicalism as workers tried to recoup lost standards of living in the inflationary postwar years. Charles E. Ruthenberg, Communist Party candidate for mayor in 1917, won nearly a third of the vote. Foreign born workers participated in a major strike in 1919 at the American Steel and Wire Company, and in the May Day parade that year which touched off a nine-hour riot, resulting in two deaths before the police arrested hundreds of suspected agitators and at last brought the melee under control. In June, the city was shocked when Mayor Harry L. Davis's home was bombed, another violent event blamed, like many others, on foreign born working class radicals.[4]

African-Americans were targets too. Only 8 percent of Cleveland's 1930 population was black, but nearly a quarter of those who moved into the city between 1916 and 1931 were black. Ninety percent of Cleveland's black population of 71,899 lived in a newly forming Central area ghetto on the city's near east side. When the Arthur Hill family left the ghetto in 1924 and attempted to occupy a house in suburban Garfield Heights, a mob of two hundred angry whites surrounded Hill's new home. The family's repeated appeals to the Garfield Heights mayor and police for protection went unheeded, and the family soon returned to Central.[5]

Social geography, real estate industry business practices, and land use control policies exploited and intensified these antagonisms, antagonisms which in part made the Realty Regime's place-specific urban policy popular with the public. Zoning itself was a reactionary response to the social geography of the industrial city. As an expression of exclusionary social class, ethnic, and racial attitudes, zoning worked against annexation. Suburban zoning and restrictive covenants were the gatekeeping tactics used by the Realty Regime to keep undesirable racial, ethnic, and religious groups out of suburbia.[6]

The state legislature supported suburban separation by enacting new laws which made incorporation easier. The scores of new suburban villages and municipalities sanctioned by the state legislature and planned and built by real estate developers showed little interest in annexing to the city of Cleveland. Annexation referenda held in Cleveland suburbs after 1910 were consistently rejected by suburbanites. The Cleveland Chamber of Commerce formed its Committee on Annexation in 1915 only to find its pro-annexation recommendations shunned by suburban residents, suburban elected officials, and realtors. Stunned by the negative reaction, the chamber and the local press protested that Cleveland's greatness was achieved through annexations.[7] These boosterish appeals to historic traditions of civic pride fell on deaf ears.

The reality of superior suburban services was more compelling than appeals to civic pride in Cleveland. Suburban police and fire departments were emancipated from patronage and prompt to respond to citizens' calls. Streets were cleaned and garbage was picked up with greater frequency and efficiency than in Cleveland. Schools were the most important public service, and the suburbs established public school systems unmatched in quality by the Cleveland Public School System. These services were costly, but upper and middle class suburban taxpayers were willing to pay.[8]

Utilities, transportation, and water were services that the city might have used to harness the independence of the suburbs, but the nexus of policy, politics, state statute, and business all worked against Cleveland. Following the time honored assumption that the city would eventually annex outlying settlements, Cleveland officials, prodded by the county commissioners and realty interests, extended streets and water mains beyond the corporate limits. County roads, state highways, and the commuter rail and bus network were also extended to the suburbs. Gas, electric, and telephone service were in the domain of private enterprise. But encouraged by the county commissioners, realty interests, and the quest for

Chapter 12: The Balkanized Metropolis   205

profit, these private utilities companies extended their services to the suburbs, actions which also helped create not only independent suburbs but also place-specific urban policy making.

The Failure of Regional Planning and Metro Government Movements

The chamber's Committee on Annexations' annual report for 1922 pronounced annexation dead and heralded regional planning and metropolitan government as the antidotes to regional political balkanization. During the next ten years, the Chamber and the Citizens League threw their weight behind no less than five schemes designed to lead the county to regional planning and metropolitan government. They included county home rule, a county planning commission, a county planning congress, a regional government committee, and a voter referendum. All failed.

The chamber and the Citizens' League joined like-minded Cincinnati civic organizations to lobby the state legislature for county home rule legislation in 1922. County home rule charters were granted, but because county governments were created as state administrative units, they were not easily adapted as regional municipal governments.[9] Home rule charters allowed county commissioners to appoint county planning commissions, and Cuyahoga County appointed one in 1924, but it was spurned by the Realty Regime. City and suburban officials and influential citizen representatives of fading corporate and emerging realty regimes were appointed to serve on the county planning commission. All parties paid solemn lip service to the importance of regional planning, but Realty Regime commission members were unwilling to make the commitments necessary to make regional planning a success. Suburban municipalities without fanfare withheld operating monies from the county planning commission, and it died a slow, unmourned death.[10]

A new but equally ineffective tack was taken in 1927 when the advisory County Planning Congress was formed. The members of the advisory Congress were primarily the part-time suburban mayors (who were full-time real estate developers) and their city engineers who hoped to link their suburbs to Cleveland's central business district by the network of highways that might be planned and built by a regional transportation agency. The Cleveland Real Estate Board endorsed the Congress's idea, and in the 1930s the advisory organization evolved into a regional transportation planning agency supported by county, state, and federal funds. In the 1920s, however, the County Planning Congress barely registered on the policy making scale.[11]

Stung by the rejection of county planning, the Chamber and the Citizens' League allied in 1928 to support the Regional Government Committee made up of representatives of four hundred public and private organizations. At the very outset, the Regional Government Committee pledged that it posed no threat to "purely local matters such as zoning and public education" while at the same time it created subcommittees to study the various components of regional government. One such subcommittee worked to amend the state constitution to allow the restructuring of counties as workable regional governments, an effort hotly opposed by a coalition of rural, suburban, and core city politicians.

Undeterred, regional government proponents next financed a public relations campaign aimed at winning suburbanites over to regional government. The metro government publicity campaign insisted that the city of Cleveland offered superior services and lower taxes than those found anywhere in the suburbs. The appeal rang false.[12] It was true that suburbs carried a large per capita burden of municipal debt and that residents of the newer suburbs especially paid more in taxes than Cleveland residents. Residents of the newer Cleveland Heights and Shaker Heights suburbs paid nearly double the tax rates of Clevelanders, reflecting the recently acquired debt and the higher cost of superior services. But large debts and high taxes were only temporary as the two oldest suburbs in the county—East Cleveland and Lakewood—were proving. By the mid 1920s, as debts were retired, taxes in these two suburbs were nearly identical to those paid by Cleveland residents.

Yet in all suburbs, whatever the tax burden, residents were convinced that Cleveland's services were not on a par with their own. In these smaller communities, citizens had a direct impact on their elected officials and were better able to choose their own standard of services, something they could not hope to achieve in the city. Thanks to zoning laws and the real estate industry's exclusionary practices, suburbs were graded by class, status, and ethnicity. Each suburb selected and paid for its own preferred grade of services. Suburbanites enjoyed having these choices, and regional government threatened suburban independence as service providers.[13]

When fiscal incentives to regional government failed to persuade suburbanites, the Regional Government Committee debated alternative forms of regional government, searching for one in the mix that would prove appealing to suburbanites. County government itself was a poor model because it had a plural executive and no representative legislature. Representation in the legislative branch of government, so long an issue at all levels of American government, was also a contentious issue in regional government debates. Specialists in municipal law and political scientists recommended an "at large" system of representation, which they claimed, no doubt rightly, would allow for middle class domination of the legislature. Middle class suburbanites, however, feared that regional government would be the shoddy anti–middle class politics of Cleveland writ large. On the other hand, inner city working class, ethnic, and racial minorities feared that at-large representation would squeeze them out of elective politics altogether at the county level.[14]

As the decade drew to a close, regional government advocates sought a compromise which allowed a clearly specified degree of autonomy for each of the region's municipalities. This proved an elusive goal, and the final form regional government would take had not been determined when the Great Depression settled over Cleveland and brought the Realty Regime and suburbanization itself to a close. Failed referenda on metro government schemes in each decade from the 1930s to the 1980s demonstrated that regional government remained unpopular.[15]

THE NEW ORDERING OF POLICY

Growth Policy

The failure of regionalism and the victory in the Ambler case gave the Realty Regime a free hand to shape urban growth policy. The Realty Regime, despite its opposition to regional institutions of governance, nonetheless cherished an expansive geographic vision. They pictured three major land use districts in the urban region: the inner city, the outer city, and the suburb. The Realty Regime was satisfied with the way market economics performed in the inner and outer city, but social status aspirations came into play in the suburbs, forces not necessarily compatible with free market economics. The solution was a place-specific urban growth policy, allowing the market a free hand in the inner and outer city. In the suburbs, however, the regime orchestrated status outcomes by means of an urban growth policy of place-specific master planning and exclusionary zoning to create a surrounding network of suburbs graded by class.[16]

Realty Regime rhetoric hailed the sanctity of market forces, but their actions belied their words, actions which show scant faith in the doctrines they advocated. Realtors in time embraced land use controls even though the very idea of land use controls ran counter to the free market creed. They came round to the idea that markets could be manipulated through institutional policy and law, including land use controls. The market in suburban land was thus manipulated to achieve income- and class-graded suburbs.

The Realty Regime, in the beginning, opposed land use controls. The free market supposedly dictated who got what parcels of real estate for which purpose and who did not. The Realty Regime precociously saw the subtle shadings of the free market at work but only slowly comprehended how the market in land might be manipulated and purged of its imperfections. In Millionaires Row and University Circle, realtors found a market too narrow and finite. In slums they found no market at all, unless the prevailing land use could be radically and massively overhauled. The Realty Regime sought a middle ground of urban land use where money, lots of it, could be made. They found that middle ground in the suburbs after realizing that people who shared the same levels of power, taste, culture, and income did not care to share urban space with those otherwise endowed.[17]

How to achieve these exclusionary economic and social ends? The methodological tools, once again, were city planning and zoning, but in the late 1910s they were in the hands of the rival Corporate Regime. For this reason, many realtors—especially small-scale real estate operators—expressed blanket opposition to planning and zoning, viewing them as twin obstacles blocking the pristine functioning of the market in land.

Stanley L. McMichael and Robert Bingham, important industry opinion makers, argued that "while old sections of existing cities may vastly be improved, greater progress will be made in the planning and directing the development of new and outlying districts."[18] McMichael and Bingham were advocates of laissez faire land use allocation in the inner and outer city and land use controls for the suburbs. They eventually embraced the City Efficient planning movement as the best means to achieve this because it would create a region-wide circulation system which was imperative if suburbs were to develop. Additionally, place-specific City Efficient master planning would treat other taxonomies of land use as if the market were functioning perfectly.

Stanley L. McMichael eventually became an advocate of zoning. Most realtors opposed zoning on economic grounds because zoning ordinances created a regulated market in land. McMichael felt that zoning could be made more appealing to realtors by subordinating the zone plan to a comprehensive City Efficient master plan and allowing a zoning appeals process. The advantages were that nuisance land uses, especially in the suburbs, could be zoned out. Zoning, in this manner, acted as a stabilizing influence by placing a floor under land values, offering protection to buyer and seller against extreme downside swings in the residential real estate business cycle.[19]

In the end, however, it was sociology rather than economics that effected a compromise between industry leaders such as McMichael and

Bingham and the rank and file of realtors. The middle class purchaser who constituted the major market for residential real estate viewed his social status as a reward for a battle well fought. In the city of industry and autos, those who emerged victorious in the marketplace struggle chose to live at greatest remove from the precincts hosting the competitive fray. This meant the suburbs. This sort of home buyer wanted a pristine haven unsullied by social conflict. Planning and zoning, municipality by municipality, fulfilled these dreams.

A predictable economic and social environment became the essence of suburban marketing. State home rule law made it possible for the real estate industry to incorporate their suburban developments as villages and municipalities. Each suburban municipality formed its own city planning commission for purposes of tailoring a City Efficient master plan, and the suburban city councils enacted zoning ordinances compatible with the municipal master plan and the preferred social outcomes of the real estate industry and suburban home buyers. Zoning laws could keep residences in and factories out. Zoning laws could keep the unwashed at bay by mandating single family houses on large lots here, single family houses on small lots there, multiple family residences in their own separate district, and retailing and services in another zone altogether. Realtors embraced suburb-by-suburb planning and zoning with a passion. To ensure this result, realtors added a new wrinkle, a new land use control—the restrictive covenant. The restrictive covenant, an addendum placed on purchase agreements and deeds, stated in plain language that the property could not be sold to specified ethnic, religious, or racial groups. Suburban planning, zoning, and restrictive covenants made the Realty Regime the gatekeepers to the good life in suburbia.[20]

The Balkanization of Distribution and Redistribution

The Realty Regime made haste to install place-specific service distribution and wealth redistribution policies, although both ranked behind urban growth policy in priority. Service distribution, because of its cost, was assigned a low priority in the city of Cleveland; in the suburbs, though, the Realty Regime damned the cost and stood four square for quality services, and these became an integral part of the sales pitch for suburban homes. The public system of wealth redistribution was spurned everywhere because it transferred tax dollars directly to deceitful clients and funded padded municipal payrolls. The private charity system was not held in high regard either, but public censure of it was considered indecorous and possibly bad for business. In any case, the costs of voluntary charity could be quietly evaded.

Here it is useful to remember that service distribution and wealth redistribution take on different shadings of meaning depending on one's place in the system of social stratification. The upper and middle classes made self-conscious distinctions between the two policies. Service distribution, while benefiting all, had an upper and middle class constituency. Wealth redistribution benefits the lower orders only, yet others pay for it.

To working and lower class people distinctions between service distribution and wealth redistribution are not so finely drawn. For example, the middle class defined municipal government housekeeping activities as distributive services, while the lower orders tended to see them as agents for wealth redistribution, or employment opportunities dispensed to members of the lower orders by the patronage network. Garbage generated by the middle class household was picked up by the working class patronage appointee.

More important was the fact that upper and middle class families demanded more higher-order services than the working and lower classes could ever hope to win for themselves. As long as the more affluent classes remained in the city, the working and lower classes received the piggy-back benefits of superior services because the cost was shouldered by upper and middle class households. The balkanized suburbs eliminated that benefit for Cleveland residents.

Public Education

Public education blurred the distinctions between service distribution and wealth redistribution. For those on the higher rungs of the social ladder, education was a distributive service. For those clinging to the lower rungs, public education was a tool for wealth redistribution. Because public education involved not just money and but also curricula, the various education constituencies could not agree on an educational philosophy, agenda, or fiscal policy.

By the 1920s Cleveland area students were served by a four-tiered region-wide school system that separated children by class, culture, and race. The system consisted of private schools, suburban public schools, parochial schools, and the Cleveland Public Schools.

The private schools served upper class neighborhoods and mimicked the eastern preparatory schools in curricula. Private schools prepared boys for private colleges and universities, often Yale, where a large number of

Cleveland's mercantile elite matriculated. The trustees and headmasters of these schools formulated an educational curriculum that intertwined traditional college preparatory classes rooted uncompromisingly in the classics complemented by a vigorous athletics program. Student–teacher ratios were set at 6 to 1, driving the cost of an education to a level no other class of people in the region could afford.[21]

Suburban public schools served the corporate middle class. Although they were coeducational, boys were taught a college preparatory program while girls were tutored in finishing school competencies. At a time when only 56 percent of Clevelanders in the 14–17 age cohort were attending high schools of any sort—preparatory, commercial, or vocational—fully 90 percent of suburban youth were enrolled in high schools, the vast majority of which offered college preparatory programs only. Suburban teachers had four year degrees from four year colleges and universities. Most Cleveland teachers, by contrast, held two year teaching certificates awarded in most cases by the in-house normal school. Suburban schools were generously funded from real property tax monies, reflected in the student–teacher ratios which ranged from a low of 17:1 in Shaker Heights to a high of 22:1 in Lakewood. Suburban public schools curricula and attendant instructional delivery strategies were carefully tailored to reflect the values and aspirations of their middle class constituencies.[22]

The inner city parochial schools offered an educational alternative for the children of upwardly mobile lower-middle and working class immigrants. They were people with traditional values and orthodox beliefs who sought reinforcement of these values in their schools. Parochial schools taught the three R's by rote and an uncomplicated orthodoxy in religion. Students were carefully screened academically and directed into appropriate educational programs. Discipline was crucial in a school system with a 40:1 student-teacher ratio, and the corporal punishments liberally meted out by the revered clerics who served as administrators and teachers summoned few complaints from parents.

All of this did not auger well for the Cleveland Public School System. It could not compete either in terms of educational quality or dollars spent delivering services. It could not offer curricula acceptable to the demands of all the classes and cultures of the population, nor could it afford to pay the tariff. This failure, reflected in the declining elementary school enrollments recorded throughout the 1920s, testifies to the exodus of the upwardly mobile from the Cleveland Public School System to one of the three regional educational alternatives. Those moving to suburbia realized that public education in Cleveland was a wealth redistributive service, and they refused to pay high taxes to educate poor kids.[23]

The real estate industry took advantage of this regional multitrack system of place-specific education. Both new and used housing was advertised in terms of its proximity to private, parochial, or suburban schools. Education was typical of the distributive and redistributive urban policies of the Realty Regime. It was based on the decentralization of policy setting factions and the making of place-specific service distribution and wealth redistribution policies. The beneficiaries were the upper and middle classes. The losers were the socially immobile who were forced to remain in the city and fight over a declining fiscal base to fund social services and wealth redistribution.[24]

Wealth Redistribution Avoided: Charities

Private charities transfer wealth from the affluent to the needy, and wealthy people prefer to control the transfer mechanisms themselves. The charity system inherited by the Realty Regime, masterminded by the Corporate Regime during the first two decades of the twentieth century, raised money through the Community Chest and imposed management and fiscal accountability on the private-sector charitable and welfare agencies via the Welfare Federation.[25] The Corporate Regime's charitable system did not entirely replace the Populist public charity network of direct assistance to individuals and patronage jobs. A semblance of a dual redistribution system persisted, providing some measure of incentive for the Corporate Regime to shift the burden of the property tax so that real property paid the lion's share of local taxes.[26]

The Populist wealth redistribution system was held in low regard by the Realty Regime because it was funded by real estate taxes and administered by corrupt politicians. The Realty Regime responded by shifting the burden of the real estate tax from large to small property holders, fighting tax increases, forcing fiscal parsimony on the municipality, and railing at every opportunity against real and imagined corruption in government.[27] Most significantly, the Realty Regime encouraged people to move from city to suburb where government transfers of wealth could be avoided altogether.

Opposing the Community Chest and Welfare Federation system was a more awkward matter. It was embarrassing to publicly criticize the system because the public relations experts hired by the Community Chest hyped this philanthropic form of wealth transfer as a community-wide moral imperative. In truth, the private redistribution system cost the Realty Regime very little. For the self-employed realtor contributions were voluntary and could easily be satisfied with a token contribution or simply ignored. The unsung benefactors of the Community Chest were those on corporate payrolls who were encouraged by their employers to make "voluntary" contributions pegged to a percentage of their annual earnings. The tithes attached to individual salaried employees were not matched by proportional tithes of corporate gross revenues or even net profits. In the real estate industry payrolls were small, so there was little grousing from employees. With only minor programmatic variations in Welfare Federation activities from year to year, seldom was there an issue or a cause to which public opposition could be rallied.[28]

CONCLUSION

Realty Regime policy was comprehensive in neither its goals nor its beneficiaries. It scarcely mattered that the Realty Regime failed to understand economic development policy because economic development was largely out of its hands after the rise of the vertically integrated national corporation. The Realty Regime supported bridge and highway improvements to open the way to suburban settlement by the middle and upper classes in place of attracting new industries. Infrastructure building was urban growth, not economic development policy.

No other regime devoted more of its energies to urban growth policy than the Realty Regime, and no other regime won more far-reaching results in consequence. The Realty Regime opposed regional institutions of governance in almost every instance, save transportation planning. The balkanized urban region of multiple polities was its creation. Policy making in the balkanized urban region was place specific and specific to class, ethnicity, and culture. Because balkanized political institutions were created in the 1920s and because the regime successfully tainted the idea of regionalism, the die was cast for the mass suburban exodus following World War II.

CONCLUSION

PATHS TO THE PRESENT
A Post Mortem

POST MORTEM

Changing the course of urban policy required time, forbearance, and coalition building. Regimes are coalitions of organizations which over the long term agree more than they disagree about the direction urban policy should take. Cleveland's regimes collapsed, one after another, because of unpopular policy priorities and internal clashes of values as between merchants and populists, professionals and populists, and professionals and entrepreneurs. In their place new regimes emerged which were willing to make long-term commitments to changing urban policy priorities.

An examination of regime coalitions highlights the roles various kinds of institutions play in urban policy making. Decisions in economic development, urban growth, service distribution, and wealth redistribution are all economic in one way or another and to one degree or another. But these decisions are not driven by market forces, as the politicians and economists like to claim. Instead, they derive from choices made by institutions, and from these choices emerge those illusory market "forces."

Urban economic development, for example, was determined by out-of-town institutions, and Cleveland's economic development policy amounted to a response by local institutions seeking to control what was unleashed by the outsiders. The Merchant Regime came closest to shaping its own destiny in economic development, but even then, the shadow of the outside institutions loomed large: in this case, the state legislature and a motley host of buccaneering railroad companies. But Cleveland's Merchant Regime did understand that the city's economic future was tied to the new technologies emerging in national system of transportation. The canals and rails the merchants brought to the city made Cleveland a grain and milling transshipment center. After the Civil War lumber and oil followed. These were nondurable goods industries, and, once the war was over, this same transportation network enabled agricultural and lumber products industries to move west and oil refining to leave Cleveland for cities closer to final markets.

But the national transportation network in the late nineteenth century placed such cities as Chicago, Cleveland, and Pittsburgh nearly equidistant from sources of iron and coal, the foundations for an enduring durable goods metals industry which blossomed in these entrepotal cities. Briefly, the fate of Cleveland's economic development became tied to locally owned business organizations which manufactured durable goods. Within two decades, however, many pivotal businesses were merged into national corporations with headquarters often in distant cities. At this point, Cleveland policy making regimes lost control over the direction economic development would take.[1] Cleveland remained an important manufacturing center through the first three-quarters of the twentieth century only because national corporations in key industries decided that Cleveland was an advantageous site for branch plant operations.

Market forces did play a leading role in shaping urban growth policy, yet even here the hand of institutional decision making was visible. The Merchant Regime persuaded the municipal government to annex land, and the market in this land shaped the processes of urbanization and urban policy for decades to come. One of the unanticipated outcomes of annexation was increased demand for distributive services, a demand so ineptly answered that it brought down the Merchant Regime and ushered in the Populist Regime, which halted municipal land annexations and vainly tried to curb the costs of services by franchising and contracting for them. When these practices proved corrupt and inefficient, the Populist Regime went under.

The Corporate Regime condemned the institutional inadequacies of mercantile and populist era land use controls as too laissez faire. Corporate Regime leaders preferred public and quasi-public land use controls, culminating in city planning and zoning, institutional mechanisms which the Corporate Regime, late in its tenure, attempted to extend to the metropolitan region. These mechanisms aroused the opposition of the real estate industry, a dissenting chorus which coalesced as the implacably anti-regional Realty Regime. This coalition replaced Corporate Regime institutional mechanisms with market driven land use decision making. In the end, the Realty Regime buried regional land use controls and established hegemony over a metropolitan network of balkanized suburban municipalities, governance institutions which guided urban growth policy toward the outcomes preferred by the regime.

Expansive urban growth policies created new developments that required infrastructure and services. Both were dauntingly expensive and inflicted heavy damage on municipal budgets. Moreover, popular demand for more and better services escalated with the passage of time and the growing sophistication of urban residents.

The annexation policy of the Merchant Regime made it necessary to provide at least rudimentary safety and housekeeping services. That the regime failed to do so accounts in large measure for the emergence of the Populist Regime. Populists played catch-up and faced escalating demands for services originating from business and labor alike for new communications and transportation technologies and from the growing middle class preoccupation with public health. The populists resorted to a variety of dubious schemes to provide the services without worsening the fiscal crisis, including, fatefully, corrupt and inefficient franchising and contracting for services.

The management-oriented businessmen and professionals in the Corporate Regime abandoned these practices and brought efficiencies to the delivery of services unimagined by the populists. Professionals in the regime, especially those lured into public service by mayors Johnson and Baker, introduced line and staff systems of management and accountability as well as civil service testing and promotions to attract competent people to government employment.

The prosperity of the 1920s prompted a new round of escalation in the demand for high quality services. The affluent now demanded urban amenities paid for by the public purse, as the demand for services became a matter of taste and therefore increasingly more class specific. In response, the Realty Regime waged a successful war against regional governance that balkanized the metro area and enabled the tastes of the residents of each suburb to dictate the quality and cost of services.

Public education provides a good case study of the balkanized pattern of service delivery. In the merchant era, the goal of public schooling was simply defined as an education in civics and moral responsibility. By 1910, however, when the wave of migration to the city crested, the consensus on public education's mission had long since evaporated. Good citizenship seemed no longer enough or even central to the mission of the public schools. From the Populist Regime to the Corporate Regime, the Cleveland Public School System tried to be all things to all people as it strove to meet demands for more grades, compulsory attendance, language instruction for the foreign born, evening and weekend classes, college preparatory, trade, and commercial curricula, and testing and tracking, all within the context of fiscal responsibility and business-like management. Everyman, it was said, rallied to the support of the public school system.

The Realty Regime and its successors exposed this claim for the sham it was. Given the opportunity to flee the city and its public school system, upper and middle class families departed in droves during the 1920s when the real estate industry opened suburban enclaves for them. Private and parochial schools had long existed as alternatives to the Cleveland Public School System. In some decades before the opening of suburbia, parochial schools enrolled as many as 30 percent of the school-age children. The consensus on the public school system's mission was always more rhetorical than real. Suburbia made that fact highly visible.

Suburban schools made no attempt to be all things to all people. The public schools in the first suburbs offered a college preparatory curriculum only. The diversity of the curriculum and class size determined costs and consequently real estate taxes. Cleveland's suburbs tailored a curriculum to a specific class and its values. The Cleveland Public School System offered all educational choices but could not match the quality of the suburbs in any single service delivered. As public schools became a suburban marketing tool, Cleveland schools (and its other services) were made to look inferior. The rhetoric of suburban marketing became a self-fulfilling prophecy.

As for wealth redistribution policies, all four regimes relied heavily on private institutions of wealth redistribution and the nearly unanimous opposition to wealth redistribution by public agencies supported by local taxes. Even the populists, who transferred tax monies to fund outdoor relief and padded municipal payrolls, did little to disturb the philanthropic system of charity bequeathed from the Merchant Regime. The Corporate Regime did what it could to end the public welfare system initiated by the populists, but devoted most of its energies and creativity to making the private system less segmented and sectarian and more efficient and business-like with a secure financial base and eligibility standards to weed out fraudulent claimants. The system of wealth redistribution remained, as always, in the private sector. The Realty Regime railed against the remnants of the populist system and did what it could, *sotto voce*, to evade the costs of the private system. At the close of the Realty Regime, however, the system of wealth redistribution was essentially unchanged.

Increasingly in American society, the dependent classes have become the beneficiaries of wealth transfers, and the adoption of these wealth transfers by federal government in the 1930s relieved cities of the direct costs of redistribution. In 1929, at the close of the Realty Regime, no more than 4 percent of gross national product was spent by industrial nations on transfer payments to dependent populations. Such transfer payments as existed were in-kind transfers or transfers of funds donated by private individuals to religious and voluntary sector agencies for distribution to the needy.

In the sixty years since local regimes made policy, the amount diverted from GNP to redistributive transfer payments rose from 4 to 30 percent. Wealth redistribution shifted from the localities to national governments and from national government, through intergovernmental transfers, back to the localities. The expansion of recipients and the "nationalization" of wealth transfers had the positive effect of cushioning large segments of the population from cyclical slumps in the economy, but at the same time, control of wealth redistribution policy passed from the locality to the federal government.

Finally, taxation was the albatross around the neck of urban policy from the mid nineteenth century into the 1920s. Each of Cleveland's regimes made efforts at tax reform, a misnomer because tax reform in reality meant tax avoidance and tax burden shifting. A clear line emerges from past to present: Wealthy individuals and businesses paid less in taxes and middle and lower income people paid more. Heavily taxed holders of personalty in the nineteenth century were able to shift the burden of taxation to large holders of commercial realty, who in the twentieth century shifted the burden to small holders of residential realty. Increasingly, the gap in local revenues has been made up with user taxes, sales taxes, and payroll taxes, regressive measures all, taxing most heavily the salaried and wage earning public.

PATHS TO THE PRESENT

The urban growth policies of the Realty Regime initiated a *de facto* urban region. Reformers today champion a *de jure* urban region. But the definition of regional political unity too often is defined as the home county. Ideally, regional government should be coterminous with the boundaries of settlement, or it too will become a balkanized network of warring polities. The Census Bureau's CMSAs might be a good place to start.[2] With a truly regional government, how independent could a locality be in making policy? Probably not as independent as one might hope. Cities are and will be dependencies, unable to achieve the historically elusive goal of home rule.

Nowhere is this more evident than in economic development policy. To be sure, a regional government could eliminate or at least referee the destructive tax abatement fratricide between neighboring municipalities to attract new development, industrial, commercial, or retail. With or without a regional polity, however, economic development policy is still in the hands of institutional players, multinational corporations, financiers, and governments outside the control of local policy makers. Under regional urban government, economic development policy probably would be no different than it is now.

Urban growth policy is a more intricate affair. Growth policy is a mix of private and governmental elements. Urbanized regions exist not simply because of Realty Regime policies but also, since the Great Depressions and World War II, because of federal policies encouraging out-migration from the core city.[3] The federal government's leadership in consumer credit schemes and the massive freeway program did much to midwife the mobile middle class that populates the urbanized region. Residential decisions shaped the locational decisions of service providers and industrial, commercial, and retail employers. It would be very difficult for regional policy makers to swim against the tide of policy originating in Washington, D.C., but within these currents much could be accomplished by a truly regional government. Portland, Oregon's, attempts to regulate sprawl by controlling regional settlement densities is worthy of emulation. Land use controls achieved by regional master planning, zoning, and highway planning could be mandated by a regional government; at least the appearance and efficiency of cities could be much improved.

Regional government's greatest gains could be made in service distribution by simply eliminating the senseless and costly duplication of services. The practical politics of this, however, is daunting.

The wealth distribution debate continues almost unchanged since the dawn of the industrial era, only now it is a state and federal level debate. Perhaps in this area the dependent status of cities is a blessing.

APPENDIX A

MAYORS OF CLEVELAND

THE MERCHANT REGIME, 1836–1878

John W. Willey, 1836–1837
Joshua Mills, 1838–1839, 1842
Nicholas Dockstadter, 1840
John W. Allen, 1841
Nelson Hayward, 1843
Samuel Starkweather, 1844–1845, 1857–1858
George Hoadly, 1846
Josiah Harris, 1847
Lorenzo A. Kelsey, 1848
Flavel W. Bingham, 1849
William Case, 1850–1851
Abner C. Brownell, 1852–1854
William B. Castle, 1855–1856
George B. Senter, 1859–1860, 1864
Edward S. Flint, 1861–1862
Irvine U. Masters, 1863–1864
Herman M. Chapin, 1865–1866
Stephen Buhrer, 1867–1870
Frederick W. Pelton, 1871–1872
Charles A. Otis, 1873–1874
Nathan P. Payne, 1875–1876
William G. Rose, 1877–1878, 1891–1892

Appendix A

THE POPULIST REGIME, 1878–1901

Rensselaer R. Herrick, 1879–1882
John H. Farley, 1883–1884, 1899–1900
George W. Gardner, 1885–1886, 1889–1890
Brenton D. Babcock, 1887–1888
Robert Blee, 1893–1894
Robert E. McKisson, 1895–1898

THE CORPORATE REGIME, 1901–1919

Tom L. Johnson, 1901–1909
Herman C. Baehr, 1910–1911
Newton D. Baker, 1912–1915
Harry L. Davis, 1916–1919, 1934–1935
William S. Fitzgerald, 1920–1921
Fred Kohler, 1922–1923

THE REALTY REGIME, 1919–1929

William R. Hopkins, 1924–1929 (City Manager)

APPENDIX B

ANNEXATIONS BY REGIME

Regime	Square Miles
Merchant Regime	26.273
Populist Regime	6.177
Corporate Regime	22.3
Realty Regime	14.351
Total	69.101

Source: City of Cleveland, Division of Engineering & Construction, 1954.

METHODOLOGICAL NOTES

INTRODUCTION

This study rests on two kinds of research: (1) qualitative sources such as books, articles, reports, and the like, which are cited, *Chicago* style, in the endnotes; and (2) quantitative sources, the numbers collected by a variety of public and private agencies. Scattered through the endnotes are references to the Methodological Notes. These notes explain how these numbers from quantitative sources were compiled and manipulated. Historians of my generation were trained to take notes from literary sources on 4 by 6 note cards. That is what is cited in the endnotes. From quantitative sources, I usually make a series of amateurishly rendered tables, charts, timelines, and tracing paper maps. These are the note cards I use for observations on the economy, budgets, local demographics, including residential location, and city structure. Since many readers (including me) do not like to wade through tables, charts, and other quantitative apparatus, none of this appears in the text; yet it needs to be cited. What follows is some of the theory and arithmetic that underpin the tables, charts, and so forth.

NOTE 1: BUDGET TIME LINE SERIES

This book relies heavily on analyses of public spending because: (1) the allocation of money is an important aid in understanding the policy priorities of each regime; and (2) abrupt changes in public spending reliably signal regime change. Both can be tracked in the municipal budgets. Spending changed dramatically over time, both in overall amount and the things on which government spent its money. During the century covered in this study, public spending matured from necessities to conveniences to amenities. These are matters of choice, and urban policy making regimes made these choices.

Observations in table 3.1 and in the text about regime succession and changing policy priorities rest heavily on inferences drawn from municipal budget time line analysis, 1860–1930. Nineteenth century budgets are annoyingly inconsistent; budget categories and line items change and mutate over time, some vanishing as others are added. Capital and operating budgets were initially combined, but in the 1870s, thankfully, they became separate accounts. To achieve consistency and make budgets a meaningful barometer of change, I have taken all budget line items for the years 1860–1930 and rearranged them in spreadsheets under budget taxonomies corresponding to the four areas of urban policy: economic development, urban growth, service distribution, and wealth redistribution. Totals can then be tabulated for each of the policy taxonomies year by year, resolving the problem of changing line items. The annual budgets reconfigured by policy taxonomy show the changes in policy priorities over time. When examined in the context of mayoral and city council election results, budget priorities are remarkably accurate in detecting regime succession and subsequent new policy priorities. In addition, the budgets make possible the calculation of such useful shorthand measurements as spending per capita, debt per capita, and rates of taxation per capita, which can also be derived on a consistent time line basis. These can then be compared with other cities.

A frustrating omission, transcending regimes and party affiliation, is that budgets studiously avoid reporting the number of employees on the municipal payroll. In some instances, the number of employees can be gleaned from other sources, such as a newspaper account or a Chamber of Commerce report. To estimate the number of city employees, I have used a system borrowed from public administrators and business accountants which assumes that 80 percent of an operating budget is spent on salaries. Average salaries taken from census data and divided into 80 percent of the operating budget yield a reasonable estimate of the number of municipal employees. These estimates check out well when real data are available. Decennial census reports showing the number of public employees were also used as counterweights.

The data for the municipal budget time lines are drawn from the following sources: City of Cleveland, *Annual Reports,* "Message of the Mayor," 1860–1930; "Report of the Comptroller," 1880–1930; Cleveland City Council, *Proceedings,* 1860–1913; Cleveland City Council, *The City Record,* 1914–1930; Cuyahoga County, *Annual Report,* "Report of the County Auditor," 1860–1930; State of Ohio, *Ohio Statistics,* 1880–1900; Charles C. Williamson, *The Finances of Cleveland* (New York: Columbia University, 1907), esp. Appendices B and C, pp. 229–255. See also Gail Radford's helpful guide through the thicket of municipal finance in "From Municipal Socialism to Public Authorities: Institutional Factors in the Shaping of American Public Enterprise," *Journal of American History,* 30 (December, 2003), 863–890.

NOTE 2: THE SYSTEM OF SOCIAL STRATIFICATION

The commentary in the text on social stratification in Cleveland was derived in the following manner.

The social stratification time lines (1860–1930) are based on occupational data. I compiled a time series of tables showing classes for each census year, and a political ward level map showing the residential location of each class for each census year. The classes are derived from seven occupational categories: (1) Proprietors, managers, and officials; (2) Professionals; (3) Clerical workers; (4) Skilled workers; (5) Semiskilled workers; (6) Unskilled workers; and (7) Personal and domestic servants. The seven categories are the same as those used by Kenneth L. Kusmer, *A Ghetto Takes Shape: Black Cleveland, 1870–1930* (Urbana: University of Illinois Press, 1976), see Appendix I; and Ronald R. Weiner and Carol A Beale, "The Sixth City: Cleveland in Three Stages of Urbanization," in Thomas F. Campbell and Edward M. Miggins (eds.), *The Birth of*

Methodological Notes 227

Modern Cleveland, 1865–1930 (Cleveland: Western Reserve Historical Society, 1988), pp. 19–53. A similar classification scheme is offered by Donald A. Deskins, Jr., *Residential Mobility of Negroes in Detroit, 1837–1965* (Ann Arbor: Department of Geography, University of Michigan, 1972), Table A1.1. A somewhat more sophisticated system is used by Olivier Zunz, *The Changing Face of Inequality: Urbanization, Industrial Development, and Immigrants in Detroit, 1880–1920* (Chicago: University of Chicago Press, 1982), see Appendix 3. Zunz's system allows for a more detailed accounting of white collar occupations, important for the turn of the century period when modern commercial, government, and corporate bureaucracies emerged. On this topic, see also Zunz, *Making America Corporate, 1870–1920* (Chicago: University of Chicago Press, 1989). I have used the less detailed version because it makes data and observations in this work consistent with Kusmer's earlier work in Cleveland and Deskins's in Detroit.

The data sources for the tables and maps are: samples taken from the 1870 and 1900 Manuscript Census (Microfilm); ten year samples taken from *Cleveland City Directory* (various publishers, 1860–1930); the printed U.S. decennial census, 1860–1930 [especially valuable for the period when the Populist Regime was succeeding the Merchant Regime is U.S. Census, *Report on the Social Statistics of Cities* (1880)]. For the twentieth century, see the valuable series of census tract reports prepared by Howard Whipple Green for the Cleveland Real Property Inventory (under various titles, 1910–1936). The Cleveland Public Library has preserved the annual wall size *City Directory* street and ward maps which were used as the base for my own pencil/tracing paper maps. Page size ward maps are found in David D. Van Tassel and John J. Grabowski (eds.), *The Encyclopedia of Cleveland History* (Bloomington: Indiana University Press, 1987), pp. 211–218.

Two measurements were used to gauge the concentration of each occupational group in a given ward. The first technique requires calculating means and standard deviations of each occupational group. Any ward with a concentration of a single occupational group more than one standard deviation above the group's mean may be described as a residential quarter for that group. The maps show the number of standard deviations each group is above the mean. These maps are also useful for showing the "class" support for political candidates when compared with ward level election results. The second technique is that used by sociologists to show residential segregation, variously called the Index of Dissimilarity or Index of Segregation. The technique is used by Kuzmer, Zunz, and Deskins for their purposes but is most succinctly explained in Charles M. Dollar and Richard J. Jensen, *Historian's Guide to Statistics: Quantitative Analysis and Historical Research* (New York: Holt, Rinehart and Winston, 1971), pp. 121–126. These indices were calculated for each census year by ward, and after 1910 by census tract, and yield results similar to the mean/standard deviation technique. See Weiner and Beale, "Sixth City," pp. 43–50. One can then make an observation like the following: "Tom L. Johnson in five municipal elections never ran well in working class wards." This statement is based on ward maps of Johnson's elections and ward maps showing where people of various occupational groups lived.

NOTE 3: CITY STRUCTURE

Urban growth policy was formulated by the various regimes for a city under constant structural change. Cleveland, while passing from Merchant to Populist to Corporate to

Realty regimes, simultaneously advanced through three distinct stages of city structure: (1) the mercantile or walking city, (2) the industrial, streetcar, or hub and spoke city, and (3) the automobile or multinucleated city. The Merchant Regime made urban growth policy for the walking city; the Populist and Corporate regimes called the shots for the streetcar city; and the Realty Regime presided over the transition from the streetcar to the multinucleated automobile city.

University of Chicago sociologists Robert E. Park, E. W. Burgess, and R. D. McKenzie in *The City* (Chicago: University of Chicago Press, 1925), 47–62 devised the concentric zone model which provides, perhaps unintentionally, a fair representation of how urban land was used in the mercantile era. Economist Homer Hoyt's *The Structure and Growth of Residential Neighborhoods in American Cities* (Washington: U.S. Government Printing Office, 1939) creates the sector model for the streetcar era industrial city. Geographers Chauncy D. Harris and Edward L. Ullman in "The Nature of Cities," *The Annals of the American Academy of Political and Social Science*, CCXLII (1945), 7–17 supply the multiple nuclei model for the automobile city.

Park, Burgess, and McKenzie were the creators of the Concentric Ring Model. At its center is the central business district (CBD) around which all other land uses form. Modified for the walking city of the merchant era city, the CBD nucleus hosts all manner of business enterprise surrounded by a ring of affluent housing, a second ring of middle income housing, and a third ring of lower income housing at the periphery of settlement. In the mercantile era, Cleveland's CBD was in the Flats, the surrounding ring east and west housed the city's most affluent residents, the next ring the middle class, and a third the working class ring of settlement.

Homer Hoyt's Sector Model uses railroad tracks and streetcar lines as the skeleton of the city. Specific land uses form around these lines, giving rise to a city of a segregated economic and social geography. The CBD is still the city's nucleus, but it houses only retail, financial, and service activities dependent on face-to-face contact with customers. Light and heavy industries locate in sectors paralleling rail lines. Wholesaling clusters near the CBD. The population segregates by class, made possible by the streetcar lines. High income groups live at the periphery of settlement in sectors at the end of streetcar lines. Following the streetcar lines inward toward the CBD are sectors housing middle income families, and, last, nearest the CBD and the factory districts, are the sectors containing the working classes and the poor. This is the classic formulation of the industrial era city. This is the city for which the Populist and Corporate regimes made policy.

The Multiple Nuclei Model created by Harris and Ullman uses the automobile street and highway system as the city's skeleton. The nodes where major streets and highways intersect become the city's nuclei, replacing the single CBD-nucleus mercantile and industrial era cities. In the automobile city, the CBD is just one of several nodal focal points. The scale of the city, of course, is also larger, spreading from the original political city to the suburbs and exurbs beyond. It is a regional model superimposed on the old industrial city. Inner city land uses remain much the same, but industrial nuclei form in the suburbs and the working class follows. High income residences cluster around high grade retail and service nodes. The multinucleated regional city was a creation of the Realty Regime. The Realty Regime's Stanley L. McMichael noticed the effects on the CBD in the 1920s and subsequently forecast the demise of the CBD as a retail center.

The three models are useful for interpreting the empirical data collected for Cleveland. The data come from samples taken from the business listings of the *Cleveland City*

Directory for 1860, 1870, 1880, 1890, 1900, 1910, 1920, and 1930. The entries were sorted into categories conforming to the federal government's Standard Industrial Classifications (SIC) and were assigned a number from the SIC 4-digit scheme. For example:

Division D Manufacturing
  D2 Nondurables
    201 Meat Products
      2011 Meat Packing Plants

The addresses of the SIC-coded businesses were also coded with a geographical identifier. A quarter-mile grid was spread over a *City Directory* Street and Ward Map, and each address from the sample was given an x-y grid coordinate corresponding to its street address. To illustrate, the Acme Meat Packing Plant (SIC 2011) at 500 Front Street might have an x-y coordinate of N2. Once done, all businesses in each of the SIC categories were sorted into their matching x-y cells on the grid. The resulting eight grids (1860, 1870, etc.) can then be compared for changes in business location, e.g., manufacturing, wholesale, retail, services, the professions, etc., over time. The whole can be transferred to graph paper maps for easy viewing. The result is an extraordinary overview of Cleveland's evolving city structure through merchant, industrial, and automobile eras. The three land use models provide a template for understanding these land use patterns.

This methodology is an adaptation of Donald R. Deskins, "Race, Residence, and Workplace in Detroit, 1880–1965," *Economic Geography* 48 (January, 1972), 79–94; Maurice Yeates, *An Introduction to Quantitative Analysis in Human Geography* (New York: McGraw-Hill, 1974), pp. 29–35; and Leslie J. King, *Statistical Analysis in Geography* (Englewood Cliffs, NJ: Prentice Hall, 1969), pp. 20–30, 117–148.

NOTE 4: CENTROGRAPHIC TECHNIQUES

Movement of SIC-coded businesses, occupational groups, ethnic and racial groups, and classes of people can be tracked using centrographic techniques. Centrography establishes the mean center of a population, e.g., wholesale businesses, professionals, Irish and African-Americans, or the *Cleveland Social Register* population. American historians are familiar with centrography from textbook maps showing the mean center of the American population in each census year, a time series of dots showing the center of population advancing from Cumberland, Maryland to Danville, Illinois and so on. For the purposes of this book the mean centers of the above mentioned populations were tracked each decade from 1870 to 1930. Centrography charts changes in city structure and social geography. The centrographic methodology was first used by the American Census Bureau in the 1870s to establish the mean center of the American population. The methodology had a briefer acceptance among Soviet geographers, surviving until Joseph Stalin discovered that none of the animals, minerals, or vegetables were to be found at their mean centers. The Soviet Centrographical Laboratory was summarily purged.

The literature on centrography is as follows: J. E. Hilgard, "The Advance of Population in the United States," *Scribner's Monthly*, IV (June, 1872), 214–218; Francis Amasa

Walker, "The Progress of the Nation—1790–1870," *Statistical Atlas of the United States, Part III: Vital Statistics* (New York: Julius Bierr, 1874), p. 5; John F. Hayford, "What is the Center of an Area, or the Center of a Population?" *Journal of the American Statistical Association*, VII, No. 58 (June, 1902), 47–58; Charles S. Sloane, *Center of Population and Median Lines and Centers of Area, Agriculture, Manufactures, and Cotton* (Washington: U.S. Government Printing Office, 1923), p. 3; Walter Crosby Eells, "A Mistaken Conception of the Center of Population," *Journal of the American Statistical Association*, XXV (March, 1930), 33–40; D. Welty LeFever, "Measuring Geographic Concentrations by Means of the Standard Deviational Ellipse," *American Journal of Sociology*, XXXII, No. 1 (July, 1926), 88–94; E. E. Sviatlovsky and Walter Crosby Eells, "The Centrographical Method and Regional Analysis," *Geographical Review*, XXVII (April, 1937), 252; Donald R. Deskins, "Race, Residence, and Workplace in Detroit, 1880–1965," *Economic Geography*, LXVIII (January, 1972), 79–94.

NOTE 5: ECONOMIC DEVELOPMENT

I have taken pains in the text to separate economic development from urban growth policy because each addresses a separate economic issue. Economic development policy addresses the export sector of the economy, and urban growth policy guides the local sector of the economy, land use in particular. I have tried to draw careful distinctions between the two because today they are at times willfully confused. Urban growth policy is often substituted for economic development policy.

For the past decade, Cleveland has been engaged in building sports palaces for its professional teams, one each for the Indians, Cavaliers, and Browns. When principal, interest, and fees are at last paid, sometime in the first quarter of the new century, the cost will approach a billion dollars, most of which will come from the pockets of taxpayers in the form of a regressive sales tax on cigarettes and liquor, known locally as the "Sin Tax."

To sell these projects to local taxpayers, the regime in power, a reincarnated realty regime, explained to a public reeling from the loss of thousands of manufacturing jobs that these projects were being built in the interest of economic development, the hot button new jobs issue. Here is a classic case of the policy makers willfully or ignorantly misleading the electorate. The stadiums are about urban growth policy, not economic development policy.

Although these distinctions are made at various places in the text, perhaps a restatement here coupled with the methodology employed will serve to clarify the matter.

An urban economy is dualistic: It has an export sector and a local sector. The export sector produces goods and services for sale outside the region. The sale of such goods and services brings new (other people's) money into the economy, which can then be invested in a variety of things, including new plant and still more jobs. Economic development policy is the conscious attempt by local leaders to add capacity to the export sector. This was initially done in Cleveland by the Merchant Regime when it connected Cleveland to national markets via a transportation system so that local enterprises could sell their products outside the immediate region. Succeeding regimes tried to encourage the growth of backward and forward linkages from initial export-sector industries, for example, chemicals as a forward linkage from the oil industry. The three stadiums built during the 1990s do not meet these criteria because they fail to bring in other people's money; as entertainment venues, they merely recycle the money already in the local economy. And they are not the forward or backward linkages of any local industry.

Data on firms from the federal Census of Manufactures and occupational data from the Census of Population was tabulated by SIC industrial category for the years 1860, 1870, 1880, 1890, 1900, 1910, 1920, and 1930 in a time-line series. Distinctions were made between export and local industries and between durable and nondurable goods industries in each census year.

This allows for two important calculations: the first is the basic–nonbasic ratio, which is a ratio between export-sector and local-sector industries. If the economy is developing rather than merely growing, a declining basic to nonbasic ratio will occur. Secondly, distinctions are made between durable and nondurable goods industries. Nondurable goods industries are tied to forestry and agriculture. If a city's economy is to develop, it must escape from the tether of nondurable goods industries. The constant (usually westward) movement of agricultural staples and forestry gives rise to new cities (such as Toledo, Grand Rapids, Detroit, Chicago, and Milwaukee) with greater short-term ability to produce cheaper nondurables derived from these products. Durable goods industries have the advantage of offering greater long-term stability, considerably larger employment opportunities, and local value-added spending by the firm. However, if the city's economy is to develop rather than merely grow, forward-linkage industries must be spun off from the original durable goods industries.

Tabulating manufacturing and employment data by SIC category establishes the trends from which these observations can be drawn. Judgments on the wisdom of the four regime's economic development policies can also be made. The Merchant Regime's economic development policy of long-distance transportation connections allowed Cleveland to make the transition from nondurable to durable goods production. The hesitant Populist Regime and more enthusiastic Corporate Regime spent enough on bridges, dredging, and docking facilities to ensure the permanence of durable goods industries, but Corporate and Realty regimes refused to direct capital to forward-linkage industries. And there Cleveland's economy drifted on the eve of the Great Depression.

Cleveland's economy was a cork bobbing and swaying amongst the waves, rhythms, and cycles of nineteenth and twentieth century economic history. These oscillations are the subject of Bryan J. L. Berry, *Long Range Rhythms in Economic Development and Political Behavior* (Baltimore: The Johns Hopkins University Press, 1991) and David Hackett Fischer, *The Great Wave: Price Revolutions and the Rhythm of History* (New York: Oxford University Press, 1996). These works enable the local historian to place Cleveland's economic development in a national and international context.

To chart the course of Cleveland's economic development, I have pirated the data from the tables in Naphtali Hoffman, "The Process of Economic Development in Cleveland, 1825–1920" (Ph.D. diss., Case Western Reserve University, 1980). The argumentative text of the dissertation is a plodding decade-by-decade exposition drawn from the tables which takes interpretive issue with Richard V. Knight, *Employment Expansion and Metropolitan Trade* (New York: Praeger, 1973). Knight's thesis asserts that economic development occurs (rather than mere growth) when high Value Added per Employee (VAPE) develop and spin off other high VAPE backward- and forward-linkage industries. The essential comparison is that local VAPE must be significantly higher than national VAPE for the same industries. Hoffman argues that while Cleveland's economy did develop rather than grow, Knight's "High VAPE thesis" fails to explain it. Hoffman concludes that (1) VAPE in manufacturing in Cleveland was not increasing during the period 1825–1920, (2) the city's leading industries did not experience significant growth in VAPE during the period, and (3) VAPE for Cleveland's manufacturing sector was not significantly higher than manufacturing VAPE for the United States during the same period.

I have reshuffled these same data to reach somewhat different conclusions. Using Hoffman's tables and the Census Bureau's decennial *Reports on the Manufactures of the United States*, I have sorted all data by industry into Standard Industrial Classification (SIC) categories (4-digit level) for the years 1825–1930. I then aggregated all industries into either durable or nondurable goods producers and calculated VAPE for both. This rendering of the data, represented in tables 3.2, 3.3, and 3.4, yields rather different results. Durable goods industries, including primary metals and forward-linkage fabricated metal products industries, did increase in VAPE during the period, though both were fatefully stagnant during the Populist Regime (1878–1895), and VAPE in all durable goods industries was significantly higher than national averages. Hoffman's VAPE manufacturing averages were dragged down by the declining VAPE in nondurable goods, also shown in tables 3.2 and 3.3. We both reach the same conclusion: that Cleveland's economy developed rather than grew during the period, but Richard Knight's "High VAPE thesis" does explain why. Knight's methodology is useful to historians because value-added data was so commonly collected and published in the nineteenth century and because VAPE is a measurement that nineteenth century businessmen and decision makers so readily understood.

See also Allan R. Pred, *The Spatial Dynamics of U.S. Urban Industrial Growth, 1800–1914* (Cambridge: MIT Press, 1966); Wilbur R. Thompson, *A Preface to Urban Economics* (Baltimore: The Johns Hopkins University Press, 1965); William D. Ellis, *Ninety Thousand Men and a Hundred of Wind: The Story of 100 Years of Iron and Steel in Ohio* (Cleveland: unpublished manuscript, 1973); and Kenneth Warren, *The American Steel Industry, 1850–1970: A Geographical Interpretation* (Oxford: Oxford University Press, 1973).

NOTES TO CHAPTERS

NOTES TO INTRODUCTION

1. In the 104-year period covered by this study, there were 52 municipal elections, 26 during the Merchant Regime alone, 11 more during the Populist Regime, 10 Corporate Regime elections, and another 5 during the decade when the Realty Regime made policy.
2. David Harvey, *The Urban Experience* (Baltimore: The Johns Hopkins University Press, 1989), pp. 125–164.
3. The sheer volume of periodical literature on regime theory defies citation in this space, but three influential books make commendable use of it: Paul E. Peterson, *City Limits* (Chicago: The University of Chicago Press, 1981); Dennis R. Judd, *The Politics of American Cities: Private Power and Public Policy* (Glenview, IL: Scott, Foresman and Company, 3rd ed., 1988); Paul Kantor, *The Dependent City: The Changing Political Economy of Urban America* (Glenview, IL: Scott, Foresman and Company, 1988).
4. After 1933, regime formation took a dramatic new turn. Franklin D. Roosevelt's New Deal introduced the federal government as a participant in local policy making. The four pre–New Deal regimes that are the subject of this book, in contrast, were purely local in character.
5. Policy categories are defined in the above cited books by Peterson, Judd, and Kantor. Following the differentiation in urban economies between export sectors and local sectors, distinctions made by location economists and urban geographers, I have identified two forms of economic policy: economic development policy, which follows the export sector, and urban growth policy, which follows the local sector. The economic distinctions are conveniently drawn in Edwin S. Mills and Bruce W. Hamilton, *Urban Economics* (New York: HarperCollins College Publishers, 5th ed., 1994); Wilbur R. Thompson, *A Preface to Urban Economics* (Baltimore: The Johns Hopkins University Press, 1965); August Losch, *The Economics of Location* (New Haven: Yale University Press, 2nd ed., 1952); Truman A. Hartshorn, *Interpreting the City: An Urban Geography* (New York: John Wiley & Sons, 1980); and Paul L. Knox, *Urbanization: An Introduction to Urban Geography* (Englewood Cliffs, NJ: Prentice Hall, 1994).
6. Losch, pp. 3–16; Thompson, pp. 11–26; Mills, pp. 33–37; Hartshorn, pp. 40–58; Knox, pp. 36–41.
7. Kenneth E. Boulding, *The Economy of Love and Fear: A Preface to Grants Economics* (Belmont, CA: Wadsworth, 1973), pp. 1–14, 89–102; Alvin E. Schorr, *Common*

Decency: Domestic Policies After Reagan (New Haven: Yale University Press, 1986), pp. 20–48; Peter Edelman, "The Worst Thing Bill Clinton Has Done, The Atlantic Monthly, March 1997, pp. 43–58.
 8. www.cleveland.com/quietcrisis.

NOTES TO CHAPTER 1

1. A valuable survey of the merchant era is Michael J. McTighe, *A Measure of Success: Protestants and Public Culture in Antebellum Cleveland* (Albany, NY: State University of New York Press, 1994), esp. pp. 57–72. McTighe identifies the merchants' policy making efforts as "public culture," the outgrowth of their struggle to reconcile the moral demands of Protestantism and the small businessman's mid-nineteenth century boosterism, the eternal struggle between God and Mammon. The merchants, McTighe concludes, would have it both ways. The seeds of New England Protestant culture, the tendrils of which sprouted in merchant era Cleveland, are explained in David Hackett Fischer, *Albion's Seed: Four British Folkways in America* (New York: Oxford University Press, 1989), pp. 13–206; and Daniel Boorstin's, *The Americans: The National Experience* (New York: Random House, 1965), pp. 113–168, which remains the most engaging account of boosterism.

2. R. Carlye Buley, *The Old Northwest: Pioneer Period, 1815–1840*, Vol. I (Bloomington: University of Indiana Press, 1950), pp. 490–508; Ralph H. Brown, *Historical Geography of the United States* (New York: Harcourt, Brace & World, 1948), pp. 212–235; D. W. Meinig, *The Shaping of America: A Geographical Perspective on 500 Years of History*, Vol. II: *Continental America, 1800–1867* (New Haven: Yale University Press, 1993), pp. 264–273.

3. Lois Kimball Mathews, *The Expansion of New England: The Spread of New England Settlement and Institutions to the Mississippi River, 1620–1865* (Boston: Houghton Mifflin, 1909); Elbert Jay Benton, *Cleveland: Cultural Study of an American City*, Part III: *During the Canal Days* (Cleveland: Western Reserve Historical Society, 1944), pp. 7–13; Helen Mabel Strong, "The Geography of Cleveland" (Ph.D. diss., University of Chicago, 1927), pp. 1–8.

4. Benton, ibid.; Carol Poh Miller and Robert Wheeler, *Cleveland: A Concise History, 1796–1990* (Bloomington: University of Indiana Press, 1990), pp. 7–20.

5. Economic development policy follows the economic base concept devised by geographers: "the reason for both the existence and growth of a city lies in the goods and services it produces and sells beyond its borders." Those industries producing such goods are called basic industries (economists label them export industries), which are the objects of economic development policy. Economic base is explained in all urban geography texts; among the most widely available are: Maurice Yates and Barry Garner, *The North American City*, 3rd ed. (New York: Harper & Row, 1980), pp. 74–76; Truman A. Hartshorn, *Interpreting the City: An Urban Geography* (New York: John Wiley & Sons, 1980), pp. 41–42; Paul L. Knox, *Urbanization: An Introduction to Urban Geography* (Englewood Cliffs, NJ: Prentice Hall, Inc., 1994), pp. 37–41.

6. David D. Van Tassel and John J. Grabowski (Eds.), *The Encyclopedia of Cleveland History* (Bloomington: Indiana University Press, 1987), p. 589.

7. Miller and Wheeler, pp. 25–31; *Encyclopedia*, pp. 589–590.

8. Harry N. Scheiber, *Ohio Canal Era: A Case Study of Government and the Econ-

omy, 1820–1861 (Athens, OH: Ohio University Press, 1969), p. 9; Miller and Wheeler, pp. 49–50

9. Miller and Wheeler, p. 51

10. Buley, I, pp. 517–535; H.R. 46th Cong., 3rd Session, V.16 #7, pp. 5–6, 42, 103; Edward J. Taaffe and Howard L. Gauthier, Jr., *The Geography of Transportation* (Englewood Cliffs, NJ: Prentice Hall, 1973), pp. 121–131.

11. Alfred D. Chandler Jr., *The Visible Hand: The Managerial Revolution in American Business* (Cambridge: The Belknap Press of Harvard University Press, 1977), pp. 79–121; C. Joseph Pusateri, *A History of American Business*, 2nd ed. (Arlington Heights, IL: Harlan Davidson, 1988), pp. 167–196; Olivier Zunz, *Making America Corporate, 1870–1920* (Chicago: The University of Chicago Press, 1990), pp. 38–40; Harold C. Livesay, "From Steeples to Smokestacks: The Birth of the Modern Corporation in Cleveland," in Thomas F. Campbell and Edward M. Miggins (eds.), *The Birth of Modern Cleveland, 1865–1930* (Cleveland: Western Reserve Historical Society, 1988), pp. 55–56.

12. Robert Wheeler, "Commercial Village to Commercial City, 1825–1860," in *Encyclopedia of Cleveland History*, p. xxv.

13. Wheeler, *Encyclopedia*, "Commercial City," pp. xxv–xxvi.

14. Hinterland agricultural production, raw materials sourcing, and nineteenth century transportation innovations form the core of William Cronon's *Nature's Metropolis: Chicago and the Great West* (New York: W.W. Norton & Company, 1991). The pre–metals making Cleveland export sector parallels these developments.

15. Miller and Wheeler, pp. 51–52, 70–72.

16. Roger H. Hinderliter, "The Origins of Commercial Banking in the Fourth Federal Reserve District," *Economic Review/Annual Report* (Cleveland: Federal Reserve Bank of Cleveland, 1976), pp. 18–22.

17. There are three capital circuits: primary, secondary, and tertiary. Primary circuit capital is that invested in raw materials, manufacturing equipment, labor, and transportation vehicles; secondary capital is invested in land and buildings; and tertiary capital is invested in science, technology, education, and culture. The capital circuits distinction was originally drawn by Henri Lefebrve, *Every Day Life in the Modern World* (New York: Harper & Row, 1971), and applied by David Harvey, *The Urbanization of Capital* (Baltimore: The Johns Hopkins University Press, 1985) and is conveniently summarized in Mark Gottdiener, *The New Urban Sociology* (New York: McGraw-Hill, Inc., 1994), pp. 126–128 and Joe R. Feagin and Robert Parker, *Building American Cities: The Urban Real Estate Game* (Englewood Cliffs, NJ: Prentice Hall, 2nd ed., 1990), pp. 13–14.

18. William Ganson Rose, *Cleveland: The Making of a City* (Cleveland: World Publishing Company, 1950), p. 225; Edmund H. Chapman, *Cleveland: Village to Metropolis* (Cleveland: Case Western Reserve University Press, 1964), p. 98.

19. Kenneth T. Jackson, *Crabgrass Frontier: The Suburbanization of the United States* (New York: Oxford University Press, 1985), pp. 140–146.

20. Land use patterns from the 1850s to the turn of the century are ably discussed in Chapman, *Cleveland: Village to Metropolis*, see esp. pp. 97–116; the chronology can be traced in City of Cleveland, Division of Engineering, Annexations to the City of Cleveland (for use with wall map) (1954), n.p.; City of Cleveland, Division of Engineering, Annexations to the City of Cleveland, Annexations to the City of Cleveland Wall Map (1954); "City Attained Greatness by Annexations," Cleveland *Plain Dealer*, 13

August 1920; "Fifty Villages Fringe Cleveland Proper, but Annexation Has Lagged," Cleveland *Plain Dealer*, 31 December 1927.

21. City of Cleveland. Annexation Wall Map.

22. *Encyclopedia of Cleveland History*, pp. 735–736.

23. Ibid.; *Atlas of Cuyahoga County, Ohio* (Philadelphia: Titus, Simmons & Titus, 1874); Celia Frances Beck, "From Grist Mill to Steel Mill: The Story of Newburgh, Now Part of Cleveland" (M.A. thesis, School of Applied Social Sciences, Western Reserve University, 1929).

24. City of Cleveland. Annual Reports, 1877, 1881.

25. The local real estate industry was deftly explained by Mayor Charles A. Otis in City of Cleveland, Annual Report, "The Annual Message of Mayor Charles A. Otis" (1873), pp. 17–21.

26. *Encyclopedia of Cleveland History*, pp. 124–125; *The Plain Dealer*, 1 March 1997.

27. The Panic of 1873 marked the beginning of the end of the Merchant Regime. David Hackett Fischer's *The Great Wave: Price Revolutions and the Rhythm of History* (New York: Oxford University Press, 1996), pp. 156–179 argues that the Panic of 1873 was a temporary downward blip in an otherwise stable era of prices, and Bryan J. L. Berry, *Long Range Rhythms in Economic Development and Political Behavior* (Baltimore: The Johns Hopkins University Press, 1991), p. 5 [fig. 3] and p. 76 [fig. 43] interprets the Panic of 1873 as the beginning of a downward Kuznets Cycle embedded within a downward Kondratief Wave which began in 1864–65. However severe, the local effects were politically damaging to the Merchant Regime, even if short-lived economically; see esp., City of Cleveland, Annual Report, "The Inaugural Address of Mayor Rensselear Russell Herrick" (1878), pp. 56–57; City of Cleveland, Annual Report, Mayor's Message, 1873–1878; Annual Report, Report of the Comptroller, 1873–1878.

28. Sam Bass Warner, Jr., *The Private City: Philadelphia in Three Periods of Its Growth* (Philadelphia: University of Pennsylvania Press, 1968), pp. ix–xii; Jon C. Teaford, *The Unheralded Triumph: City Government in America, 1870–1900* (Baltimore: The Johns Hopkins University Press, 1984), pp. 4–6; James F. Richardson, "To Control the City: The New York Police in Historical Perspective," in Kenneth T. Jackson and Stanley K. Schultz (eds.), *Cities in American History* (New York: Alfred A. Knopf, 1972), pp. 272–274; Martin V. Melosi, *Garbage in the Cities: Refuse, Reform, and the Environment, 1880–1980* (Chicago: The Dorsey Press, 1981), pp. 16–20.

29. Marian J. Morton, "Temperance Reform in the 'Providential Environment:' Cleveland, 1830–1930," in David D. Van Tassel and John J. Grabowski (eds.), *Cleveland: A Tradition of Reform* (Kent, OH: The Kent State University Press, 1986), pp. 50–56; Michael V. Wells, "Crime," in *Encyclopedia of Cleveland History*, p. 306.

30. City of Cleveland, *Ordinances of the City of Cleveland* (Cleveland: Clark-Britton Printing Co., 1890); Wells, "Crime," *Encyclopedia of Cleveland History*, p. 306; James F. Richardson, "Public Safety," in *Encyclopedia of Cleveland History*, pp. 807–809.

31. Wells, ibid.; Richardson, ibid.; Teaford, *The Unheralded Triumph*, pp. 66–67.

32. William A. Gould, "Remarks to the Cleveland Chapter of the American Institute of Town Planners," 16 June 1969.

33. *Encyclopedia of Cleveland History*, pp. 232–233.

34. Teaford, *The Unheralded Triumph*, pp. 163–166.

35. Adna Ferrin Weber, *The Growth of Cities in the Nineteenth Century: A Study in Statistics* (Ithaca, NY: Cornell University Press, 1967 [c. 1899]), pp. 343–365.

36. Chapman, *Village to Metropolis*, pp. 116–117.

37. Willis E. Sibley, "Water System," *Encyclopedia of Cleveland History*, pp. 1029–1032.
38. City of Cleveland, Division of Public Health, "Births and Deaths Recorded in the City of Cleveland, 1836–1980."
39. Sibley, ibid.
40. Annual Report, "Mayor's Message," 1865–1880.
41. Ibid.
42. "Births and Deaths Recorded in the City of Cleveland."
43. See Methodological Note 1.
44. McTighe, *A Measure of Success*, pp. 8, 73–75.
45. U.S., Manuscript Census, 1870 (Microfilm) reveals that virtually every worker in Cleveland's industrial wards was laid off for periods of as little as two weeks and as long as two months. Skilled workers experienced the shortest periods of downtime, while unskilled workers could expect longer layoffs.
46. The transition of rural to urban working classes was first noted in E.P. Thompson, *The Making of the English Working Class* (New York: Vintage Books, 1966); Gareth Stedman Jones, *Outcast London* (Oxford: Clarendon Press, 1971); G. E. Mingay, *Rural Life in Victorian England* (London: Fortuna Publications Limited); and in America, Robert E. Gallman, "The Agricultural Sector and the Pace of Economic Growth: The U.S. Experience in the Nineteenth Century," in David C. Klingaman and Richard K. Vedder (eds.), *Essays in Nineteenth Century Economic History: The Old Northwest* (Athens, OH: Ohio University Press, 1975), pp. 35–76.
47. Michael J. McTighe, "Leading Men, True Women, Protestant Churches, and the Shape of Antebellum Benevolence," in David D. Van Tassel and John J. Grabowski (eds.), *Cleveland: A Tradition of Reform* (Kent, OH: The Kent State University Press, 1986), pp. 20–22; McTighe, *A Measure of Success*, pp. 82–84.
48. Edward M. Miggins, "The Search for the One Best System: Cleveland Public Schools and Educational Reform, 1836–1920," in *Cleveland: A Tradition of Reform*, pp. 137–140.
49. McTighe, *A Measure of Success*, pp. 73–96.
50. Ibid.
51. Walter I. Trattner, *From Poor Law to Welfare State: A History of Social Welfare in America*, (New York: The Free Press, 3rd ed., 1984), pp. viii–ix; Leiby James, "Social Welfare Institutions and the Poor," *Social Casework* 49 (February, 1968), pp. 90–95.
52. Michael J. McTighe, "Babel and Babylon on the Cuyahoga: Religious Diversity in Cleveland," in Thomas F. Campbell and Edward M. Miggins (eds.), *The Birth of Modern Cleveland, 1865–1930* (Cleveland: Western Reserve Historical Society, 1988), pp. 234–236.
53. *Measure of Success*, pp. 76–79.
54. Ibid., pp. 90–96.
55. Morton, "Providential Environment," pp. 50–66; *Measure of Success*, pp. 97–124.
56. McTighe, "Leading Men, True Women," pp. 22–28; Methodological Note 1.
57. McTighe, "Antebellum Benevolence," pp. 22–23; Methodological Note 1 (Annual Budget, 1870).
58. "Antebellum Benevolence," p. 21.
59. Ibid., pp. 22–24.
60. Ibid.
61. Methodological Note 2.

62. Ibid.
63. Methodological Note 3.
64. City of Cleveland, *Annual Report*, 1870–1880; City of Cleveland, *Council Proceedings*, 1870–1880.
65. Ibid.
66. The "Mayor's Annual Message" in City of Cleveland, *Annual Reports*, 1870–1890 contain frequent expressions of frustration with the charter and their inability to control the bureaucracy. See esp., John H. Farley, "Annual Message," 1884; and James B. Whipple, "Cleveland in Conflict: A Study in Urban Adolescence, 1876–1900" (Ph.D. dissertation, Western Reserve University, 1951), pp. 340–343.
67. *City of Cleveland Directory,* 1870–1880, lists school board members by ward, occupation, and place of residence; see also Edward M. Miggins, "Becoming American: Americanization and the Reform of the Cleveland Public Schools," in Thomas F. Campbell and Edward M. Miggins (eds.), *The Birth of Modern Cleveland, 1865–1930* (Cleveland: Western Reserve Historical Society, 1988), pp. 345–373 and Edward M. Miggins, "The Search for the One Best System: Cleveland Public Schools and Educational Reform, 1836–1920," in David D. Van Tassel and John J. Grabowski (eds.), *Cleveland: A Tradition of Reform* (Kent, OH: The Kent State University Press, 1986), pp. 136–155.
68. Trattner, *From Poor Law to Welfare State*, pp. 77–107; Michael J. McTighe, "Leading Men, True Women, Protestant Churches, and the Shape of Antebellum Benevolence," in David D. Van Tassel and John J. Grabowski (eds.), *Cleveland: A Tradition of Reform* (Kent, OH: The Kent State University Press, 1988), pp. 13–28; John J. Grabowski, "Social Reform and Philanthropic Order in Cleveland, 1896–1920," in *Tradition of Reform,* pp. 30–32; David C. Hammack, "The Development of Nonprofit Organizations in Cleveland," a paper presented at Case Western Reserve University American Studies Program: Tenth Annual Western Reserve Studies Symposium (October 6–7, 1995), pp. 13–14.

NOTES TO CHAPTER 2

1. The discussion of the professional ideal in this and subsequent chapters draws primarily on Robert Wiebe, *The Search for Order, 1877–1920* (New York: Hill and Wang, 1967); Kenneth E. Boulding, *The Organizational Revolution: A Study in the Ethics of Economic Organization* (Chicago: Quadrangle Books, 1968 [c. 1953]); John Kenneth Galbraith, *The New Industrial State* (Boston: Houghton-Mifflin, 1967); Alfred D. Chandler, Jr.'s two books, *The Visible Hand: The Managerial Revolution in American Business* (Cambridge: The Belknap Press of Harvard University Press, 1977) and *Scale and Scope: The Dynamics of Industrial Capitalism* (Cambridge: The Belknap Press of Harvard University Press, 1990); Harold Perkin, *The Rise of Professional Society: England Since 1880* (London: Routledge, 1989); Gareth Morgan, *Images of Organization* (Newbury Park, CA: Sage Publications, 1986); and Olivier Zunz, *Making America Corporate, 1870–1920* (Chicago: The University of Chicago Press, 1990).

2. My conception of working class culture and the working class ideal draws on Christopher Lasch, *The True and Only Heaven: Progress and Its Critics* (New York: W.W. Norton, 1991); E. P. Thompson, *The Making of the English Working Class* (New York: Vintage Books, 1966 [c. 1963]); Herbert Gutman, *Work, Culture, and Society in Industrializing America* (New York: Vintage Books, 1977); Harold Perkin's *Origins of Modern*

English Society (London: Routledge, 1969) and the previously cited *The Rise of Professional Society: England Since 1880*; Melvyn Dubofsky, *When Workers Organize: New York City in the Progressive Era* (Amherst, MA: The University of Massachusetts Press, 1968); and Harry Braverman, *Labor and Monopoly Capital: The Degradation of Work in the Twentieth Century* (New York: Monthly Review Press, 1974).

3. Lasch, pp. 47–49.
4. Ibid., pp. 223–225.
5. Ibid., pp. 135–147.
6. Melvyn Dubofsky, *Industrialism and the American Worker, 1865–1920* (New York: Thomas Y. Crowell 1975), pp. 29–71.
7. Perkin, *The Rise of Professional Society*, pp. 101–114; Gutman, pp. 13–32.
8. Raymond Mohl, *The New City: Urban America in the Industrial Age, 1860–1920* (Arlington Heights, IL: Harlan Davidson, 1985), pp. 180–193; Olivier Zunz, *The Changing Face of Inequality: The Changing Face of Inequality in Detroit, 1880–1920* (Chicago: The University of Chicago Press, 1982), pp. 81–88; Josef J. Barton, *Peasants and Strangers: Italians, Rumanians, and Slovaks in an American City, 1890–1950* (Cambridge: Harvard University Press, 1975), pp. 48–63; Lasch, pp. 120–167.
9. Glenn Porter and Harold Livesay, *Merchants and Manufacturers: Studies in the Changing Structure of Nineteenth Century Marketing* (Baltimore: The Johns Hopkins University Press, 1971), pp. 13–78.
10. Ibid., pp. 79–95; *Visible Hand*, pp. 13–65.
11. *Scale and Scope*, pp. 13–46; *Images of Organization*, pp. 19–38; Anthony Sampson, *Company Man: The Rise and Fall of Corporate Life* (New York: Random House, 1995), pp. 35–51.
12. *Origins of Modern English Society*, pp. 218–272; *Making America Corporate*, pp. 67–102.
13. Jon C. Teaford, *The Unheralded Triumph: City Government in America, 1870–1900* (Baltimore: The Johns Hopkins University Press, 1984), pp. 132–173.
14. Annual Report, "Annual Message of Mayor C. A. Otis," (1873), pp. 17–21.
15. Max Weber, *Economy and Society*, edited by Guenther Roth and Claus Wittich, 2 vols. (Berkeley: University of California Press, 1978), I, pp. 360–362.
16. Methodological Note 3.
17. An illuminating discussion of social theory and social geography is found in Ira Katznelson, *Marxism and the City* (Oxford: Oxford University Press, 1991), pp. 1–27; Raymond Mohl's previously cited *The New City*, pp. 180–189 discusses neighborhoods and working class culture, as does Howard M. Gitelman, *Workingmen of Waltham: Mobility in American Urban Industrial Development, 1850–1890* (Baltimore: The Johns Hopkins University Press, 1974), pp. 132–163. The Cleveland experience is documented in Barton's *Peasants and Strangers*, pp. 48–90; a series of articles by Wellington G. Fordyce, "Immigrant Colonies in Cleveland," *Ohio State Archaeological and Historical Quarterly*, LXL (October, 1936), 320–340; "Immigrant Institutions in Cleveland," *Ohio State Archaeological and Historical Quarterly*, XLVII (April, 1938), 87–103; "Nationality Groups in Cleveland Politics," *Ohio State Archaeological and Historical Quarterly*, XLVI (April, 1937), 109–120; Kenneth L. Kusmer, *A Ghetto Takes Shape: Black Cleveland, 1870–1930* (Urbana: The University of Illinois Press, 1976), pp. 35–52; and the research cited in Methodological Note 3.
18. *City Council Proceedings*, 1870–1880; "Mayor R.R. Herrick Inaugural Address," (1878), p. 55.

19. James B. Whipple, "Cleveland in Conflict: A Study in Urban Adolescence, 1876–1900," (Ph.D. dissertation, Western Reserve University, 1951), pp. 337–345. Every Cleveland mayor from Charles A. Otis (1873–1874) to George W. Gardner (1889–1890) complained about the weak mayor system: *Annual Reports* (1873–1891), *passim*.
20. *Annual Report*, "Annual Message of Mayor Benton D. Babcock," (1888), p. ix.
21. *Annual Report*, "Annual Message of Mayor Charles A. Otis," (1873), p. 24.
22. *Annual Report*, "Annual Message of Mayor Nathan Perry Payne," (1874), p. xvi.
23. *Annual Report*, "Annual Message of Mayor R. R. Herrick," (1878), p. 55.
24. Farley served two terms as mayor of Cleveland, 1883–1883 and 1899–1900.
25. *Annual Report*, "Annual Message of Mayor John H. Farley," (1883), n.p.
26. *Annual Report*, "Annual Message of Mayor George Gardner," (1886), p. xxv.
27. *Annual Report*, "The Farewell Address of Mayor Brenton D. Babcock," (1888), p. ix.
28. Ibid.
29. Whipple, pp. 345–346.
30. *Annual Reports*, Payne (1873), p. xxix; Rose (1876), p. 47; Farley (1884), n.p.; Gardner (1886), p. x; Gardner (1889), pp. x–xi; "Annual Message of Mayor Robert Blee," (1893), p. ix.
31. Whipple, p. 348; Gardner (1886), p. x; Farley (1884), p. xii.
32. Farley (1884), p. xiii.
33. Farley (1883), p. x.
34. Ibid.
35. Thomas F. Campbell, "Mounting Crisis and Reform: Cleveland's Political Development," in Thomas F. Campbell and Edward M. Miggins (eds.), *The Birth of Modern Cleveland, 1865–1930* (Cleveland: Western Reserve Historical Society, 1988), p. 301; Thomas F. Campbell, "Background for Progressivism: Machine Politics in the Administration of Robert E. McKisson, Mayor of Cleveland, 1895–1899" (M.A. Thesis, Western Reserve University, 1960), pp. 17–18; Whipple, "Cleveland in Conflict," pp. 353.
36. Ibid.
37. Campbell, "Mounting Crisis and Reform," pp. 309–315; James F. Richardson, "Political Reform in Cleveland," in David D. Van Tassel and John J. Grabowski (eds.), *Cleveland: A Tradition of Reform* (Kent, OH: The Kent State University Press, 1986), p. 158.

NOTES TO CHAPTER 3

1. See Methodological Note 1.
2. Glenn Porter, *The Rise of Big Business, 1860–1910* (New York: Thomas Y. Crowell 1973), pp. 29–37; C. Joseph Pusateri, *A History of American Business*, 2nd ed. (Arlington Heights, IL: Harlan Davidson, 1988), pp. 199–228; Alfred D. Chandler, *The Visible Hand: The Managerial Revolution in American Business* (Cambridge, MA: The Belknap Press of Harvard University Press, 1977), pp. 13–78, 287–314.
3. Naphtali Hoffman, "The Process of Economic Development in Cleveland, 1825–1920" (Ph.D. dissertation, Case Western Reserve University, 1980), ch. 3, pp. 1–69.
4. See Methodological Note 5.
5. Hoffman, ch. 4, pp. 4–14.
6. See Methodological Note 5.

7. *Visible Hand*, pp. 36–47.
8. Hoffman, ch. 4, pp. 12–14.
9. Gunnar Alexandersson, *Geography of Manufacturing* (Englewood Cliffs, NJ: Prentice Hall, 1967), pp. 32–138; Wilbur R. Thompson, *A Preface to Urban Economics* (Baltimore: The Johns Hopkins Press, 1965), pp. 28–33.
10. Hoffman, ch. 3, p. 13.
11. See Methodological Note 1.
12. City of Cleveland, *Annual Report*, Inaugural Address of Mayor Nathan Perry Payne (1873), p. xxvii; Annual Message of Mayor W. G. Rose (1876), p. 9; Inaugural Address of Mayor R. R. Herrick (1878), p. 57.
13. See Methodological Note 1.
14. William Cronon, *Nature's Metropolis: Chicago and the Great West* (New York: W.W. Norton, 1991), pp. 97–147; Hoffman, ch. 2, pp. 10–27.
15. Harold C. Livesay, "From Steeples to Smokestacks: The Birth of the Modern Corporation in Cleveland," in Thomas F. Campbell and Edward M. Miggins (eds.), *The Birth of Modern Cleveland, 1865–1830* (Cleveland: The Western Reserve Historical Society, 1988), pp. 55–56; Cronon, *Nature's Metropolis*, pp. 148–206; Hoffman, ch. 3, pp. 15–17.
16. Hoffman, ch.3, p. 22, 37–44.
17. *Annual Reports*, N. P. Payne (1873), pp. xxvi–xxvii; W. G. Rose (1876), p. 9; R. R. Herrick (1878), p. 59; J. H. Farley (1883), p. xvii; G. W. Gardner (1886), p. xvi; W. G. Rose (1891), pp. xxii–xxiv.
18. Ibid.
19. Farley (1883), p. xvii.
20. Gardner (1886), p. xvi.
21. Ibid.
22. Rose (1891), p. xxiv.
23. Blee (1893), p. xv; McKisson (1895), p. xii.
24. Whipple, p. 345.
25. Maurice Yeates and Barry Garner, *The North American City*, 3rd. ed. (New York: Harper & Row, 1980), p. 462; Truman A. Hartshorn, *Interpreting the City: An Urban Geography* (New York: John Wiley & Sons, 1980), pp. 40–41; Paul L. Knox, *Urbanization: An Introduction to Urban Geography* (Englewood Cliffs, NJ: Prentice Hall, 1994), pp. 393–394.
26. Allan R. Pred, *The Spatial Dynamics of U.S. Urban Industrial Growth, 1800–1914* (Cambridge: MIT Press, 1966), ch. 4; Wilbur R. Thompson, *A Preface to Urban Economics* (Baltimore: The Johns Hopkins Press, 1965), pp. 11–18; Edwin S. Mills and Bruce W. Hamilton, *Urban Economics*, 5th ed. (New York: HarperCollins College Publishers, 1994), pp. 7–30.
27. Methodological Note 1.
28. W. G. Rose (1877), p. 20.
29. R. R. Herrick (1878), pp. 56–57.
30. Otis (1873), pp. 20–21.
31. Methodological Note 1; City of Cleveland, *City Council Proceedings*, 16 April 1877; Herrick (1878), pp. 56–57.
32. Payne (1876), p. xxvi.
33. Ibid.
34. Ibid.; Herrick (1878), pp. 56–57; Herrick (1880), pp. 22–25; Herrick (1881),

p.16.
35. Otis (1873), pp. 19–21.
36. Ibid.; Rose (1878), pp. 56–57; City of Cleveland, Division of Engineering and Construction, *Annexations to City of Cleveland* (for use with wall map) (1954).
37. *Council Proceedings,* 16 April 1877.
38. Otis (1873), pp. 20–21.
39. *Annexations.*

NOTES TO CHAPTER 4

1. Jon C. Teaford, *The Unheralded Triumph: City Government in America, 1870–1900* (Baltimore: The Johns Hopkins University Press, 1984), pp. 218–219.
2. James B. Whipple, "Cleveland in Conflict: A Study of Urban Adolescence, 1876–1900" (Ph.D. diss., Western Reserve University, 1951); Thomas F. Campbell, "Background for Progressivism: Machine Politics in the Administration of Mayor Robert E. McKisson, 1895–1899" (M.A. Thesis, Western Reserve University, 1960).
3. See chapters 2 and 3.
4. *The Encyclopedia of Cleveland History,* David D. Van Tassel and John J. Grabowski, eds. (Bloomington: Indiana University Press, 1987), p. 133.
5. Darwin H. Stapleton, "The City Industrious: How Technology Transformed Cleveland," in Thomas F. Campbell and Edward M. Miggins (eds.), *The Birth of Modern Cleveland, 1865–1930* (Cleveland: Western Reserve Historical Society, 1988), pp. 78–81.
6. For the gas industry, see City of Cleveland, "Citizens Gas Light Company," Ordinance, 6 April 1854; *Ordinances* (1872), pp. 149–150; (1890), pp. 145–155; *Annual Report,* "Annual Message of Mayor George W. Gardner," (1886), n.p.
7. City of Cleveland, *Revised Ordinances* (1907), p. 671.
8. *Encyclopedia,* pp. 369–371; 230; Thomas F. Campbell, "Municipal Ownership," pp 699–703.
9. David Ward, *Cities and Immigrants: A Geography of Change in Nineteenth Century America* (New York: Oxford University Press, 1971), pp. 125–139; Edmund H. Chapman, *Cleveland: Village to Metropolis: A Case Study of Problems of Urban Development in Nineteenth Century America* (Cleveland: The Western Reserve Historical Society, 1964), pp. 112–114.
10. City of Cleveland, *Municipal Ordinances* (1853).
11. Ibid.
12. City of Cleveland, *Special Ordinances* (1890), p. 675.
13. Campbell, "Municipal Ownership," p. 700; David R. Goldfield and Blaine A. Brownell, *Urban America,* 2nd ed., (Boston: Houghton Mifflin Company, 1990), p. 263; Howard P. Chudacoff, *The Evolution of American Society,* 2nd ed.,(Englewood Cliffs, NJ: Prentice Hall, Inc., 1981), p. 80. State legislators deemed municipal ownership unwise because of its cost. The street railway industry had to raise large amounts of capital to meet operating expenses and capital equipment purchases. Financial uncertainty was further magnified by rapidly changing technology. Each technological change prompted a new round of capital investment. The state legislature had no confidence that strained municipal treasuries and fledgling municipal bureaucracies could meet these challenges.
14. *Special Ordinances* (1890), pp. 669–888.

15. Ibid.
16. Ibid., p. 329.
17. For the 1899 Cleveland streetcar strike, see *Encyclopedia*, p. 230; Shelton Stromquist, "The Crucible of Class: Cleveland Politics and the Origins of Municipal Reform in the Progressive Era," *Journal of Urban History* 23 (January, 1997), 200–203; Jean Y. Tussey, "An Introduction to the History of the Cleveland Labor Movement, 1865–1929," A Special Reprint for the Cleveland Bicentennial Year from *The Cleveland Citizen* (March–May, 1995), pp. 10–11.
18. *Special Ordinances* (1890), pp. 669–888 contains the text of the grants made to 17 of the city's street railways between 1869 and 1900.
19. Ibid.; Whipple, p. 362; Farley (1883), p. xxii.
20. *Special Ordinances* (1890), p. 669; *Encyclopedia*, pp. 230, 1005; Whipple, pp. 361–362.
21. City of Cleveland, *City Charter* (1852).
22. Goldfield and Brownell, p. 263; Monkkonen, pp. 80–81; *Special Ordinances*, p. 329.
23. Municipal Association of Cleveland, *Bulletin of the Municipal Association: The City of Cleveland and the Street Railway Question* [by Frederic C. Howe] (15 November 1897), p. 16.
24. *Special Ordinances* (1890), pp. 669–888; *Encyclopedia*, pp. 230, 1003; Whipple, p. 81.
25. Whipple, pp. 361–362.
26. Ibid.
27. Campbell, "Background for Progressivism," pp. 36–97; Campbell, "Mounting Crisis and Reform, pp. 300–303; Frederic C. Howe, *Confessions of a Reformer*, intro. by John Braeman (Chicago: Quadrangle, 1967), pp. 85–87.
28. See the full citation in note 23.
29. Howe, *Street Railway Question*, p. 15.
30. Ibid.
31. Ibid., p. 16.
32. Howe, *Street Railway Question*, pp. 11–16.
33. Ibid., p. 11.
34. Ibid., p. 6.
35. Whipple, p. 362.
36. Ibid.; *Council Proceedings* (5 February 1900); Whipple, pp. 360–361.
37. Campbell, "Background for Progressivism," pp. 37–97; Campbell, "Mounting Crisis," pp. 300–303.
38. Ibid.
39. Municipal Association of Cleveland, *Concerning the Republican and Democratic Candidates for Mayor at the City Election*, Bulletin No. 11 (3 April 1899); Howe, *Confessions*, pp. 85–86.
40. *Council Proceedings* (4 March 1901), p. 447.
41. Ibid.
42. A century after the fall of the Populist Regime, in yet another era of fiscal constraint, contracting is again in vogue but is known by the more modern euphemisms "privatization" and "outsourcing," which appear to be old garbage in new pails.
43. Martin V. Melosi, *Garbage in the Cities: Refuse, Reform, and the Environment, 1880–1980* (Chicago: The Dorsey Press, 1981), pp. 29–30.
44. City of Cleveland, *Annual Report*, "Annual Message of Mayor R. R. Herrick"

(1880), p. 22.
45. Melosi, pp. 45–46.
46. Mayor B. D. Babcock (1887), p. xii.
47. Bulletin No. 11, pp. 32–33; Whipple, p. 347.
48. Whipple, p. 347.
49. Melosi, pp. 113–159; on the volume of horse manure and urine, see Teaford, p. 231, a statistic confirmed by the Republican National Committee, an organization whose authority on the substances in question is unassailable.
50. Melosi, pp. 113–159.
51. Ibid., p. 113.
52. The *Annual Reports* and the *Council Proceedings* make repeated references to the issue: a sampling is offered in N. P. Payne (1873), p. xxix; *Council Proceedings* (20 May 1878); Farley (1882), n.p.; Farley (1884), p. x; Gardner (1889), pp. x–xi; Blee (1893), p. ix; McKisson (1898), n.p.; Bulletin No. 11, p. 7.
53. Bulletin No. 11, pp. 5–6.
54. Farley (1882), n.p.; Gardner (1886), p. x; Whipple, pp. 337–343.
55. Bulletin No. 11, p. 33; Whipple, p. 348.
56. Brian Harrison, "Pubs," in H. J. Dyos and Michael Wolff (eds.), *The Victorian City: Images and Realities*, 2 vols. (London: Routledge & Kegan Paul, 1973), I, pp. 161–190.
57. Bulletin No. 11, pp. 5, 33.
58. Miggins, "Education Reform," pp. 142–143; Miggins, "Becoming American: Americanization and the Reform of the Cleveland Public Schools," in Thomas F. Campbell and Edward M. Miggins (eds.), *The Birth of Modern Cleveland, 1865–1930* (Cleveland: Western Reserve Historical Society, 1988), pp. 345–349.
59. Ibid.; school board demographics are taken from the *Cleveland City Directory* (1885).
60. Miggins, "Becoming American," pp. 350–352.
61. Ibid.
62. *Cleveland City Directory* (1892–1893).
63. "Becoming American," pp. 350–353; "Educational Reform," pp. 144–148.
64. "Becoming American," pp. 351–354.
65. Harold Perkin, *Origins of Modern English Society* (London: Routledge, 1969), pp. 263–264, 446–448 and *The Rise of Professional Society: England Since 1880* (London: Routledge, 1989), pp. 123–125; Walter I. Trattner, *From Poor Law to Welfare State: A History of Social Welfare in America*, 3rd ed. (New York: Free Press, 1984), pp. 77–107; Edward M. Miggins, "A City of 'Uplifting Influences': From 'Sweet Charity' to Modern Social Welfare and Philanthropy," in Campbell and Miggins (eds.), *The Birth of Modern Cleveland, 1865–1930*, pp. 141–153; John J. Grabowski, "Social Reform and Philanthropic Order in Cleveland, 1896–1920, in Van Tassel and Grabowski (eds.), *Cleveland: A Tradition of Reform*, pp. 30–33.
66. Michael J. McTighe, *A Measure of Success: Protestants and Public Culture in Antebellum Cleveland* (Albany: State University of New York Press, 1994), pp. 73–96.
67. Methodological Note 1.
68. The criticism was acknowledged in official publications, for example: City of Cleveland, *Annual Report*, "The Annual Report of the Police Commissioners (1873), pp. 328–33; "The Annual Message of Mayor W. G. Rose" (1876), p. 36; *Council Proceedings* (16 April 1877); *Annual Report* (1880), pp. 393–393; "The Annual Message of Mayor G.

W. Gardner (1885), pp. xxx–xxxix; "Annual Report of the Department of Charities and Corrections" (1893–1899). The 1894 Charities and Corrections report shows that the number of families served increased from 1,841 in 1891 to 6,011 in the 1894 recession year but that the amount spent per family decreased from $13.18 to $8.15.

69. See Methodological Note 1; Whipple, "Cleveland in Crisis," pp. 337–343. In 2003, the city of Cleveland had 9,400 employees serving a population of approximately 490,000, or a ratio of 1 to 52. *Plain Dealer*, 10 September 2003.

70. Municipal Association, Bulletin No. 11, pp. 5–17.

NOTES TO CHAPTER 5

1. The individualist/collectivist distinction is made in Harold Perkin *Origins of Modern English Society* (London: Routledge, 1969), pp. 221–229. Perkin traces individualism to preindustrial society, and so too does Ira Katznelson, *Marxism and the City* (Oxford: Clarendon Press, 1992), p. 10–11. Katznelson further notes that collective identities, such as that manifested by professionals, were the product of the nineteenth century industrial city. In these renderings, the individualistic entrepreneur, paradoxically, was at odds with the city he had done much to create.

2. *Origins of Modern English Society*, pp. 312–313; Perkin, *Rise of Professional Society*, pp. 135–141.

3. *Origins of Modern English Society*, pp. 319–321; Robert H. Wiebe, *The Search for Order, 1877–1920* (New York: Hill and Wang, 1967), pp. 111–132.

4. Cleveland Chamber of Commerce, *Annual Report* (1895), pp. 114–121.

5. Murdock, *Tom Johnson*, pp. 23–30; Peter d'A. Jones, *Henry George and British Socialism* (New York: Garland, 1991), pp. 121–123.

6. The positions are clearly stated in City of Cleveland, "Mayor's Message [Tom L. Johnson, 21 April 1902]" *Annual Report* (1901), p. x; Cleveland Chamber of Commerce, *Annual Report* (1908), pp. 83–84.

7. Frederic C. Howe, "Cleveland's Education Through Its Chamber of Commerce," *Outlook*, LXXXIII (July 28, 1906), 745; J. J. Sullivan and F. A. Scott, "Chamber of Commerce," *Harper's Weekly*, XLVIII (April 23, 1904), 628.

8. Cleveland Chamber of Commerce, "Minutes," 20 December 1899.

9. Cleveland Chamber of Commerce, *Serving Cleveland since 1848*.

10. Cleveland Chamber of Commerce, *Annual Reports* (1899–1919).

11. Ibid.

12. CCC, *Annual Report* (1895), pp. 115–121.

13. Ibid, pp. 116–117.

14. CCC, Minutes, 20 December 1899.

15. Citizens League of Cleveland, *75 Years of Doing Good: The Story of the Citizens League* (1971), pp. 7–14.

16. The various Bulletins of the organization make this point clear, particularly the famous Bulletin No.11 denouncing the McKisson administration.

17. Eugene C. Murdock, *Tom Johnson of Cleveland* (Dayton, OH: Wright State University Press, 1994), pp. 177–184; Kenneth Finegold, *Experts and Politicians: Reform Challenges to Machine Politics in New York, Cleveland, and Chicago* (Princeton: Princeton University Press, 1995), pp. 69–118. Finegold characterizes Johnson as a populist reformer who made ample use of experts in his administration. I identify Johnson as an

entrepreneur, owner of street rail companies and a steel mill, who was accustomed to working with professionals in his business enterprises. It was natural that he would govern with them. Johnson was part of the Corporate Regime, not the Populist Regime. The mantra of his administration was honesty and efficiency, something decidedly lacking in the Populist Regime which preceded him.

18. *75 Years*, pp. 7–14; *Encyclopedia of Cleveland History*, pp. 184–185.

19. The tax reform label may be a misnomer because implied in the concept of reform is improvement by removal of abuses. Some abuses were removed during the Corporate Regime, but in the main what was achieved under the rubric of tax reform in the Corporate and Realty eras was tax burden shifting from the several varieties of capital to the home owner.

20. Perkin, *Origins of Modern English Society*, pp. 222–237.

21. Tom L. Johnson fulminated mightily against the tax code's favoritism toward inactive, passive, and monopoly capital. See his *My Story*, ed. by Elizabeth Hauser (Kent, OH: Kent State University Press, 1993 [c. 1911]), passim; Frederic C. Howe, *The Confessions of a Reformer* (Chicago: Quadrangle Books, 1967 [c. 1925]), pp. 225–230; and Johnson's annual address, City of Cleveland, *Annual Report*, "Mayor's Message," 4 May 1904. The Cleveland Chamber of Commerce made similar distinctions between types of capital and the taxation of each and expressed similar sentiments in *Annual Report* (1895), p. 52; *AR* (1905), p. 74; *AR* (1908), pp. 83–84; *AR* (1912), p. 110.

22. Ibid.

23. *My Story*, pp. 125–131; "Mayor's Message," 21 April 1902; 4 May 1904; 1 May 1905; *Confessions*, pp. 225–230; William W. Suit, "Tom Loftin Johnson: Businessman Reformer" (Ph.D. diss. , Kent State University, 1988), pp. 170–182; Murdock, pp. 177–184.

24. *My Story*, pp. 125–31, and Mayor's Messages just cited.

25. "Mayor's Message," 21 April 1902; 4 May 1904; Suit, pp. 170–182; Robert H. Bremner, "The Single Tax Philosophy in Cleveland and Toledo," *American Journal of Economics and Sociology*, IX, No. 3 (April, 1949), 369–376; Robert H. Bremner, "Tax Equalization in Cleveland," *American Journal of Economics and Sociology*, X, No. 3 (April, 1951), 301–312.

26. *Confessions*, pp. 225–230; Murdock, pp. 89–103.

27. Johnson's position is explained in his "Mayor's Messages," 1901; *My Story*, pp. 125–131; Frederic C. Howe's *Confessions of a Reformer*, pp. 225–230; Suit, pp. 170–182. The Cleveland Chamber of Commerce addressed the tax issue in its previously cited *Annual Reports* in 1895, 1908, and 1914.

28. The Cleveland Chamber of Commerce did not reject municipal ownership until 1914. The Chamber was divided on the issue until the streetcar crisis of the Johnson administration and Mayor Baker's drive for a municipal light plant forced the organization to choose between regulation and public ownership. The Chamber, however, agreed with Johnson, Howe, and Baker that the transit and utilities companies should be taxed more heavily than they were. Early in the Corporate Regime, when the chamber was dominated by entrepreneurs such as Samuel Mather, municipal ownership was given a fair hearing largely because English entrepreneur Joseph Chamberlain had been successful with it when he was mayor of Birmingham.

29. Several bridge schemes and minor buildings in the Group Plan were repeatedly rejected by home owning voters during the Corporate Regime.

30. Even now, forty years after its publication, the flow of American society in the

industrial era is still most deftly explained in Samuel P. Hays, *The Response to Industrialism, 1885–1914* (Chicago: University of Chicago Press, 1957), especially pp. 4–115; on the economic geography of manufacturing, see Gunnar Alexandersson, *Geography of Manufacturing* (Englewood Cliffs, NJ: Prentice Hall, 1967), pp. 32–136; on the evolving structure of the business organization, see Alfred D. Chandler, Jr., *Scale and Scope: The Dynamics of Industrial Capitalism* (Cambridge: The Belknap Press of Harvard University Press, 1990), pp. 38–49; and on the sums and parts of organizations, see Gareth Morgan, *Images of Organization* (Newbury Park: Sage Publications, 1986), pp. 19–38; Bill McKelvey, *Organizational Systematics: Taxonomy, Evolution, Classification* (Berkeley: University of California Press, 1982), pp. 34–66; W. Richard Scott, *Organizations: Rational, Natural, and Open Systems* (Englewood Cliffs: Prentice Hall, 1992), pp. 3–50.

31. Gabriel Kolko was the first historian to acknowledge the ascending scale of business–government supplication in his *Triumph of Conservatism: A Reinterpretation of American History, 1900–1916* (New York: The Free Press, 1963).

32. Alfred D. Chandler, Jr.'s previously cited *Scale and Scope* explains the merger movement by industry as does his *The Visible Hand: The Managerial Revolution in American Business* (Cambridge: The Belknap Press of Harvard University Press, 1977), while the local manifestations of the merger movement can be traced in the company histories found in David D. Van Tassel and John J. Grabowski (eds.), *The Encyclopedia of Cleveland History* (Bloomington: University of Indiana Press, 1987). Lawyer Frederick H. Goff helped effect the mergers of local companies into multilocational corporations, and as president of Cleveland Trust bank he managed the estates of local entrepreneurs.

33. Cleveland Chamber of Commerce, *Annual Reports*, 1895–1919.

34. Ronald R. Weiner, "A History of Civic Land Use Decision Making in the Cleveland Metropolitan Area, 1880–1930," (Ph.D. diss, Kent State University, 1974), p. 74 [Table 2].

35. Occupational data was gathered from the U.S. Census and sorted in Standard Industrial Classifications for the years 1880, 1890, 1900, 1910, 1920, and 1930 in a time line series, hereinafter cited as Occupational Time Line Series. U.S. Census (1880), I, *Population*, Table XXVI, 872; U.S. Census (1890), II, *Population*, Table 117, 628–629; U.S. Census (1900), II, *Population*, Table 94, 558; U.S. Census (1910), III, *Population*, Table VIII, 548–550; U.S. Census (1920), IV, *Population*, Table 19, 150–166; U.S. Census (1930), IV, *Population*, Table 3, 1240–1248.

36. Ibid.

37. Ibid.

38. See note 33 above.

39. Alan R. Pred, *The Spatial Dynamics of U.S. Urban-Industrial Growth, 1800–1914* (Cambridge: MIT Press, 1966).

40. *Encyclopedia*, p. 133.

41. Ibid., p. 1042.

42. Harold C. Livesay, "From Steeples to Smokestacks: The Birth of the Modern Corporation in Cleveland," in Thomas F. Campbell and Edward M. Miggins (eds.), *The Birth of Modern Cleveland, 1865–1930* (Cleveland: Western Reserve Historical Society, 1988), pp. 67–69.

43. Occupational Time Line Series, 1880–1930.

44. Ibid.

45. CCC, *AR* (1895), p. 61, 111; (1903), pp. 5–6.

46. CCC, *AR* (1905), p. 114.
47. CCC, *AR* (1903), pp. 118–122.
48. CCC, *AR* (1913), p. 226; (1908), p. 178.
49. CCC, *AR* (1905), p. 114.
50. CCC, *AR* (1911), pp. 144–148.
51. CCC, *AR* (1909).
52. CCC, *AR* (1911), pp. 144–148.
53. CCC, *AR* (1913), p. 99.
54. CCC, *AR* (1911), pp. 72–73; (1911), pp. 72–73; (1913), pp. 163–170.

NOTES TO CHAPTER 6

1. David Schuyler, *The New Urban Landscape: The Redefinition of City Form in Nineteenth-Century America* (Baltimore: The Johns Hopkins University Press, 1986), pp. 59–76.

2. Leslie F. Speir, *Cleveland: Our Community and Its Development* (Cleveland: Cleveland Public Schools, 1941), pp. 96–101; Carol Poh Miller, "Parks," in David D. Van Tassel and John J. Grabowski (eds.), *The Encyclopedia of Cleveland History* (Bloomington: University of Indiana Press, 1987), pp. 752–754.

3. Ibid.
4. Ibid.
5. Miller, "Parks," p. 753.
6. Spier, *Cleveland*, p. 96.
7. *Encyclopedia*, p. 926.

8. Paul Boyer, *Urban Masses and Moral Order in America, 1820–1920* (Cambridge: Harvard University Press, 1976), p. 224; D. W. Meinig, "Symbolic Landscapes: Models of American Community, in D. W. Meinig (ed.), *The Interpretation of Ordinary Landscapes: Geographical Essays* (New York: Oxford University Press, 1979), pp. 164–192.

9. *New Urban Landscape*, p. 144; Speir, *Cleveland*, p. 69; Metropolitan Park District, *First Annual Report* (1917–1918), p. 49.

10. Speir, *Cleveland*, p. 69.
11. Ohio Laws 459.

12. Works Progress Administration, *Cuyahoga County Archives Guide* (Washington: U.S. Government Printing Office, 1938), p. 275.

13. Ibid.; Metropolitan Parks Board, *First Annual Report*, p. 9; *Cleveland News* (29 December 1929).

14. Ibid.; William Ganson Rose, *Cleveland: The Making of a City* (Cleveland: World Publishing, 1950), p. 701.

15. *New Urban Landscape*, p. 174; *Urban Masses*, pp. 233–251.
16. Ohio Laws 65.

17. O.L. 65; 113 O.L. 659; 108 O.L. 1098; WPA, *Guide*, p. 275; MPD, *First Annual Report*, pp. 7–9; Cleveland *Plain Dealer* (31 December 1964).

18. *Plain Dealer* (31 December 1964).

19. The standard treatments of parks include Mel Scott, *American City Planning Since 1890* (Berkeley: University of California Press, 1969), pp. 10–30; John W. Reps, *The Making of Urban America: A History of City Planning in the United States* (Prince-

Notes to Chapter 6

ton: Princeton University Press, 1965), pp. 325–348; and the previously cited, David Schuyler, *The New Urban Landscape*, pp. 59–148; and Paul Boyer, *Urban Masses and Moral Order*, pp. 220–251; and for comment critical of Schuyler, see W. Edward Orser, "The Contested Terrain of 19th century Urban Landscape Design," *American Quarterly,* v. 10, no. 4 (December, 1988), 550–555.

20. CCC, "Minutes" (20 October 1896), pp. 2–7.
21. Speir, *Cleveland*, pp. 96–101.
22. CCC, "Minutes" ([E. W. Bowditch Speech] 20 October 1896), pp. 2–7.
23. Ibid.; Geoffrey Blodgett, "Frederick Law Olmsted: Landscape Architecture as Conservative Reform," *Journal of American History,* LXII, No. 4 (March, 1976), 883––888.
24. Ibid.
25. Board of Park Commissioners, *Annual Report* (1897), frontispiece, n.p.
26. BPC, *Annual Report* (1895), p. 32.
27. Miller, "Parks," p. 753; Robert H. Bremner, "Humanizing Cleveland and Toledo," *American Journal of Economics and Sociology,* XIII, No. 2 (January, 1953), 179–190; Thomas F. Campbell, *Daniel Morgan, 1877–1949: The Good Citizen in Politics* (Cleveland: Western Reserve University Press, 1966), pp. 40–41.
28. See Methodological Note 1.
29. See chapter 5.
30. Murdock, *Tom Johnson,* p. 173; *Plain Dealer* (24 March 1913).
31. Ibid.
32. CCC, Municipal Art and Architecture Committee, "Minutes" (16 January 1911); (12 June 1912).
33. "A Recreation Plan for Cleveland," *The Survey,* 26 (12 August 1911), 690.
34. George Burnap, *Parks: Their Design, Equipment, and Use* (Philadelphia: Lippincott, 1916); see also Boyer, *Urban Masses,* pp. 241–244.
35. Ibid.; John J. Grabowski, "Social Reform and Philanthropic Order in Cleveland, 1896–1920," in David D. Van Tassel and John J. Grabowski, (eds.) *Cleveland: A Tradition of Reform* (Kent, OH: The Kent State University Press, 1986), pp. 30–49.
36. Miller, "Parks," pp. 752–753.
37. Frederick Law Olmsted, "Cleveland's Planning Needs: Radial Thoroughfares and County Parks," *Proceedings of the Eighth Annual Conference on City Planning, Cleveland, June 5–7, 1916* (New York: National Conference on City Planning, 1916), pp. 8–13.
38. Ibid.; Cleveland Metropolitan Park System, Board of Park Commissioners, *Annual Report* (1917–1918), p. 13.
39. "Cleveland's Planning Needs," p. 11.
40. Ibid., pp. 8–13.
41. CMPS, Board of Park Commissioners, *Annual Report* (1929), map; *Cleveland Press* (4 July 1930).
42. Ibid.
43. CMPS, *Annual Report* (1929), n.p.; WPA, *County Archives Guide,* p. 275.
44. The anti-regionalism of the Realty Regime is explained in chapter 12.
45. *State ex. rel. Stanton,* 108 Ohio St. 497, 141 NE 322; *Cleveland News* (26 December 1929).
46. *Pontiac Improvement Company vs. Cleveland Metropolitan Park District,* 104 Ohio St. 447, 135, NE 635, 23 ALR 866.

NOTES TO CHAPTER 7

1. Mel Scott, *American City Planning Since 1890* (Berkeley: University of California Press, 1969), pp. 47–182; John W. Reps, *The Making of Urban America: A History of City Planning in the United States* (Princeton: Princeton University Press, 1965), pp. 497–526; Anthony Sutcliffe, *Towards the Planned City: Germany, Britain, the United States and France* (Oxford: Basil Blackwell, 1981); Jon A. Peterson, "The City Beautiful Movement: Forgotten Origins and Lost Meanings," *Journal of Urban History* 2 (August 1976), 415–434; David Schuyler, *The New Urban Landscape: The Redefinition of City Form in the Nineteenth Century* (Baltimore: The Johns Hopkins University Press, 1986), pp. 180–195.

2. Ronald R. Weiner, "A History of Civic Land Use Decision Making in the Cleveland Metropolitan Region, 1880–1930" (Ph.D. diss., Kent State University, 1974), pp. 35–43, Appendix I, Figs. 3–8.

3. Ibid.; Edmund H. Chapman, *Cleveland: Village to Metropolis: A Case Study of Problems of Urban Development in Nineteenth Century America* (Cleveland: The Western Reserve Historical Society, 1964), pp. 151–155.

4. Frederic C. Howe, *The Confessions of a Reformer* (Chicago: Quadrangle Books, 1967 [c. 1925]), pp. 80–84.

5. Ibid.; Cleveland Chamber of Commerce, "The Public Buildings of Europe," An Address by Liberty E. Holden (20 May 1901).

6. Cleveland Chamber of Commerce, Public Building Committee, "Minutes" (4 March 1899; 10 March 1899; 24 August 1899; 19 December 1899).

7. The role of the Cleveland Chamber of Commerce can be traced in the annual reports and weekly minutes of its committees: see Committee on City Plan (originally Committee on Municipal Art and Architecture), *Annual Reports* (1899–1929); see also City of Cleveland, Board of Supervision of Public Buildings and Grounds, *The Group Plan of the Buildings of the City of Cleveland: Report Made to the Hon. Tom L. Johnson, and to the Hon. Board of Public Service by Daniel Burnham, John M. Carrere, Arnold Brunner, Board of Supervision* (New York: Cheltenham Press, August, 1903); City of Cleveland, City Planning Commission, *Annual Reports* (1913–1929); City Planning Commission, "Minutes" (1 July 1913–30 December 1920); City Planning Commission, "The Cleveland Mall Forty Years After" (1 September 1936).

8. Cleveland Chamber of Commerce, "Minutes" (22 January 1902).

9. Edwin Childs Baxter, "The Grouping of Public Buildings in Cleveland," *Review of Reviews*, XXXI (May, 1905), 561–566; Ward A. Roberts, "Civic Art in Cleveland, Ohio," *Craftsman*, IX (October, 1905), 41–55.

10. Board of Supervision, *Group Plan*, pp. 9–17; Arnold M. Brunner, "Cleveland's Group Plan," *Proceedings of the Eighth Annual Conference on City Planning. Cleveland, June 5–7, 1916* (New York: National Conference on City Planning, 1916), p. 24.

11. Brunner, "Group Plan," p. 24.

12. Board of Supervision, *Group Plan*, p. 15.

13. Ibid., pp. 12–13.

14. *The Cleveland Mall Forty Years After*; Cleveland Chamber of Commerce, *The Union Station: On the Lake Front or on the Public Square* (1918).

15. Darwin H. Stapleton, "Philanthropy and Community: The Creation of University Circle in Cleveland, 1880–1930," A Paper Delivered at the Great Lakes American Studies Association Annual Conference, Cleveland, Ohio (October 12–13, 1990), pp. 1–25.

16. Ibid, pp. 5–8.
17. C. H. Cramer, *Case Western Reserve: A History of the University, 1826–1976* (Boston: Little, Brown and Company, 1976), pp. 106–114.
18. Ibid., pp. 197–220.
19. Stapleton, pp. 15–17; Prudence B. Randall, "The Making of Progressivism in Urban School Reform, 1900–1909" (Ph.D. diss., Case Western Reserve University, 1971), pp. 98–99.
20. Stanley L. McMichael, "The Romance of Real Estate in Cleveland" [pamphlet] (1919), p. 6; *Cleveland Realtor* (12 July 1926), p. 2.
21. Cleveland Chamber of Commerce, "Minutes," vol. 2, Committee on City Plan, University Circle Subcommittee (1 August 1918).
22. *Encyclopedia*, p. 530.
23. Subcommittee on University Circle (7 January 1918).
24. Cleveland *Plain Dealer*, 8 June 1926; *Cleveland Press*, 16 December 1926.
25. Cramer, pp. 106–120.
26. Cleveland *Plain Dealer*, 26 December 1926, 20 April 1959; *Cleveland News*, 8 January 1930.
27. The anthropologist Clifford Geertz has observed that "at the center of any complexly organized society there is both a governing elite and a set of symbolic forms expressing the fact that it is in truth governing"; see his *Local Knowledge: Further Essays in Interpretive Anthropology* (New York: Basic Books, 1983), p. 124.
28. For interpretation of built environments, I have been guided by the following: Pierce F. Lewis, "Axioms for Reading the Landscape: Some Guides to the American Scene," in D. W. Meinig (ed.), *The Interpretation of Ordinary Landscapes* (New York: Oxford University Press, 1979), pp. 15–27; D. W. Meinig, "Symbolic Landscapes: Models of American Community," also in Meinig (ed.), pp. 165–172; Denis Cosgrove and Stephen Daniels, "Introduction: Iconography and Landscape," in Denis Cosgrove and Stephen Daniels (eds.), *The Iconography of Landscape* (Cambridge: Cambridge University Press, 1988), pp. 1–10; David Schuyler, *The New Urban Landscape: The Redefinition of City Form in Nineteenth-Century America* (Baltimore: The Johns Hopkins University Press, 1986), pp. 180–196; "A Bourgeois Puts His World in Order: The City as a Text," which is chapter 3 in Robert Darnton, *The Great Cat Massacre and Other Episodes in French Cultural History* (New York: Vintage Books, 1985), pp. 107–143; Erwin Panofsky, *Gothic Architecture and Scholasticism* (Cleveland: A Meridian Book by the World Publishing Company, 1957).
29. Geertz, pp. 120–146.
30. Mark Gottdiener, *The New Urban Sociology* (New York: McGraw-Hill, 1994), p. 17.
31. Two contrasting contemporary views are presented by C. M. Robinson, *Modern Civic Art, or The City Made Beautiful* (New York: G.P. Putnam's Sons, 1903), p. 246 and Stanley L. McMichael and Robert F. Bingham, *City Growth and Values* (Cleveland: The Stanley McMichael Publishing Organization, 1923), p. 74.
32. Ibid.
33. Gottdiener, p. 17.
34. William H. Wilson, "The Seattle Park System and the Ideal of the City Beautiful," in Daniel Schaffer (ed.), *Two Centuries of American Planning* (Baltimore: The Johns Hopkins University Press, 1988), p. 119.
35. Brunner, op cit.; for the invention of tradition, see Eric Hobsbawm, *The Age of Empire, 1875–1914* (New York: Vintage Books, 1989 [c. 1987]), pp. 105–106.

36. Schuyler, p. 190; Walter C. Leedy, Jr., *Cleveland Builds an Art Museum: Patronage, Politics, and Architecture, 1884–1916* (Cleveland: Cleveland Museum of Art, 1991), p. 17; Walter C. Leedy, Jr., "Cleveland's Struggle for Self-Identity: Aesthetics, Economics, and Politics," in R. G. Wilson and Sidney K. Robinson (eds.), *Modern Architecture in America: Visions and Revisions* (Ames: Iowa State University Press, 1991), pp. 75–105.
37. Schuyler, pp. 190–194.
38. Ibid., pp. 149–158.
39. Schuyler, p. 192; Penelope Woolfe, "Symbol of the Second Empire: Cultural Politics and the Paris Opera House," in Cosgrove and Daniels, (eds.) *The Iconography of Landscape*, pp. 219–223; Denis Cosgrove, "The Geometry of Landscape: Practical and Speculative Arts in Sixteenth Century Venetian Land Territories," also in *The Iconography of Landscape*, p. 254.

NOTES TO CHAPTER 8

1. Frederic C. Howe, *The Confessions of a Reformer* (Chicago: Quadrangle Books, 1967 [c. 1925]); Tom L. Johnson, *My Story* (Kent, OH: Kent State University Press, 1993 [c. 1911]); Eugene C. Murdock, *Tom Johnson of Cleveland* (Dayton:Wright State University Press, 1994); Thomas F. Campbell, *Daniel E. Morgan: The Good Citizen in Politics* (Cleveland: The Press of Western Reserve University, 1966).
2. The pattern parallels that noted by David B. Tyack, *The One Best System: A History of American Education* (Cambridge: Harvard University Press, 1974), pp. 6–7.
3. Edward M. Miggins, "The Search for the One Best System: Cleveland Public Schools and Educational Reform, 1836–1920," in David D. Van Tassel and John J. Grabowski (eds.), *Cleveland: A Tradition of Reform* (Kent, OH: The Kent State University Press, 1986), pp. 136–155; Cleveland Board of Education, *Annual Reports*, 1900–1920; *Cleveland City Directory* (Cleveland: various publishers), 1901–1920.
4. Edward M. Miggins, "Becoming American: Americanization and the Reform of the Cleveland Public Schools," in Thomas F. Campbell and Edward M. Miggins (eds.), *The Birth of Modern Cleveland, 1865–1930* (Cleveland: Western Reserve Historical Society, 1988), pp. 345–373.
5. Ibid.
6. Miggins, "The One Best System," pp. 137–151.
7. Prudence B. Randall, "The Meaning of Progressivism in Urban School Reform, 1901–1909" (Ph.D. diss., Case Western Reserve University, 1971), pp. 69–84.
8. Tyack, p. 136.
9. Miggins, "The One Best System," pp. 141–150.
10. Catholic school enrollments were half that of the Cleveland Public Schools throughout the period.
11. Randall, pp. 200–222.
12. Miggins, "The One Best System," p. 151.
13. Ibid., pp. 151–155.
14. Tyack, pp. 200–217.
15. Gareth Morgan, *Images of Organization* (Newbury Park, CA: Sage Publications, 1986), pp. 19–39; Thorstein Veblen, *The Higher Learning in America: A Memorandum on the Conduct of Universities by Businessmen* (New York: B.W. Huebsh, 1918).
16. Miggins, op cit.

17. Ibid.; Edward M. Miggins, "Businessmen, Pedagogues, and Progressive Reform: The Cleveland Foundation's 1915 School Survey," (Ph.D. diss., Case Western Reserve University, 1975).
18. The phrase "one best system" is Tyack's; see above.
19. Cleveland Board of Education, *Annual Reports*, 1914–1922.
20. Ibid.
21. Cleveland Board of Education, *Annual Report*, 1925–26, p. 114; 1931, p. 65; State of Ohio, *Ohio School Report*, 1929–1931, Tables 7 and 114.
22. Kenneth E. Boulding, *The Economy of Love and Fear* (Belmont, CA: Wadsworth, 1973), pp. 1–14; by the same author, *The Organizational Revolution: A Study in the Ethics of Economic Organizations* (Chicago: Quadrangle Paperbacks, 1968 [c. 1953]), pp. xii–xxvi.
23. Thomas Robert Malthus, *An Essay on the Principle of Population* (Harmondsworth, Middlesex, England: Penguin Books, 1970 [c. 1798]), p. 98.
24. Harold Perkin, *Origins of Modern English Society* (London: Routledge, 1969), pp. 420–428.
25. Walter I. Trattner, *From Poor Law to Welfare State: A History of Social Welfare in America*, 3rd ed. (New York: The Free Press, 1984), pp. 252–254.
26. Brian Ross, "The New Philanthropy: The Reorganization of Charity in Turn of the Century Cleveland" (Ph.D. diss., Case Western Reserve University, 1989), p. vii.
27. Howe, *Confessions*, pp. 75–79.
28. Ibid.; Ross, p. 43.
29. John J. Grabowski, "A Social Settlement in a Neighborhood in Transition: Hiram House, Cleveland, Ohio, 1896–1926," (Ph.D. diss., Case Western Reserve University, 1977).
30. Ross, pp. ix, 54.
31. Cleveland Chamber of Commerce, *Annual Reports*, 1911–1918.
32. CCC, *Annual Reports*, 1911, pp. 154–159; 1913, pp. 64–67.
33. CCC, *Annual Reports*, 1919.
34. David D. Van Tassel and John J. Grabowski (eds.), *The Encyclopedia of Cleveland History* (Bloomington: Indiana University Press, 1987), pp. 997–998; Ross, p. 7.
35. James E. Cutler and Maurice Rea Dowie, *A Study in Professional Education at Western Reserve University: The School of Applied Social Sciences* (Cleveland: Western Reserve University Press, 1930); Thomas F. Campbell, *SASS: Fifty Years of Social Work Education* (Cleveland: The Press of Western Reserve University, 1967); C. H. Cramer, *Case Western Reserve: A History of the University, 1826–1976* (Boston: Little, Brown and Company, 1976), pp. 331–337.
36. School of Applied Social Sciences, *Catalogues*, 1917–1920.
37. Ibid.
38. Western Reserve University Alumni Association, *Alumni Directory: Fifty SASS Years, 1916–1966*.
39. SASS, *Catalogues*, 1920–1930; Trattner, pp. 250–254.

NOTES TO CHAPTER 9

1. The Cleveland Real Estate Board (CREB) published its membership lists in *The Realty Record* and its successor publication *The Cleveland Realtor*.

2. CREB publications also listed the officers of what it regarded as "sister organizations."

3. Stanley L. Mcmichael and Robert F. Bingham, *City Growth and Values* (Cleveland: The Stanley Mcmichael Publishing Organization, 1923), p. 132.

4. Ibid.

5. William M. Randle, "Professors, Reformers, Bureaucrats, and Cronies: The Players in Euclid v. Ambler," in Charles M. Haar and Jerold S. Kayden (eds.), *Zoning and the American Dream: Promises Still to Keep* (Chicago: American Planning Association, Planners Press, 1989), pp. 42–47.

6. Chronicled in the weekly issues of the *Realty Record* and *The Cleveland Realtor*, 1920–1930.

7. Ibid.

8. Richard T. Ely and John Wehrwein, *Land Economics* (Madison: The University of Wisconsin Press, 1964 [c. 1940]), pp. v–x; Randle, pp. 42–55; *Cleveland Realtor*, 24 February 1923.

9. See the previously cited *City Growth and Values*; the same authors' *City Growth Essentials* (n.p., n.d.); Stanley L. Mcmichael, *The Romance of Real Estate in Cleveland* (n.p., 1919); Robert F. Bingham and Elmore L. Andrews, *Financing Real Estate* (n.p., 1924).

10. See also John A. Zangerle, *Principles of Real Estate Appraisal* (n.p., 1924).

11. *Cleveland Realtor*, 14 January 1924; Zangerle, op. cit.; Herbert B. Dorau and Albert G. Hinman, *Urban Land Economics* (College Park, MD: McGrath Publishing, 1969 [1928]), pp. 509–536; Richard U. Ratcliff, *Urban Land Economics* (New York: McGraw-Hill, 1949), pp. 355–364.

12. *Cleveland Realtor*, 24 February 1923.

13. Thompson, Hine, and Flory, Office File, 1913–1930 [hereinafter, THF, Office File].

14. Arthur V. N. Brooks, "The Office File Box—Emanations from the Battlefield," in Charles M. Haar and Jerold S. Kayden (eds), *Zoning and the American Dream: Promises Still to Keep* (Chicago: American Planning Association, Planners Press, 1989), pp. 3–30.

15. Cleveland Association of Building Owners and Managers, *Bulletin #8*, 27 November 1920; THF, Office File, Amos Burt Thompson, "Brief of the Cleveland Association of Building Owners and Managers Submitted to John A. Zangerle," 29 August 1924.

16. *Finance and Industry*, 14 June 1919, 27 November 1923; *News Leader*, 14 November 1921; Robert F. Bingham, "Main Street Cleveland," *The Real Estate Outlook*, September, 1922; *Cleveland Realtor*, 11 June 1923; CABOM Brief.

17. Dorau and Hinman, pp. 224–235; Ratcliff, p. 404; *Growth and Values*, pp. 211–227; THF, Office File, Memorandum, Oscar J. Horn, et al. to John A. Zangerle, 11 May 1920.

18. *Cleveland Trust Monthly*, v. 4, #4, April 1923.

19. O. J. Horn Memorandum; CABOM Brief; *Growth and Values*, pp. 216–217.

20. *Growth and Values*, pp. 213–218; THF, Office File, A. B. Thompson Scrapbook, Robert F. Bingham undated, untitled article.

21. Bingham and Mcmichael's ideas were fully expressed in *Growth and Values*.

22. Ibid.

23. Ibid.

24. *Cleveland Trust Monthly*, March 1923; THF, Office File, "Amos Burt Thompson Speech to the Cleveland Bar Association," 5 May 1923.

25. *Cleveland Realtor,* 13 January 1930.
26. *Cleveland Trust Monthly.*
27. *Cleveland Realtor,* 24 December 1928.
28. *Plain Dealer,* 23 January 1923.
29. Ian S. Haberman, *The Van Sweringens of Cleveland: The Biography of an Empire* (Cleveland: The Western Reserve Historical Society, 1979), pp. 133–159.
30. Neal H. Atterman, "The IRS and the Municipal Bond Industry," in Frank J. Fabozzi, Sylvan G. Feldstein, Irving M. Pollack, and Frank Zarb (eds.), *The Municipal Bond Handbook* (Homewood, IL: Dow-Jones-Irwin, 1983), pp. 697–698.
31. John L. Kraft, "The Role of Legal Counsel in Public Agency Financing," in *The Municipal Bond Handbook,* pp. 505–507; David S. Kidwell and Eric N. Sorenson, "Investment Banking and the Underwriting of New Municipal Issues," in *The Municipal Bond Handbook,* pp. 170–171.
32. *Cleveland Realtor,* 13 December 1926, 17 September 1928; *Finance and Industry,* 4 February 1928.
33. *Growth and Values,* p. 345.
34. The *Annual Reports* (1919–1930) of the Cleveland Chamber of Commerce list committee members. The December issues of the *Cleveland Realtor* (1919–1930) list CREB committee members and city and suburban public officials.
35. CCC, *Annual Report,* 1926, p. 75.
36. Kammen borrowed the phrase from James Russell Lowell; see Michael Kammen, *A Machine that Would Go of Itself: The Constitution in American Culture* (New York: Vintage Books, 1987), p. 124.
37. *Finance and Industry,* 4 February 1928.
38. "Stanley L. McMichael Farewell Address," *Cleveland Realtor,* 7 October 1929.
39. *Growth and Values,* p. 328.
40. "Farewell Address."
41. CCC, *Annual Reports,* 1919–1930; *Cleveland Realtor,* 1919–1930; City of Cleveland, City Planning Commission, "Membership List," 1923–1930.
42. CCC, *Annual Reports,* 1915–1919; City Planning Commission, "Membership List," 1923–1930.
43. Thomas F. Campbell, *Daniel E. Morgan: The Good Citizen in Politics* (Cleveland: The Press of Western Reserve University, 1966), pp. 99–130.
44. *The Encyclopedia of Cleveland History,* David D. Van Tassel and John J. Grabowski (eds.), pp. 185–186, 515–519.
45. His self-serving real estate development schemes and the politicalization of his administration doomed the city manager experiment. Hopkins as city manager was the choice of the Republican Party (which he headed) and the Cleveland Real Estate Board. To make his appointment palatable to Democrats, Hopkins agreed to split patronage appointments with W. Burr Gongwer, the county chairman of the Democratic Party. The arrival of Hopkins was a visible, irrefutable symbol that a new regime was in power.
46. *Cleveland Realtor,* 27 September 1923, 12 November 1923, 14 January 1924.

NOTES TO CHAPTER 10

1. Robert Sobel, *The Great Bull Market: Wall Street in the 1920s* (New York: W.W. Norton & Company, 1968), pp. 82–83; Ian S. Haberman, *The Van Sweringens of Cleve-*

land: The Biography of an Empire (Cleveland: The Western Reserve Historical Society, 1979), pp. 65–88.

2. Brian J. L. Berry, *Long Wave Rhythms in Economic Development and Political Behavior* (Baltimore: The Johns Hopkins University Press, 1991), pp. 44–45, figs. 23 and 24.

3. *Cleveland Realtor,* 24 December 1928, 29 September 1930.

4. Ibid.

5. Ibid., 26 January 1926.

6. *Finance and Industry,* 14 April 1928; *The Encyclopedia of Cleveland History,* David D. Van Tassel and John J. Grabowski, eds. (Bloomington: Indiana University Press, 1987), p. 928.

7. Kondratieff Rhythm or Cycle. Named for Russian born economist Nikolai Kondratieff (1891–1931). The theory refers to trade cycles of long duration. Kondratieff studied American, British, and French wholesale prices and interest rates from the eighteenth century and found that peaks and troughs in economic activity fell at regular intervals. Harvard economists conducted similar work into British wheat prices from the thirteenth century and found cycles lasting fifty-four years. Brian J. L. Berry cited above and David Hackett Fischer cited below are two recent students of the phenomenon.

8. Berry, pp. 46–64.

9. Ibid., pp. 65–86; David Hackett Fischer, *The Great Wave: Price Revolutions and the Rhythm of History* (New York: Oxford University Press, 1996), pp. 188–197.

10. Alfred D. Chandler, Jr., *Scale and Scope: The Dynamics of Industrial Capitalism* (Cambridge: The Belknap Press of Harvard University Press, 1990), pp. 3–13.

11. Ibid., pp. 121–145, Appendix A.1 & A.4.

12. Ibid., pp. 36–46; John D. Rockefeller, Jr., "Brotherhood in Business," *Finance and Industry,* 24 August 1918.

13. The Cleveland Real Estate Board's "sell Cleveland" advertising campaign mentioned in the previous chapter was aimed at this residential real estate market segment.

14. *Scale and Scope,* p. 9; *Cleveland Realtor,* 13 December 1926, 15 October 1928, 7 January 1929, 17 February 1930.

15. *Cleveland Realtor,* 7 February 1927, 17 February 1930.

16. Frederic C. Howe, *The Confessions of a Reformer* (Chicago: Quadrangle Paperbacks, 1967 [c. 1925]), pp. 225–230.

17. Jon C. Teaford, *The Unheralded Triumph: City Government in America, 1870–1900* (Baltimore: The Johns Hopkins University Press, 1984), p. 301.

18. Stanley L. McMichael, *City Growth and Values* (Cleveland: The Stanley McMichael Publishing Organization, 1923), p. 281; Thompson, Hine and Flory (THF), Office File, Amos Burt Thompson, "Brief of the Cleveland Association of Building Owners and Managers Submitted to Mr. John A. Zangerle, Auditor of Cuyahoga County," 29 August 1924.

19. THF, Office File, "Testimony of Amos Burt Thompson before the Special Joint Taxation Committee," Columbus, Ohio, 30 January 1917.

20. Jon C. Teaford estimates that the personal property tax in most cities—including Cleveland—brought in no more than 4 or 5 percent of the total; see *Unheralded Triumph,* pp. 293–304.

21. *Cleveland Realtor,* 10 March 1924, 7 April 1924, 19 November 1924.

22. *Encyclopedia,* p. 1079.

23. *Cleveland Realtor,* 17 September 1923.

24. John A. Zangerle, *Who's Who and What's What in Cuyahoga County: The Need of a County Wide Re-Appraisal of Real Estate* (Cleveland: n.p., 1924), p. 10.
25. THF, Office File, "Testimony of John A. Zangerle before the Joint Tax Committee," Columbus, Ohio, 20 February 1919.
26. *Realty Record,* 20 February 1919.
27. THF, Office File, John A. Zangerle, "Why a Corporate Excess Tax in Ohio?" January, 1917.
28. "Zangerle Testimony," 20 February 1919.
29. Ibid.
30. *Growth and Values,* p. 281.
31. "Zangerle Testimony,"
32. Zangerle, "Who's Who."
33. CABOM Brief; *Growth and Values,* pp. 281–287; Herbert B. Dorau and Albert G. Hinman, *Urban Land Use Economics* (College Park, MD: McGrath Publishing, 1969 [c. 1928]), pp. 524–536.
34. *Growth and Values,* pp. 281–282.
35. Ibid., p. 265.
36. Dorau, pp. 373–376; Richard U. Ratcliff, *Urban Land Economics* (New York: McGraw-Hill, 1949), pp. 426
37. Ibid., p. 282.
38. Dorau, pp. 224–235; CABOM Brief; THF, Horn et al., Memorandum to John A. Zangerle; *Growth and Values,* pp. 216–217.
39. CABOM Brief.
40. Horn Memorandum; *Plain Dealer,* 3 September 1920; *Growth and Values,* pp. 286.
41. Ibid.
42. *Growth and Values,* p. 283.
43. *Cleveland Realtor,* 23 August 1929.
44. Ibid.
45. James F. Richardson, "Political Reform in Cleveland," in David D. Van Tassel and John J. Grabowski (eds.), *Cleveland: A Tradition of Reform* (Kent, OH: The Kent State University Press, 1986), p. 159; *Plain Dealer,* 15 September 1920.
46. Citizens League of Cleveland, *Municipal Bulletin,* December, 1914.
47. THF, Office File, "Vote Yes" [pamphlet], November, 1920.
48. *Plain Dealer,* 15 September 1920; *Cleveland News,* 24 February 1922; *Growth and Values,* p. 340.
49. *Finance and Industry,* 28 January 1928.
50. *Cleveland Realtor,* 14 January 1924, 24 November 1924.
51. CABOM Brief.
52. John L. Kraft, "The Role of Legal Counsel in Public Agency Financing," in Frank J. Fabozzi, Sylvan G. Feldstein, Irving Pollack, and Frank Zarb (eds.), *The Municipal Bond Handbook* (Homewood, IL: Dow Jones-Irwin, 1983), pp. 304–306; David S. Kidwell and Eric N. Sorenson, "Investment Banking and the Underwriting of New Municipal Issues," in *The Municipal Bond Handbook,* pp. 170–171.

NOTES TO CHAPTER 11

1. *Cleveland Realtor,* 30 August 1926.
2. Ibid., 3 May 1926.

3. Ian S. Haberman, *The Van Sweringens of Cleveland: The Biography of an Empire* (Cleveland: The Western Reserve Historical Society, 1979), pp. 12–17.

4. *Cleveland Realtor,* 31 March 1924; Stanley L. Mcmichael and Robert F. Bingham, *City Growth and Values* (Cleveland: The Stanley McMichael Publishing Organization, 1923), p. 189; David R. Goldfield and Blaine A. Brownell, *Urban America: A History,* 2nd ed. (Boston: Houghton-Mifflin, 1990), pp. 264–265.

5. *Growth and Values,* pp. 177–193.

6. Ibid., p. 50.

7. Robert H. Bremner, "The Street Railway Controversy in Cleveland," *American Journal of Economics and Sociology,* X, No. 2 (January, 1951), 203–214.

8. *Cleveland Realtor,* 21 April 1924.

9. *Plain Dealer,* 16 August 1930; a city building boom peaked in 1925, and private investment in infrastructure declined sharply thereafter: see Brian J. L. Berry, *Long Wave Rhythms in Economic Development and Political Behavior* (Baltimore: The Johns Hopkins University Press, 1991), pp. 84–86.

10. Randolph F. Sellers, *Rapid Transit and Subways for Greater Cleveland: The Problem Reviewed, 1910–1930* (Cleveland: n.p., 1930), pp. 1–6.

11. Ibid., p. 8.

12. *Cleveland Realtor,* 21 March 1924.

13. *Rapid Transit,* pp. 10–12.

14. *Cleveland Realtor,* 24 September 1928; *Rapid Transit,* pp. 12–13.

15. Cuyahoga County, Board of Elections, Election Returns, 1919–1930.

16. *Cleveland Realtor,* 28 March 1928.

17. Ibid., 13 January 1928.

18. *Growth and Values,* pp. 53–54.

19. Three seminal essays develop models of city structure. They are: Ernest W. Burgess, "The Growth of the City: An Introduction to a Research Project," in Robert E. Park, Ernest W. Burgess, Roderick D. McKenzie, (eds.), *The City* (Chicago: The University of Chicago Press, 1925); Homer Hoyt, *The Structure and Growth of Residential Neighborhoods in American Cities* (Washington, D.C.: United States Government Printing Office, 1939); Chauncy D. Harris and Edward L. Ullman, "The Nature of Cities," *The Annals of the Academy of Political and Social Science,* CCXLII (1945), 7–17. Burgess and Hoyt make the city analogous to a cell with the central business district as its nucleus; Harris and Ullman extend the analogy, noting that the unfolding highway system has given the city more than one nucleus, pointing toward the decentralization of urban functions characteristic of the post World War II urban region. Realtor Stanley L. McMichael anticipated the theoretical work of Harris and Ullman by two decades.

20. *Rapid Transit,* pp. 12–13.

21. Richard U. Ratcliff, *Urban Land Use Economics* (New York: McGraw-Hill, 1949), pp. 390–408; *Growth and Values,* pp. 316–322.

22. See chapter 6.

23. *Growth and Values,* pp. 294–300.

24. Ohio State 497; *Plain Dealer,* 29 August 1940; Thompson, Hine, and Flory, Office File, "Greater Cleveland: A Bulletin of Public Business," February, 1928.

25. See chapter 7.

26. Haberman, pp. 31–49.

27. *Plain Dealer,* 18 September 1918; Cleveland *News Leader,* 15 December 1918; Haberman, pp. 38–39.

28. The outcome illustrates regime succession. The *Plain Dealer,* which in 1918 favored the Mall site, switched positions in 1921 without so much as a word of explanation to readers, but its advertising displayed many more column inches purchased by realtors and Public Square and Euclid Avenue retailers than by export-sector corporations: *PD,* 20 July 1921, 17 September 1921, 22 September 1921, 21 December 1921; Haberman, pp. 43–48.

29. Cleveland Chamber of Commerce, Minutes of the Municipal Art and Architecture Committee, "Letter of Frederic C. Howe to the Committee, 12 November 1910."

30. Elroy McKendree Avery, *A History of Cleveland and Its Environs: The Heart of New Connecticut,* 3 vols. (New York: The Lewis Publishing Company, 1918), I, p. 472.

31. Municipal Art and Architecture Committee, "Minutes," 23 January 1913.

32. Ibid., 5 February 1914.

33. Ibid., 5 August 1914; "Memorandum of Mayor Newton D. Baker to the Municipal Art and Architecture Committee," 15 August 1914.

34. Ibid.

35. Planning Committee, Minutes, 8 January 1918, 17 January 1918; Avery, I, p. 473; *Growth and Values,* p. 306.

36. Richard F. Babcock, *The Zoning Game: Municipal Practices and Policies* (Madison: The University of Wisconsin Press, 1966); Charles M. Haar, *Land Use Planning: A Casebook on the Use, Misuse, and Reuse of Urban Land,* 2nd ed. (Boston: Little, Brown and Company, 1971); William A. Fischel, *The Economics of Zoning Laws: A Property Rights Approach to American Land Use Controls* (Baltimore: The Johns Hopkins University Press, 1985); Charles M. Haar and Jerold S. Kayden (Eds.), *Zoning and the American Dream: Promises Still to Keep* (Chicago: Planners Press, American Planning Association, 1989); Norman Krumholz, "Zoning," in *The Encyclopedia of Cleveland History,* David D. Van Tassel and John J. Grabowski, eds. (Bloomington: Indiana University Press, 1987), pp. 1081–1083.

37. Mel Scott, *American City Planning Since 1890* (Berkeley: University of California Press, 1969), pp. 160–161; CCC, Board of Directors, Minutes, 16 April 1919; *Annual Report,* "The Effect of City Planning on Estate Values," (1919).

38. *Growth and Values,* pp. 320–323.

39. *Plain Dealer,* 11 April 1926, 12 November 1926; *Cleveland Realtor,* 4 September 1927, 17 October 1927, 2 November 1927, 17 August 1928.

40. *Growth and Values,* pp. 320–323.

41. *Village of Euclid v. Ambler Realty Co.,* 272 U.S. 365, 47 Sup. Ct. 114, 71 L. Ed. 303 (1926), reprinted in Charles M. Haar, *Land Use Planning: A Casebook on the Use, Misuse, and Re-use of Urban Land* (Boston: Little, Brown and Company, 1971), pp. 165–168.

42. Ibid.

43. Ibid.

44. 316 (N.D. Ohio 1924); 297 Fed. 307.

45. William M. Randle, "Professors, Reformers, Bureaucrats, and Cronies: The Players in Euclid v. Ambler," in the previously cited *Zoning and the American Dream,* pp. 31–69.

46. Quoted in Haar, *Land Use Planning,* pp. 172–173, fn. 1.

47. Ibid.

48. *Euclid v. Ambler*

49. Ibid.

NOTES TO CHAPTER 12

1. City of Cleveland, Division of Engineering and Construction, *Annexations to the City of Cleveland* (1954); Cleveland Chamber of Commerce (CCC), Committee on Annexations, *Annual Report* (1919); Cleveland *Plain Dealer*, 13 August 1920.
2. Kenneth T. Jackson, *Crabgrass Frontier: The Suburbanization of the United States* (New York: Oxford University Press, 1985), p. 150.
3. CCC, *A City Plan for Greater Cleveland*, 19 September 1923; *Plain Dealer*, 13 August 1920.
4. Carol Poh Miller and Robert Wheeler, *Cleveland: A Concise History, 1796–1990* (Bloomington: University of Indiana Press, 1990), p. 120; Jean Y. Tussey, *An Introduction to the History of the Cleveland Labor Movement, 1865–1929* (Cleveland: A Reprint from *The Cleveland Citizen*, March–May, 1995), pp. 13–15.
5. Kenneth L. Kusmer, *A Ghetto Takes Shape: Black Cleveland, 1870–1930* (Urbana: University of Illinois Press, 1976), pp. 10, 174–189.
6. See chapter 11.
7. CCC, Committee on Annexations, *Annual Report* (1916); *Plain Dealer*, 13 August 1920.
8. *Cleveland Town Topics*, 18 February 1922.
9. CCC, City Planning Committee, *A City Plan for Greater Cleveland* (19 September 1923); Regional Government Committee, Fact Finding Committee, *Regional Planning and Zoning and Industry in the Cleveland District* (27 June 1928); William M. Randle, "Professors, Reformers, Bureaucrats, and Cronies: The Players in *Euclid v. Ambler*," in Charles M. Haar and Jerold S. Kayden (eds.), *Zoning and the American Dream: Promises Still to Keep* (Chicago: Planners Press, American Planning Association, 1989), pp. 47–49.
10. *Plain Dealer*, 13 May 1925.
11. *Plain Dealer*, 13 May 1925; *Regional Planning and Zoning*, pp. 3–4.
12. *Planning and Zoning*, pp. 1–9.
13. Several times a year the *Cleveland Realtor* and *Finance and Industry* published tables showing tax rates and bonded indebtedness by municipality.
14. James F. Richardson, "Political Reform in Cleveland," in David D. Van Tassel and John J. Grabowski (eds.), *Cleveland: A Tradition of Reform* (Kent, OH: The Kent State University Press, 1986), pp. 161–167.
15. Ibid.
16. Ibid.; Paul Kantor, *The Dependent City: The Changing Political Economy of Urban America* (Glenview, IL: Scott, Foresman and Company, 1988), pp. 269–296.
17. Michael P. Smith, *The City and Social Theory* (New York: St. Martin's Press, 1978), pp. 171–229; Katznelson, pp. 6–27.
18. Stanley L. McMichael and Robert F. Bingham, *City Growth and Values* (Cleveland: The Stanley McMichael Publishing Organization, 1923), p. 305.
19. *Growth and Values*, pp. 320–323.
20. William A. Fischel, *The Economics of Zoning Laws: A Property Rights Approach to American Land Use Controls* (Baltimore: The Johns Hopkins University Press, 1985), p. 62.
21. Miller and Wheeler, p. 96; *Encyclopedia*, passim; State of Ohio, *Ohio School Report*, 1925–1930.
22. Cleveland Public Schools, *Annual Report*, 1919–1931.

23. The exodus was temporarily halted by depression in the 1930s and war in the 1940s, but resumed with a vengeance in the 1950s.
24. CPS, *Annual Report*, 1919–1930.
25. Brian Ross, "The New Philanthropy: The Reorganization of Charity in Turn of the Century Cleveland" (Ph.D. diss., Case Western Reserve University, 1989); John J. Grabowski, "Social Reform and Philanthropic Order in Cleveland, 1896–1920," in David D. Van Tassel and John J. Grabowski (eds.), *Cleveland: A Tradition of Reform* (Kent, OH: Kent State University Press, 1986), pp. 29–49; Edward M. Miggins, "A City of 'Uplifting Influences': From 'Sweet Charity' to Modern Social Welfare and Philanthropy," in Thomas F. Campbell and Edward M. Miggins (eds.), *The Birth of Modern Cleveland* (Cleveland: The Western Reserve Historical Society, 1988), pp. 141–170.
26. Ibid.
27. See the account of the tax reform struggle in chapters 5 and 10.
28. The traditional view is expressed in *Encyclopedia*, pp. 997–998; *The Plain Dealer*, 10 September 1995.

NOTES TO CONCLUSION

1. For decades, this condition was camouflaged by the appearance of local forward-linkage industries which created a welcome agglomeration effect in Cleveland's economy. However, in time, the forward-linkage industries would also be merged into larger, national corporate entities.
2. Jon C. Teaford so argues; see his *The Unheralded Triumph: City Government in America, 1870–1900* (Baltimore: The Johns Hopkins University Press, 1984.)
3. U.S. Census Bureau, *Statistical Abstract of the United States: 2002* (Washington, D.C., 2001), table 10, p. 32.

INDEX

advertising campaigns, 164, 206, 256n13
agricultural tools industry, 14
air transportation, 173, 176
Ambler, Martha B., 108
Ambler Realty, Village of Euclid v., 158, 198–200
American Steel and Wire Company, 203
Annexation Committee, 204, 205
annexations: Corporate Regime and, 202; Merchant Regime and, 14, 16–19, 33, 46, 60–61, 63, 215–16; Populist Regime and, 63, 215; Realty Regime and, 62–63, 202–5; statistics on, 223
anti-Catholicism, 78
appraisals, 156–57, 178, 180–82
Arbuthnot, Charles C., 147
automobile industry, 95–96, 175
Axworthy, Thomas, 44
Ayres, Leonard, 138

Babcock, Brenton D., 44
Baker, Newton D., 110–11, 126, 132, 134, 149, 158, 196–97
Baker Hostettler (law firm), 158
banking/finance industry, 14, 40, 99, 118, 162–64, 173–74. *See also* capital
Beer and Skittles Club, 119–20
Bellamy, George A., 111–12, 144
Bemis, Edward W., 155
Benevolent Associations Committee, 144–45
benevolent organizations. *See* charities
Bernstein, Harry "Czar," 46, 82
Berry, Bryan J. L., 236n27

Bevan, William C., 76
Big Con(solidated) Railway, 69–70, 72
Bingham, Robert, 156, 158, 161–62, 165, 182, 194, 208–9
Black, Morris A., 119, 168
Blee, Robert, 58–59
Board of. *See specific boards (e.g.,* Control, Board of)
boosterism, 40, 164
Bowditch, E. W., 108, 119, 124, 130
Bramley, M. F., 74
bridges, 18, 174, 187–88
Broadway and Brooklyn Street Railway Company, 68–69
Brooklyn Township, 17
brothels, 76–77, 111
Brunner, Arnold W., 121–22, 128–29
Brush, Charles F., 66, 95
Brush Electric Company, 95
budgets, municipal, 48–50, 225–26; of Corporate Regime, 110; deficits in, 61–62; infrastructure needs in, 55–56; of Merchant Regime, 23, 27, 49, 55, 61–62; park system in, 110; poor relief in, 27; of Populist Regime, 49, 55, 58, 62–63; of Realty Regime, 184–86; water and sewerage system in, 23
building codes, 116, 132
Bulletin No. 11 (Municipal Association), 73, 245n16
Burgess, Ernest W., 258n19
Burnap, George, 111–12
Burnham, Daniel H., 121–22, 195

263

business organization, 39–41, 47, 50, 92–94, 174–76, 215
bus services, 190

CABOM. *See* Cleveland Association of Building Owners and Managers
Cadwallader, Starr, 144
Campbell, Dr. (health dept. physician), 76
canal development, 11–14, 214
capital: active/passive, 86, 90–92, 94, 173–74, 177; circuit flows of, 98–100, 130. *See also* banking/finance industry
Carnegie Avenue, 129
Carrere, John M., 121–22
Case, Leonard, 124–25
Case Institute of Technology, 99, 124
Center Street Bridge, 18
central business district. *See* city structure
Chadsey, Mildred, 147
Chagrin River Valley Hunt Club, 115
Chamberlain, Joseph, 86, 90, 143
Chamber of Commerce. *See* Cleveland Chamber of Commerce
charities, 25–26, 34, 80, 144–45, 212–13. *See also* wealth redistribution
Charities and Corrections, Department of, 81
Charity Organization Society (COS), 144
Chester Avenue, 158–59
churches, 25–26, 28
Citizens League, 168, 205–6
City Beautiful movement, 116, 128–31, 193–95
City Efficient movement, 116, 131–32, 195–97, 208–9
City Infirmary, 27, 80
city master plans, 116, 127–28, 132
City Plan Committee, 166, 197
City Planning Commission, 116, 132, 167–68, 196–97
city structure, 6, 117–19, 187–93, 227–29; automobile impact on, 161, 170, 190, 191–93; civic center (Group Plan), 103, 116–17, 119–23, 127–31, 194–95; hub and spoke, 42, 161; land speculation and, 63; segmentation in, 29–30; University Circle, 99, 103, 116–17, 124–31; walking city, 16, 161

Civic League, 89, 190
Civil War, 15, 51, 54
Cleveland Association of Building Owners and Managers (CABOM), 183, 187, 190–91
Cleveland Chamber of Commerce, 86–89; Annexation Committee, 204, 205; Benevolent Associations Committee, 144–45; City Efficient movement and, 116, 196; City Plan Committee, 166, 197; civic center (Group Plan) and, 120, 195; declining influence of, 166–67; economic development policy and, 97–101, 130, 149; Grouped Public Buildings Committee, 120; Industrial Development Committee, 100–101; Municipal Art and Architecture Committee, 111, 196–97; municipal ownership and, 246n28; park system and, 105, 108, 110–11; public health and, 132; regional planning and, 205–6; tax policies and, 89–92; transportation development and, 73, 173, 190; University Circle and, 126; urban growth policy and, 116, 120, 126, 166, 195, 196, 204; wealth redistribution and, 144–45
Cleveland Conference for Educational Cooperation, 127
Cleveland Electric Railway Company, 190–91
Cleveland Foundation, 134, 138, 145, 148, 150
Cleveland Heights, 185, 206
Cleveland Institute of Art, 125
Cleveland Metropolitan Park Dist. Bd. of Comm'rs, State, ex. rel. Stanton v., 114, 194
Cleveland Museum of Art, 125–26
Cleveland Orphan Asylum, 28
Cleveland Public Library, 120, 126
Cleveland Real Estate Board (CREB), 155–57, 169–70; advertising/boosterism of, 164, 256n13; bridge construction and, 188; municipal government organization and, 168–69; tax policies and, 176, 178–82; transportation development and, 173, 190–91, 205

Cleveland Realtor, The, 156, 164, 173, 253n1
Cleveland Recreation Survey, 111–12
Cleveland Trust Bank, 162
Columbus Street Bridge, 18
committees. *See specific committees* (e.g., Benevolent Associations Committee)
Commons, John R., 155
Community Chest, 145–46, 148, 212–13
ConCon Railway, 70
contracting, 74–75, 215–16
Control, Board of, 75
cooperage industry, 14
Corporate Regime, 3–4, 7, 85–150; achievements of, 148–50; annexations and, 202, 223; budgets of, 110; business organization in, 92–94; civic center (Group Plan) and, 103, 116–17, 119–23, 127–31, 195; economic development policies of, 92–101, 130, 149; ideals of, 85–86, 87–88, 102–3, 115, 131, 133–34, 141, 143–44; institutional setting of, 86–89; mayors of (list), 222; municipal government organization in, 89, 133, 149, 168–69; park system and, 103–15, 130; public education in, 99, 134–41, 149; public schools in, 134–41; service distribution policies of, 133–41, 149, 190, 216; tax policies of, 89–92, 114, 140, 177–78; University Circle and, 99, 103, 116–17, 124–31; urban growth policies of, 6, 102–32, 149, 193, 202, 215; wealth redistribution in, 133, 141–48, 150, 212, 217
countinghouses, 40
County Planning Congress, 205
courts system, 20
Cragin, Raymond T., 168, 191
Craw, James A., 21
CREB. *See* Cleveland Real Estate Board
Currency Act (1863), 14
Cutler, James Elbert, 147

Daily True Democrat, 28
Davis, Harry L., 203
Day, Lewis, 78–79
Democratic Party, 82
Department of. *See specific departments* (e.g., Charities and Corrections, Department of)
Diehl, William, 106
Draper, Andrew, 79–80, 136–37
durable goods manufacturing, 40, 50–54, 56, 175, 215

East Boulevard, 108
East Cleveland Township, 17, 185, 206
East Cleveland Village, 17
East Ohio Gas Company, 67
economic development policies, 4–5, 7, 142, 214–15, 230–32; boosterism and, 40, 164; of Corporate Regime, 92–101, 130, 149; growth pole effect and, 55, 59–60; of Merchant Regime, 11–15, 33, 50–51, 57, 93, 214; of Populist Regime, 50–60, 93; of Realty Regime, 171–76; regional government and, 218–19
Edgewater Park, 108, 111
education. *See* public education
Educational Cooperation, Cleveland Conference for, 127
elections and campaigns, 1–2, 73, 135, 203
electrical industry, 66–67, 95–96
Elson, William H., 136–37
Ely, Richard T., 155–56, 183
eminent domain, 114
entrepreneurial ideals, 85–88, 148–49; active/passive capital and, 94; business organization and, 39, 41, 47; city planning and, 116–17, 131; in park system, 102–3, 105, 115, 130; service distribution and, 133–34, 141; wealth redistribution and, 143, 145
Erie Canal, 12
ethnic antagonisms, 78, 203–4, 207, 209
Euclid Avenue, 23, 30, 118, 129, 158–60, 189
Euclid Avenue Association, 190–91
Euclid Village, 158, 198–200

Farley, John H. "Honest John," 44–45, 58–59, 73, 76, 81–82
Farnsworth, Henry M., 106, 168
"Federal" charter system, 45–46, 70, 79, 81, 104, 134–35

Federation for Charity and Philanthropy (later Federation for Community Planning). *See* Welfare Federation
Fesler, Mayo, 147
finance. *See* banking/finance industry
Finance and Industry, 167
Finegold, Kenneth, 245n17
fire protection, 21–22, 32, 204
Fischer, David Hackett, 236n27
Flats, the, 117
food products industry, 51, 53, 56
Ford, Henry, 173
Ford Motor Company, 96, 175
franchising, 66–74, 86, 91, 215–16
Frederick, James, 136–37
furniture industry, 14

gaming houses, 76–77, 111
garbage removal, 74–75, 204
Garden Society, 125
Gardner, George W., 44, 58–59
Gardner Act (1920), 185
Garfield brothers, Harry and James, 70, 82
Garfield Heights, 203–4
gas light companies, 66–67
Geertz, Clifford, 251n27
General Electric Company, 95
General Motors, 175
George, Henry, 86
Gilmour, Richard, 79
Goff, Frederick H., 138, 159–60, 162–64, 196, 247n32
Gongwer, W. Burr, 255n45
Goode, J. P., 156
Gordon, William, 110, 130
Gordon Park, 108, 111
government, county, 205–6
government, municipal: budgets of, 23, 27, 48–50, 61–63, 110, 184–86, 225–26; city manager system of, 89, 168–69; in Corporate Regime, 89, 133, 149, 168–69; "Federal" charter system of, 45–46, 70, 79, 81, 104, 134–35; home rule charters and, 196; mayors of (list), 221–22; in Merchant Regime, 31–32, 44; metro government movement and, 205–7; in Populist Regime, 42–47, 75–77, 81–82; in Realty Regime,

168–69, 205–7; "weak mayor" system of, 31, 43–44, 104
government, regional, 218–19
grains. *See* milling industry
Grange (Ohio), 156, 178, 180
Grouped Public Buildings Committee, 120
Group Plan, 103, 116–17, 119–23, 127–31, 194–95
Group Plan Commission, 120–21
growth pole effect, 55, 59–60

Hanna, Marcus A., 70–71, 73–74, 82
harbor improvements. *See* water transportation
Harris, Chauncy D., 258n19
Havens, Munson, 147
Hayden, Warren S., 147
Haydn, Hiram, 124
health. *See* public health
Herrick, Myron T., 120–21, 123
Herrick, R. R., 44, 58, 62, 74
Hill, Arthur, 203–4
Hinsdale, Burke A., 78
Hiram House, 111–12, 143
Holden, Liberty E., 120, 125
home rule charters, 196, 205
Hopkins, William R., 168–69, 190–91
House of Correction, 28
housing codes, 132
Howe, Frederic C., 70–73, 82, 91, 119, 121, 143–44, 196
Hoyt, Homer, 258n19
Hubbell, Benjamin S., 126, 129, 131

Indians, 20
indoor relief, 27, 80
Industrial Development Committee, 100–101
Industrial School, 28
infrastructure: bridges, 18, 174, 187–88; contracting for, 74–75, 215–16; franchising of, 66–74, 86, 91, 215–16; industry needs and, 51, 55–60, 100; streets and roads, 18–19, 56, 61, 62–63, 66–67, 74, 108, 113, 174, 192, 204; urban growth and, 161–62; utilities, 61, 62–63, 66–67, 91, 174, 187–88, 204

Index

insurance industry, 22

Jackson, James, 144, 146
Johnson, Tom L., 133–34, 148–49; civic center (Group Plan) and, 121; as entrepreneurial politician, 86, 88–89; park system and, 104, 110–11; political affiliation of, 82; public education and, 135; street railway system and, 74, 189; tax policies and, 90–92, 246n21
Jones, Lewis H., 136–37
judicial system, 20

Katznelson, Ira, 245n1
Kelley, Alfred, 12–15, 40
Kick, Michael, 20–21
kindergartens, 137
Kolko, Gabriel, 247n31
Kondratieff Rhythms, 256n7

labor antagonisms, 203
Lakewood, 169, 185, 206, 211
land use. *See* urban growth policies
land valuation, 156–57
Laronge, Joseph, 168
Leader, 13–14
leaseholds, 99-year, 160–61, 182
legal profession, 157–62
liquor consumption, 76–77. *See also* temperance movements
Little Con(solidated) Railway, 69–70, 72, 73
living trusts, 160, 162–63
long-wave economic rhythms, 174
Lorain-Carnegie Bridge, 187–88
low-income housing, 183–84
lumber industry, 14, 51, 53–54, 56, 215

Malthus, Thomas Robert, 143
Manual Training School, 79
manufacturing industries: in Corporate Regime, 94–97; in Merchant Regime, 13–15, 215; in 1970s, 101; in Populist Regime, 40, 50–54, 56; in Realty Regime, 175
Martha Washington and Dorcas Society, 26
Mather, Samuel, 85–86, 88, 126, 196

Mather, William Gwinn, 120, 126, 168
McKisson, Robert E. "Corky Bob": corruption in administration of, 66, 76; infrastructure needs and, 59, 75; municipal government organization and, 81; patronage network of, 46; political affiliation of, 82; street railway system and, 70, 73; tax policies and, 90
McMichael, Stanley L, 156, 161, 165, 167, 192, 194, 208
McTighe, Michael J., 234n1
Merchant Regime, 3, 7, 11–34; annexations and, 14, 16–19, 33, 46, 60–61, 63, 215–16, 223; budgets of, 23, 27, 49, 55, 61–62; economic development policies of, 11–15, 33, 50–51, 57, 93, 214; fire protection in, 21–22, 32; heralds of succession, 29–33; mayors of (list), 221; municipal government organization in, 31–32, 44; police protection in, 20–21, 32; public conveyance regulations of, 67–68; public education in, 24–25, 28, 32, 77–78, 136, 216; rowdy boys in, 24, 28–29; service distribution policies of, 19–23, 29, 33, 38, 61, 67; tax policies of, 18–19, 61; urban growth policies of, 6, 15–19, 29–30, 33, 38, 46, 60–63, 102, 215; water and sewerage in, 22–23, 32; wealth redistribution in, 23–29, 32–34, 38, 80
mergers, 69–70, 92, 98, 175
metals industries: in Corporate Regime, 95–96, 100, 215; in Merchant Regime, 14–15, 18; in Populist Regime, 51, 54, 56–57, 59–60
Metropolitan Park Commissioners, Board of, 114
Metropolitan Police Act (1866), 20
Metzenbaum, James, 168
milling industry, 12, 14, 215
Moley, Raymond, 147
monopolies, 66–67, 71, 86, 91
Moses, Louis A., 106, 167, 194
Municipal Art and Architecture Committee, 111, 196–97
Municipal Association, 70, 73, 75–77, 88–89
Musical Arts Society, 125

Nash, George K., 121
National Banking Act (1864), 14
National Real Estate Board, 155
Native Americans, 20
nativism, 78
needle trades industries, 94
Newburgh Township, 17
Nickel Plate Railroad, 172
ninety-nine-year leaseholds, 160–61, 182
9th Street, East, 118
nondurable goods industries, 40, 50–53, 56, 215
Northwest Ordinance, 24
Norton, Z. Z., 196

Ohio Canal, 12, 14
Ohio City, 12, 16–17
Ohio Grange, 156, 178, 180
oil refining industry, 53–54, 56, 215
Olmstead, Frederick Law, 108
Olmstead, Frederick Law, Jr., 112–13, 194
105th Street, East, 158, 189
orphanages, 28
Orth, Samuel P., 138
Otis, Charles A., 43, 61–63, 190, 236n25
outdoor relief, 27–28, 80–81
outsourcing, 243n42

Palmer, Carl, 169
Panic of 1873, 19, 31, 61
Park Board Reorganization Association, 104
Park Commissioners, Board of, 104, 106, 108, 110, 114, 194
park system, 103–15, 193–94; function, 110–15, 130; scale, 107–10; special purpose districts and, 106–7, 112, 114; structure, 103–7
parochial schools, 79, 99, 210–11, 217, 252n10
patronage, 32, 41–42, 44–45, 76, 79
Payne, Nathan Perry, 43, 59, 62
Perkin, Harold, 245n1
Plain Dealer, The, 156, 190, 197, 259n28
Playhouse Square, 158
Police Board, 20
Police Commission, 45
police protection, 20–21, 32, 44–45, 76–77, 204
political parties, 1–2, 46, 82, 255n45
Pontiac Improvement Company, 114
poorhouses, 27
population growth, 13, 15, 30, 46, 63, 94, 203
Populist Regime, 3, 7, 31; annexations and, 63, 215, 223; budgets of, 49, 55, 58, 62–63; business organization in, 39–41, 47, 50; economic development policies of, 50–60, 93; ideals of, 37–39, 47, 65, 76; mayors of (list), 222; municipal government organization in, 42–47, 75–77, 81–82; neighborhoods in, 42; police protection in, 44–45, 76–77; public education in, 77–80, 135; service distribution policies of, 42, 63, 65–80, 215–16; tax policies of, 58, 61–62; urban growth policies of, 6, 41, 63–64, 102, 127; wealth redistribution in, 42, 65, 80–82, 212, 217
poverty. *See* wealth redistribution
Prentiss, Francis F., 168
press, the, 74, 78
private schools, 210–11, 217
privatization, 243n42
professional ideals, 37–39, 85, 87–88, 148–49; business organization and, 41, 47; city planning and, 116–17, 131; in park system, 102–3, 105, 115, 130; service distribution and, 133–34; wealth redistribution and, 143–45
property taxes, 62, 90–92, 177–80, 182–84
Prospect Avenue, 158–59
public education, 216–17; in Corporate Regime, 99, 134–41, 149; in Merchant Regime, 24–25, 28, 32, 77–78, 136; in Populist Regime, 77–80, 135; in Realty Regime, 204, 210–12
public health, 22–23, 75, 132, 136–37
Public Square, 22, 66, 117–19, 123, 195

racial antagonisms, 203–4, 207, 209
Ragged School, The, 28, 80
railroad repair industry, 13–14, 54
railroads, 13–14, 58–59, 121, 123, 172–73, 195, 214

Rapid Transit Commission, 190
Rappe, Amadeus, 28
real estate industry, 153–64; appraisals/land valuations and, 156–57, 178, 180–82; ethical standards and, 155, 157; finance and, 162–64; legal profession and, 157–62; low-income housing and, 183–84; in Merchant Regime, 14, 17–18, 62–63; ninety-nine-year leaseholds and, 160–61, 182; park system and, 110, 113–14; street railways and, 69, 174; tax policies and, 91–92, 159–61. *See also* Cleveland Real Estate Board
Realty Regime, 4, 7, 165–219; annexations and, 62–63, 202–5, 223; budgets of, 184–86; business organization and, 174–76; city managers in (list), 222; city planning and, 128, 193–97, 208; city structure and, 187–93; economic development policies of, 171–76; municipal government organization in, 168–69, 205–7; park system and, 114; public education in, 204, 210–12; regional planning and, 114, 205–7, 216; rise of, 165–70; service distribution policies of, 187–93, 204–6, 209–10, 216; tax policies of, 159–61, 170, 176–84, 212, 246n19; transportation and, 170, 172–74, 176, 188–93; urban growth policies of, 6, 163, 176–201, 207–9, 215; wealth redistribution in, 209–10, 212–13, 217; zoning in, 158, 193, 198–200, 204, 208–9
Regional Government Committee, 206
regional planning, 132, 196, 205–7, 216
Republican Party, 1, 73, 78, 82
restrictive covenants, 209
Retail Merchants Board, 97
Reynolds Ordinance, 70–73
Rickoff, Andrew, 77–78
Ritchie, Ryerson, 87–88, 98
river improvements. *See* water transportation
Rockefeller, John D., 53, 56, 108, 130
Rose, W. G., 58–59, 62
rowdy boys, 24, 28–29
Rudolph, Max, 169

Russell Sage Foundation, 138
Ruthenberg, Charles E., 203

St. Clair Street Railway, 68
St. Lawrence Waterway Project, 173
saloons, 27, 76–77, 111
Sargent, H. Q., 79
School of Applied Social Sciences, 145–48, 150
schools. *See* public education
Scovil, Samuel, 147
service distribution policies, 6–7, 142; contracting and, 74–75, 215–16; of Corporate Regime, 133–41, 149, 216; fire protection, 21–22, 32, 204; franchising and, 66–74, 86, 91, 215–16; garbage removal, 74–75, 204; of Merchant Regime, 19–23, 29, 32, 33, 38, 61, 67; municipal ownership and, 91, 189–90; police protection, 20–21, 32, 44–45, 76–77, 204; of Populist Regime, 42, 63, 65–80, 215–16; public education, 24–25, 28, 32, 77–80, 99, 134–41, 204, 210–12; of Realty Regime, 187–93, 204–6, 209–10, 216; regional government and, 219; street railway systems, 42, 67–74, 91, 109, 117, 174, 188–90; streets and roads, 18–19, 56, 61–63, 66–67, 74, 108, 113, 192, 204; water and sewerage, 22–23, 32, 188, 204
Shaker Heights, 169, 188, 206, 211
Shaker Realty Company, 108
sidewalks. *See* streets and roads
6th Street, East, 118
Smith, John A., 104
Smith Act (1911), 184–85
Smythe, Fr. (St. Malachi's Church), 79
social order, 127–29
social stratification: antagonisms and, 203–4; neighborhoods and, 29–30, 33, 42, 226–27; in park system, 111–12, 115; suburbanization and, 204, 208–9; wealth redistribution and, 210; in workforce, 40
Society for the Relief of the Poor, 26
South Chagrin Reservation, 115
Spaulding, Frank, 137–41

special purpose districts, 106–7, 112, 114
Squire, Andrew, 167
Standard Oil Company, 179
Stanley, Joseph, 69
State, ex. rel. Stanton v. Cleveland Metropolitan Park Dist. Bd. of Comm'rs, 114, 194
Stinchcomb, William A., 104–6, 108, 111, 113–14, 147, 167, 194
Stone, Amasa, 124
Stout, William B., 173
street railway systems, 42, 67–74, 91, 109, 117, 188–90
streets and roads: contracting system and, 74; economic development and, 56; lighting of, 66–67; park system and, 108, 113; urban growth and, 18–19, 61–63, 192; 6th Street, East, 118; 9th Street, East, 118; 105th Street, East, 158, 189; Carnegie Avenue, 129; Chester Avenue, 158–59; East and West Boulevards, 108; Euclid Avenue, 23, 30, 118, 129, 158–60, 189; Prospect Avenue, 158–59; Superior Avenue, 117–18
suburbanization, 175, 185–86, 188–89, 192, 204, 208–9
subway system, 190–91
Sullivan, Jeremiah J., 97–98
Sunday Laws, 77
Superior Avenue, 117–18
Supervision, Board of, 120–21
Sutherland, George, 200
Swasey, Ambrose, 98, 196

Tax Commission, 91–92, 181
tax policies, 218; in Corporate Regime, 89–92, 114, 140, 177–78; in Merchant Regime, 18–19, 61; in Populist Regime, 58, 61–62; in Realty Regime, 159–61, 170, 176–84, 212, 246n19
Tax School, 90–92
Tayler, Robert Walker, 189
Taylor, Frederick Winslow, 138–39
Taylor Grant (1909), 189
Taylorism, 138–40
Teaford, Jon C., 256n20
temperance movements, 20, 26–27

tenement codes, 132
Thomas Houston Electric Company, 95
Thompson, Amos Burt, 158–61, 163, 178, 182, 194
Thompson, Hine, and Flory (law firm), 158
Thwing, Charles, 124, 126
Townes, Clayton C., 169
Trade, Board of, 87
transportation development, 161–62, 214–15; air, 173, 176; automobiles, 161, 170, 190, 191–93; long-distance, 172–74, 176; railroads, 13–14, 58–59, 172–73, 195; regional planning and, 205; street railway system, 42, 67–74, 91, 109, 117, 174, 188–90; streets and roads, 18–19, 56, 61–63, 66–67, 74, 108, 113, 192, 204; subway system, 190–91; water-based, 11–14, 58, 172–-73
Tuckerman, Louis B., 144

Ullman, Edward L., 258n19
University Circle, 99, 103, 116–17, 124–27, 174; assessment of, 127–31
University Improvement Company, 126–27, 131
urban growth policies, 5–7, 142, 215; annexations and, 14, 16–19, 33, 46, 60–61, 202–5, 223; of Corporate Regime, 102–32, 149, 193, 202, 215; eminent domain, 114; infrastructure for, 18, 61, 62–63; of Merchant Regime, 15–19, 29–30, 33, 38, 46, 60–63, 102, 215; park system and, 103–15; of Populist Regime, 41, 63–64, 102, 127; of Realty Regime, 163, 176–201, 207–9, 215; regional government and, 219; special purpose districts and, 106–7, 112, 114; zoning and, 116, 127–28, 132, 158, 166, 193, 198–200, 204, 208–9. *See also* city structure; tax policies
utilities, 61–63, 66–67, 91, 174, 187–88, 204

value added per employee (VAPE), 52–54, 57

Van Aken, William, 166, 169
Van Sweringen brothers, M. J. and O. P.:
    city planning and, 166, 168, 197; creative loan making and, 163; railroad interests of, 158–59, 172–73, 195; street railways and, 188, 190–91
Village of Euclid v. Ambler Realty, 158, 198–200
Vinson, Robert E., 126
Vitality Index, 23
vocational education, 28, 78–79, 136–37

Wade, Jeptha H., 110, 124, 130, 196
Wade, Jeptha H., II, 124, 125
Wade Park, 108–9
Wade Realty, 124–25, 127, 131
Wannamaker, R. M., 114
water and sewerage, 22–23, 32, 188, 204
water transportation, 11–14, 58, 172–73
"weak mayor" system, 31, 43–44, 104
wealth redistribution, 6–7, 217–18; in Corporate Regime, 133, 141–48, 150, 212; in Merchant Regime, 23–29, 32–34, 38, 80; in Populist Regime, 42, 65, 80–82, 212; in Realty Regime, 209–10, 212–13; regional government and, 219. *See also* tax policies
Weigand, Edward A., 169
Welfare Federation, 145–46, 148, 150, 212–13
West Boulevard, 108
Western Reserve Historical Society, 125
Western Reserve University, 99, 124, 126, 146
Westinghouse, George, 95–96
Westinghouse Company, 95–96
West Park, 185
Wholesale Merchants Board, 97
Witt, Peter, 189, 191
working class, 109, 112, 207; ideals of, 37–39, 41, 47

Zangerle, John A., 104, 156, 178–80
zoning, 116, 127–28, 132, 166, 193; legal cases on, 158, 198–200; suburbanization and, 204, 208–9

URBAN LIFE AND URBAN LANDSCAPE
Zane L. Miller, Series Editor

The series examines the history of urban life and the development of the urban landscape through works that place social, economic, and political issues in the intellectual and cultural context of their times.

High Stakes: Big Time Sports and Downtown Redevelopment
TIMOTHY JON CURRY, KENT SCHWIRIAN, AND RACHAEL A. WOLDOFF

Suburban Steel: The Magnificent Failure of the Lustron Corporation, 1945–1951
DOUGLAS KNERR

New York City: An Outsider's Inside View
MARIO MAFFI

Merchant of Illusion: James Rouse, America's Salesman of the Businessman's Utopia
NICHOLAS DAGEN BLOOM

The Failure of Planning: Permitting Sprawl in San Diego Suburbs, 1970–1999
RICHARD HOGAN

Faith and Action: A History of the Catholic Archdiocese of Cincinnati, 1821–1996
ROGER FORTIN

Regionalism and Reform: Art and Class Formation in Antebellum Cincinnati
WENDY JEAN KATZ

Making Sense of the City: Local Government, Civic Culture, and Community Life in Urban America
EDITED BY ROBERT B. FAIRBANKS AND PATRICIA MOONEY-MELVIN

Visions of Place: The City, Neighborhoods, Suburbs, and Cincinnati's Clifton, 1850–2000
ZANE L. MILLER

Suburban Alchemy: 1960s New Towns and the Transformation of the American Dream
NICHOLAS DAGEN BLOOM

A Right to Representation: Proportional Election Systems for the Twenty-First Century
KATHLEEN L. BARBER

Boss Cox's Cincinnati: Urban Politics in the Progressive Era
ZANE L. MILLER

Columbus, Ohio: A Personal Geography
HENRY L. HUNKER

Lancaster, Ohio, 1800–2000: Frontier Town to Edge City
DAVID R. CONTOSTA

Domesticating the Street: The Reform of Public Space in Hartford, 1850–1930
PETER C. BALDWIN

Cincinnati in 1840: The Social and Functional Organization of an Urban Community during the Pre–Civil War Period
WALTER STIX GLAZER

The Rise of the City, 1878–1898
ARTHUR MEIER SCHLESINGER

History in Urban Places: The Historic Districts of the United States
DAVID HAMER

Getting around Brown: Desegregation, Development, and the Columbus Public Schools
GREGORY S. JACOBS

For the City as a Whole: Planning, Politics, and the Public Interest in Dallas, Texas, 1900–1965
ROBERT B. FAIRBANKS

Changing Plans for America's Inner Cities: Cincinnati's Over-the-Rhine and Twentieth-Century Urbanism
ZANE L. MILLER AND BRUCE TUCKER

Main Street Blues: The Decline of Small-Town America
RICHARD O. DAVIES

Visions of Eden: Environmentalism, Urban Planning, and City Building in St. Petersburg, Florida, 1900–1995
R. BRUCE STEPHENSON

Designing Modern America: The Regional Planning Association of America and Its Members
EDWARD K. SPANN

The Poetics of Cities: Designing Neighborhoods That Work
MIKE GREENBERG

Welcome to Heights High: The Crippling Politics of Restructuring America's Public Schools
DIANA TITTLE

The Mysteries of the Great City: The Politics of Urban Design, 1877–1937
JOHN D. FAIRFIELD

The Lost Dream: Businessmen and City Planning on the Pacific Coast, 1890–1920
MANSEL G. BLACKFORD

The New York Approach: Robert Moses, Urban Liberals, and Redevelopment of the Inner City
JOEL SCHWARTZ

Suburb in the City: Chestnut Hill, Philadelphia, 1850–1990
DAVID R. CONTOSTA

Cincinnati: Queen City of the West, 1819–1838
DANIEL AARON

Cincinnati Observed: Architecture and History
JOHN CLUBBE

Fragments of Cities: The New American Downtowns and Neighborhoods
LARRY BENNETT

www.ingramcontent.com/pod-product-compliance
Lightning Source LLC
Chambersburg PA
CBHW020943230426
43666CB00005B/150